Power and Change in Canada

Power and Change in Canada

edited by Richard J. Ossenberg

McCLELLAND AND STEWART

McClelland and Stewart Limited
The Canadian Publishers
25 Hollinger Road
Toronto Ontario
M4B 3G2

CANADIAN CATALOGUING IN PUBLICATION DATA

Main entry under title:

Power and change in Canada
Includes bibliographies and index.

ISBN 0-7710-6904-9

1. Canada – Social conditions.   2. Power (Social
sciences)   3. Elite (Social sciences)   I. Ossenberg,
Richard J., 1934-

HN110.Z9P66   303.3'4'0971   C80-094135-7

Manufactured in Canada by Webcom Limited

Contents

Acknowledgements   *vi*

Preface   7

Chapter One: Approaches to Power and Change: A Selected Overview and Interpretation/Richard J. Ossenberg, Queen's University   *14*

PART I: Political Economy: The Dynamics of Change   *27*

Editor's Introduction   *29*

Chapter Two: Unity in Diversity: The Political Economy of Subordination in Canada/Daniel Glenday, Brock University   *34*

Chapter Three: Canadian Labour and the Capital Crisis: The Dynamics of Conflict/Paul Willox   *65*

PART II: Class, Culture, and Legitimation   *101*

Editor's Introduction   *103*

Chapter Four: Education, Class, and Power in Canada/Robert M. Pike, Queen's University   *106*

Chapter Five: Power and Play in Canadian Society/Richard S. Gruneau, Queen's University   *146*

PART III: Control and Coercion   *195*

Editor's Introduction   *197*

Chapter Six: A Critical Perspective on Law in the Canadian State: Delinquency and Corporate Crime/D. Laureen Snider, Queen's University, and W. Gordon West, University of Guelph   *199*

Chapter Seven: Social Control and the Military in Canada/ Terry C. Willett, Queen's University   *246*

Index   *285*

ACKNOWLEDGEMENTS

To Fred

I want to thank all of my colleagues who joined me in the completion of this book. I am grateful for their cooperation, assistance, and encouragement throughout the development of this project, which involved my requests for several revisions. Without the cooperative and collective spirit we shared, despite our varying approaches to the topic, the project would not have come to fruition.

Peter Milroy and Peter Saunders, along with W. Gordon West, initiated the idea for this volume, and I thank them for inviting me to bring together a diversity of currents of thought about social life in Canada as viewed in the context of power and change. A special thanks is due Richard Gruneau, who was a constant source of encouragement and suggestions for organizational and editorial changes, and Peter Milroy, who was tireless in his efforts to see the project through.

My sincere thanks to the secretaries who did the "real" work on the project, not only for their technical expertise, but for their true involvement and encouragement, and willing replies to my numerous calls for assistance—often at the last moment. For the time being, a humble thank you must suffice for the invaluable assistance of Christine Zippi, Amanda Vance, Julia Stevenhaagen, and Shirley Fraser.

My appreciation is extended to the Department of Sociology at Queen's, to the School of Graduate Studies and Research (for financial assistance in support of research, much of it relevant to this book), and to the Queen's University community in general, for providing a congenial and supportive atmosphere in which to work.

Richard J. Ossenberg
Kingston, Ontario, 1979

PREFACE

Richard J. Ossenberg

The Theme

Among the most fundamental and basic realities of social life are the universal and omnipresent need to make decisions and the changes that occur because of people's decisions. Yet, as in so many aspects of the human condition, the apparently elementary structures, processes, and events seem to be the most difficult to understand. In the case of *social power*, it is perhaps widely assumed that decision-making (potential power) and the realization of these decisions (actual power) are simply inevitable and "natural" events; that it is self-evident that some people or groups have more power than others, regardless of our individual hopes and aspirations; and, therefore, that it is redundant to analyze and impossible to control the distribution of power.

And what of *social change*? Everyone is aware of and affected by changes, especially in relatively urbanized and industrialized societies such as Canada – but, as in the case of the weather, very few pretend to have any influence over change. After all, to cite but a few examples, if people throughout the world are populating urban centres, depending on the mass media for information and entertainment, alarmed by crime and social upheaval, or resigned to environmental disaster, are we not simply paying the price for progress and civilization? An increasing number of people are obviously not willing to answer this question in the affirmative; there is either general uneasiness over the present human condition or definitive social action directed toward changing it. But both the uneasiness and the attempts to change inevitably encounter the perplexing problem of *power structures* which are

7

inherent in all societies: groups of people and institutions which have the "real" power to promote or inhibit change and who have a vested interest in doing so, with or without the willing consent of people without such power.

What is a power structure, and how does it relate to social change in Canada? This is the basic question and problem addressed in this book. The definition of this problem becomes increasingly focused throughout the book: it is generally oriented around the rather general but cogent observation of C. Wright Mills, who stated that:

> "Power", as the term is now generally used in social science, has to do with whatever decisions [people] make about the arrangements under which they live, and about the events which make up the history of their period. . . . social arrangements do change without benefit of explicit decision. But in so far as such decisions are made ... the problem of who is involved in making them (or not making them) is the basic problem of power. (1961: 40)

This view of power and change appears reasonable; it is unlikely that many would take issue with it. However, it is but a preliminary statement that leads to a further assumption, which is the focus for study by all of the authors in this volume and one which in "liberal-democratic" societies such as Canada many might object to, or at least feel some discomfort about:

> We cannot assume today that [people] must in the last resort be governed by their own consent. Among the means of power that now prevail is the power to manage and to manipulate the consent of [people] ... much power today is successfully employed without the sanction of the reason or the conscience of the obedient. (Mills, 1961: 40-41)

This assumption clearly implies that in all societies where social inequalities are evident social order is obtained not merely by some degree of consensus (general and willing agreement about ways and means to achieve the most desirable ends), but often by manipulation (socialization) or, in the extreme, by brutal force (the police and the military). Both means are manifestations of power. We take issue with the view that such use of power is both natural and inevitable; indeed, we question both the legitimacy and the morality of the use of power in maintaining social inequalities which are not derivative of the innate talents and abilities of individuals within a society.

The vast majority of writings by sociologists and social scientists, generally, have acknowledged the existence of social inequalities. Very few writers, for example, would deny the existence of a social-class structure in Canada, or racial, ethnic, and regional inequalities. Yet, only the exceptional publication has dealt explicitly with the problem of power, including the question of whether the actions and decisions of the groups in power are legitimate in the sense of being consistent with the interests and aspirations of the majority without power. Especially, few publications have considered whether changes occur because or in spite of groups in power.

The relationship between the powerful and the powerless is essentially dialectical; that is, it involves a reciprocal relationship between them. The powerless *react* to the actions and decisions of the powerful in a number of ways, including compliance (genuinely, or simply through fatalistic resolve), modified acceptance, protest, or revolution. The powerful, in turn, reply to the reaction through force, conciliation, manipulation, or capitulation, thus initiating yet another set of reciprocal relationships. It is in the context of this ongoing dynamic dialectical relationship that change is inevitable; hence, the theme of this book. All of the authors deal explicitly with the problem of power and its coercive and manipulative dimensions insofar as they relate to the "holding-together" of Canadian society. The authors also consider the relationship between power and change in its manifold complexities.

Having adopted this basic position, we further agree there are two ways in which a small group of people who hold power (a power-elite) can profoundly influence the general course of events *and* the fate of individual members of the majority. The one method may be referred to as the "soft" or subtle form of social control, i.e., socialization or manipulation. This method is aptly characterized by Parkin:

... one of the central aims of any dominant class is to make the rules governing the distribution of rewards seem legitimate in the eyes of all, including those who stand to gain least from such rules. The greater the extent to which this is achieved, the more stable the political order is likely to be, and the less the need for recourse to coercive means. (1971: 48)

Thus, it is incumbent on the power-elite, either wittingly or simply through actions which are the natural and uncontemplated manifestations of their social-class position, to influence all of the institutions of socialization, ranging from government and the legal system to the family, and including the school system and the mass media. The dominant norms of society, the deeply held beliefs and values which govern appropriate behaviour and impose sanctions against deviations, must be made to appear synonymous with, or at least a reasonable facsimile of, their own norms. But soft or subtle social control, highly effective as it is, cannot stand by itself without the potential threat or actual implementation (buttressed by legal sanctions) of the direct use of force or coercion in support of the norms of those in power, whether or not those norms correspond to those of the majority. Thus, the second method of social control is the "hard" use of coercion and force through the police and the military with the implicit or active support of those in power, including the government and the private but powerful interest groups that often influence the government to a much greater extent than the majority are able to do through either the electoral process or social protest movements. "Soft" socialization is never in itself effective enough to prevent the periodic and often continuous social upheavals, which challenge conventional and traditional wisdom and, in so doing, threaten to erode or destroy the authority and influence of those in power.

This book was planned to analyze both forms of the use of power, with greater stress in some of the essays on the one than on the other. Of course, both forms of social control operate congruently, and the high visible use of military and police force directed against certain individuals or groups (usually publicized for its alleged "deterrent" value) is often a last resort in the face of failure to maintain social order through the "soft" forms of socialization.

The Theoretical Orientation

As is the case with any topic of study, there are many different theoretical approaches to the analysis of power. Although the authors present different philosophical and personal approaches in this book, *the theoretical orientation is conflict theory.* Some of the authors whole-heartedly embrace conflict theory in their essays; others modify it; and still others bring its relevance into question. But all of the authors acknowledge the importance of conflict theory, and even the critical views are tempered by a recognition of at least some validity to the use of this theory in sociological study. Thus, the book is both a theoretical endorsement and critical assessment of conflict theory. This theoretical orientation links the essays together, although some of the authors have attempted to show that other perspectives such as *order theory,* or the philosophy of liberalism, are also pertinent to a full understanding of power and change.

Conflict theory is a perspective of social life emphasizing three basic assumptions: (1) that most societies are held together through the power and influence of a small number of people; (2) that this situation is undesirable and detrimental to individuals and groups who have little or no impact on the course of events; and (3) that this must be changed to bring about greater equality and general access to power. Until this "ideal" is reached, societies will always be marked by conflict between the powerful and the powerless.

Another important aspect of conflict theory, according to Horton, is that

> Social problems and social change arise from the exploitive and alienating practices of dominant groups; they are responses to the discrepancy between what is and what is in the process of becoming. Social problems, therefore, reflect, not the administrative problems of the social system, nor the failure of individuals to perform their system roles in the order explanation, but the adaptive failure of society to meet changing individual needs. (1966: 704)

This view of society stands in sharp contrast to that of the *order* or *consensus* perspective which, with few exceptions, accepts and often rationalizes the need for social inequalities. In general, the order perspective does not challenge or confront the status quo; it assumes that societies are integrated through the willing and widespread agreement and cooperation of the public (normative-integration), with the necessity of a power-elite provided that there are opportunities for individuals to become members of the elite. Another aspect of the order perspective is the notion that the major conflicts, especially class and race and ethnic conflicts, are *exceptional* instead of *continuous* features of all societies, and are therefore viewed as "pathological."*

The Essays
All of the authors have incorporated certain common themes which illustrate many of the characteristics of conflict theory. These themes include:

1. *The historical background* to the topic being discussed, in the belief that we do not know where we are or where we are going unless we know where we have come from.

2. A *macroscopic analysis* (general overview) in order to portray the "large picture" within which more specific events occur, with the assumption that the more specific events are largely affected by organizations such as governments and multi-national corporations, and are not simply the consequences of individual personalities, as some writers would hold. (In this connection, the observation of C. Wright Mills (1961: 20) seems particularly appropriate: "My conception stands opposed to social science . . . which inhibit[s] social inquiry by 'methodological' pretentions, which congest such work by obscurantist conceptions, or which trivialize it by concern with minor problems unconnected with publicly relevant issues.")

3. Discussion of *contemporary and emerging trends*, with an emphasis on social issues and problems.

4. *The role that individuals can play* in bringing about changes in the nature of the "larger picture" and thereby have greater

---

*A full discussion of the contrasts between the order and conflict theories is provided by Horton, 1966.

control over their own destinies.

The essays in this volume are the end result of frequent informal discussions between the editor and the authors over the past three years. The concept of power and change emerged from these discussions as the central focus. We felt that the topic had not been sufficiently treated in existing publications and it soon became apparent there was a need for a book which would both deal with the theoretical aspects and apply these aspects to specific topics, some of which appeared, on the surface, to be only remotely related to or affected by social power.

All of the essays, in spite of the specialized areas implied by the titles, relate to many other topics simply because of their macroscopic nature; moreover, because of their consistent and in-depth evaluations, the modes of analysis can certainly be seen to relate, if not directly apply, to topics which have not been specifically covered. It is my hope that we, and others who may find in this book a new perspective for looking at the nature of Canadian society, will continue to work in this direction, to the extent that every conceivable topic in sociology may be seen in the context of power and change.

REFERENCES

Horton, John
   1966 "Order and Conflict Theories of Social Problems," *American Journal of Sociology* (May): 701-13.
Mills, C. Wright
   1961 *The Sociological Imagination*. New York.
Parkin, F.
   1971 *Class, Inequality and Political Order*. London.

CHAPTER ONE

Approaches to Power and Change: A Selected Overview and Interpretation
by Richard J. Ossenberg

The relationship of power, social organization, and change has long been the concern of many social scientists and philosophers. A few of the pioneers in this tradition who have written about the topic from differing ideological perspectives have had a considerable influence on contemporary thought. In order to provide some background to our concern in this book with the context of power and change in Canada, I have chosen to discuss some relevant contributions of three social scientists whose works have become classics: Karl Marx (1818-1883), Vilfredo Pareto (1848-1923), and Emile Durkheim (1858-1917).

Each of these writers presents a somewhat different philosophy about the nature of society; together, they provide a range of possible points of view (ideologies) in evaluating the importance and validity of the use of power in keeping a society together and inhibiting or encouraging change. The most striking contrast in interpretation can be seen in the works of Marx and Durkheim. Marx, whose views were instrumental in the development of conflict theory, considered the use of force a necessity in societies where great disparities in wealth and power exist, but he argued that such situations were undesirable and should be eliminated through either major social change or revolution. This supposedly would bring about a classless society, where the use of force would be replaced with communal cooperation.

A summary of the views of Marx (and Friedrich Engels) on power and social change can be found in *The Communist Manifesto*:

The history of all hitherto existing society is the history of class struggles.

Freeman and slave, patrician and plebian, lord and serf, guildmaster and journeyman, in a word, *oppressor and oppressed*, stood in constant opposition to one another, carried on an uninterrupted, now hidden, now open fight, a fight that each time ended, either in a revolutionary reconstitution of society at large, or in the common ruin of the struggling classes.

In the earlier epochs of history, we find almost everywhere a complicated arrangement of society into various orders, a manifold gradation of social rank. In ancient Rome we have patricians, knights, plebians, slaves; in the Middle Ages, feudal lords, vassals, guildmasters, journeymen, apprentices, serfs; and in almost all of these particular classes, again, other subordinate gradations.

The modern bourgeois society that has sprouted from the ruins of feudal society has not done away with class antagonisms. It has only established new classes, *new conditions of oppression*, new forms of struggle in place of the old ones. (1964: 57-8; italics mine)

Marx envisioned that this struggle ultimately would lead to a classless society:

Political power, properly so called, is merely the organized power of one class for oppressing another. If the proletariat during its contest with the bourgeoisie is compelled, by the force of circumstances, to organize itself as a class, if, by means of revolution, it makes itself the ruling class, and, as such sweeps away by force the old conditions of production, then it will, along with these conditions, have swept away the conditions for class antagonisms and of classes generally, and will thereby have abolished its own supremacy as a class. In place of the old bourgeois society, with its classes and class antagonisms, we shall have an *association* in which the free development of each is the condition for the free development of all. (*ibid.*: 95; italics mine)

Marx, then, viewed the use of force as a form of oppression alien to the natural condition of human society, but concluded that it was generally through the use of force by the oppressed (revolution) that the need for force could be eliminated.

Durkheim, in contrast to Marx, while not dealing with the concept of social classes, considered that a "division of labour" was both necessary and inevitable for the "health" of any society. Indeed, he argued that it was only through a distinct division of labour (social classes) that societies could advance technologically, become densely populated, and remain integrated (1893). One of the means of maintaining social integration or "social solidarity," according to Durkheim, was by assuring that all societies have a built-in and often ritualized (public) system of social control through various degrees of punishment (depending on the severity of the "offence") directed toward individuals and groups who depart from the norms and therefore threaten the cohesiveness of the "collective-conscience" (society in general). This system is essential, Durkheim thought, because it functions as a continuous and dramatic reminder of the norms to be observed and is especially crucial during times of uncertainty concerning "appropriate" social behaviour, when either the status quo or the continuing smooth functioning of the social order is in potential jeopardy; therefore, deviation or criminality *and* punishment are inevitable and inherent features of all societies. The former is potentially dangerous, but it provokes the latter, which serves as a reminder of the importance of the norms that are being violated and thereby reinforces a sense of social solidarity.

Although Durkheim felt that certain forms of crime are not in themselves "pathological" but deviations from the collective-conscience which could lead to more healthy forms of social integration, his main emphasis was on the inevitability of crime and the necessity for reaction to it. According to Durkheim:

> . . . since there cannot be a society in which the individuals do not differ more or less from the collective type, it is also inevitable that, among these divergences, there are some with a criminal character. What confers this character upon them is not the intrinsic quality of a given act but that definition which the collective conscience lends them. If the collective conscience

is stronger, if it has enough *authority* practically to *suppress these divergences*, it will also be more sensitive, more exacting: and, reacting against the slightest deviations with the energy it otherwise displays only against more considerable infractions, it will attribute them the same gravity as formerly to crimes. (1938: 70; italics mine)

Durkheim took great pains to avoid simplification of this concept and argued, for example, that the use of power and suppression could exceed "normal boundaries"; nevertheless, an obvious conclusion to be derived from the writings of Durkheim is the inevitability of punishment expressed by the "collectivity" (society in general) through its representatives, i.e., the state, and its defenders, i.e., the police and the military.

The position taken by Pareto is somewhat different from that expressed in either the progressive leftist perspective of Marx or the ideological conservatism of Durkheim. Pareto's thesis is that the use of force and power is inevitable in any society, but, unlike Durkheim, he did not deny the validity of revolution or rapid structural changes in society. In this sense, there is some similarity to the position of Marx. On the other hand, contrary to Marxist thought, Pareto held that it would *always* be a relatively small proportion of the population (a power-elite) which, through force, would assure the ongoing functioning of society. This group might be the government in power, or if the strength of that government falters, it would be the insurgent group that replaces it and subsequently assumes leadership, again, through the use of power. Pareto (1935) makes this point explicit in proclaiming that:

. . . when a governing class divests itself too completely of the sentiments of group-persistence, it easily reaches a point where it is unfit to defend, let alone its own power, what is far worse, the independence of its country. In such a case, if the independence is to be deemed an advantage, it must also be deemed an advantage to be rid of a class that has become incompetent to perform the functions of defence. As a rule, it is from the subject class that individuals come with faith *and the resolve to use force* and save a country. (1935: 595; italics mine)

The analyses of the use of force and coercion represented in the works of Marx, Durkheim, and Pareto illustrate different ideological positions, some related aspects of which are discussed by authors of the essays in this book.

Power and Change in Canada: An Overview of Theories

In Canada, a number of writers have stressed the use of power and force; although they do not represent the positions of the major schools of thought in social science, they have provided a basis for a new perspective. Among these writers, the economic historian, Stanley B. Ryerson, has made the most important contribution to a theoretical approach conforming basically to a Marxist orientation. It is especially in Ryerson's book, *The Founding of Canada* (1960), that a clear and consistent theoretical analysis of the use of power and coercion in Canada's history can be seen, but it is also reflected, in a more complex version, in his *Unequal Union* (1968), where he emphasizes the extent to which the aspirations of French Canadians have been consistently suppressed through the power of the Anglophone majority.

But it is the emphasis on social-class conflict and the exploitation of the underclasses that has been characteristic of the writings of Ryerson. For example, he states that:

All of the feverish abandon of the landowner-capitalist elites in their scramble for pelf and power, for public monies and resources, all their legalized public theft and illicit bribery and political corruption, depended in the last resort on the extraction of surplus values [relative increase in profits compared to increase in wages] from the living labour. Without the productive labour of working people in town and countryside (starting with Indian trappers, later embracing pioneer settlers and "mechanics," workers in the factories and mines of the metropolis and the railway-building and growing manufacturers of the colonies), there could not have taken place the initial accumulation of capital and its subsequent self-expansion through re-invested profits. (1972: xvi)

Ryerson discusses the development of Canada as a series of conflicts between contending groups, beginning especially with

European colonization and the annihilation of native peoples or the exploitation of their labour during the time that the fur trade was the basis of the Canadian economy. The ascendency of a merchant class through the fur trade was associated with the rapid decline in the power of the native peoples, for they became workers for the early fur-trade companies, such as the Northwest Company and the Hudson's Bay Company, and lost not only their capacity for self-sufficiency but also their traditional culture and social organization. And as the fur trade was replaced by the wheat economy, the labour of native peoples became virtually superfluous. Ryerson contends that with the development of industrialization and urbanization, racial conflicts (between European colonists and native peoples), social-class conflicts, including the struggle for power between the French and the English, and the numerous conflicts between the industrial capitalists (bourgeoisie) and the working class culminated in most instances in the suppression of the demands and aspirations of the workers through police or military force (often with the explicit approval of the Canadian government).

Gustavus Myers, another economic historian, must also be cited as having made an important contribution to the development of conflict interpretations of Canadian society. His emphasis on social classes, class conflict, and the exploitation of Canada's peoples and natural resources by a closed network of a small number of members of the merchant and capitalist elites was so controversial and threatening to the established order that his writings on these topics, published originally in Chicago in 1914, were not published in Canada until 1972.

The use of power by elites during the earlier development of Canada (erroneously referred to as the "feudal period") is documented by Myers; for example:

That the seigneurs, both French and English, enforced every iota of their feudal rights against their tenants is evident from the statement of the number of executions [civil and criminal charges] lodged in the sheriff's office at Montreal at the insistence of the seigneurs. From October 5, 1839, to October 5, 1842, there was a total of 3,440 executions. In turn, the sheriffs extorted fortunes in fees from the misfortunes of these

impoverished peasants and manual workers. . . . In other official reports further facts are set forth as to the merciless rigidity
with which hard laws were enforced against the poor; at every
turn the impoverished peasant and labourer were harshly proceeded against. (Myers, 1972: 112)

What is of interest in Myers' account is not simply the use of
power but the extent to which there was widespread discontent
among the underclasses with the norms and expectations of those
in power; in other words, a basic class conflict situation existed.

Both Ryerson and Myers, in different ways, analyzed Canadian
society in a Marxist perspective. There are other writers who,
while acknowledging the existence of power and conflict in Canada, tend toward a perspective which is more closely related to
the concepts of Durkheim and Pareto. The Canadian sociologist
and noted social historian, S. Delbert Clark, has documented the
existence of conflict and the use of force in the development of
Canada in his *Movements of Political Protest in Canada* (1959) and
in *The Social Development of Canada* (1942).

Clark, however, underplays the concept of social-class antagonisms and emphasizes instead political, regional, ethnic, and
religious conflicts and deviations. Clark appears to endorse the
legitimacy of the use of force for suppressing those deviations
that constitute a distinct threat to the continued integration of society. Indeed, Clark has suggested that the use of force through
the significant role that the police and the military have played in
the history of Canada has been vital to the relatively "peaceful"
development of Canadian society, especially in the early development of Canada's "frontiers."

In his discussion of the analysis of social history, Clark states
that:

. . . what is required is a model of society as it has become or is
becoming. Within such a framework of analysis interest shifts
from those disturbances within the social order which, while
imposing stress and strain upon the structure, are contained
and *brought under control by forces finding support within the
vested interests of the order* to the disturbances which result in a
change in the basic character of the order. Whether a particular

disturbance is considered one producing stress and strain within the order or one bringing about a change of the order depends upon how the society's basic character has been defined. (1968: 301; italics mine)

It seems unlikely that Clark would grant legitimacy to revolution as a form of social change; while being critical of theories of evolution (gradual and smooth change), Clark generally stresses the need for some kind of continuing (although changing) forms of social integration.

The continuing use of power and the existence of social classes in contemporary Canada is well-documented. Professor John Porter, in *The Vertical Mosaic* (1965), shows that Canada continues to be characterized by power-elites and by great divergences in personal incomes, by regional economic disparities as well as by great economic differences between ethnic groups. One of Porter's main conclusions is that the economic elite of Canada (less than two per cent of the population) are not representative of the population. With few exceptions, they are white, Anglo-Saxon, Protestant men who comprise a closed social network through friendship, similar experiences in education, membership in elite clubs, and marriage within the group. According to Porter, there has been little or no chance of people outside this network becoming members of the economic elite. While deploring this situation, Porter denies the validity of a Marxist concept of class struggle and revolution. In doing so, he is generally oriented to an order concept of the nature of society. Porter states, for example, that:

Power arises because of the general social need for order. Sets of ordered relationships distinguish a social system from a disorganized mass of human beings. Whenever human beings find themselves together, they begin very quickly to establish a set of ordered relationships so that they are able to make some predictions about how other people are going to behave. Everyone in society has a set of expectations about how others will behave. Without ordered relationships which provide expectations, it would be impossible to live. Among these ordered relationships are those which grant the right to a few people to make decisions on behalf of the group. (1965: 202)

It should not be inferred from this quotation that Porter advocates an authoritarian or monopolistic view of the natural order of society. Indeed, Porter stressed the need for considerable modification of the power structure – but without changing the necessary conditions for leadership. He states:

> Although it has a class structure peculiar to its own history and geography, Canada is probably not unlike other western industrial nations in relying heavily on its elite groups to make major decisions and to determine the shape and direction of its development. The nineteenth-century notion of a liberal citizen-participating democracy is obviously not a satisfactory model by which to examine the process of decision-making in either the economic or political contexts. Given the complexities of modern societies, it is unlikely that widespread participation can develop without very great changes and institutional experimentation. If power and decision-making must always rest with elite groups, there can at least be open recruitment from all classes into the elites. (1965: 558)

This concept of the essential requirement for power-elites, provided that there is continuous "circulation of elites" to stimulate innovation from different and refreshing perspectives, is closely related to the concept of power developed by Mosca (1939) and is in many ways similar to the analysis of Pareto.

Porter's position regarding the existence of social classes and a power-elite was later supported by Clement (1975), who discovered that recruitment into the economic elite had not increased (indeed, in some respects, it had decreased) and that the economic elite, which was the essential focus of study by Porter, largely controlled the sources of information through the mass media – newspaper, radio, magazine, and television. This situation can be referred to as elite institutional "overlap," and is probably characteristic of all aspects of life in Canada, including the control over organized sports and leisure, a theme developed in this book by Gruneau.

In contrast to Porter's visions of Canada as a liberal democracy with the potential for political pluralism (all interest groups having an opportunity to influence the shape and directions of a society), Clement, adhering more to a conflict perspective, suggests that:

> Pluralists generally focus on "consensus" and the idea of a "balance" of social forces. It ignores the systematic biases evident in class based societies and the reflection these have on relations between the state and corporate worlds. The pluralist model assumes "free willed" individuals who will come together when they detect injustice and voice their concerns through the many "access points" in the state. What this ignores is the fact that individuals are not "free willed" but subject to dominant ideological systems; what it fails to acknowledge is the unequal allocations of resources necessary to mobilize and realize concerns. (1975: 259)

No review of the Canadian literature, brief as it may be, can neglect the singular contribution of Harold Innis who, in *The Fur Trade in Canada*, established a theory of the social, political, and economic structure of Canada, which has been the one theory most referred to by other authors in this area, whether supportive or critical. In this extraordinary, ambitious, and scholarly work, Innis develops what is normally referred to as the "staples theory" of Canada's origin and growth. While there have been many different interpretations of this theory, it can be described basically as the concept that Canada was not created as a reaction to American expansionism (as many writers would argue), but that it emerged because of French and British dependence on a series of geographically determined staples for export, beginning with fish and continuing with fur, lumber, and wheat. According to Innis, the unified, centralized fur trade made it easy, later on, for Canadian industry, finance, and transportation to develop under private or mixed enterprise.

One of the major consequences of this early economic structure was the development of "metropolis-hinterland" distinctions in Canada which continue to account for regional conflicts. It was in the metropolis, such as Montreal and Toronto, that merchants, bankers, and capitalists were (and remain) concentrated. They profited from the sale of staples provided, with relatively little reward, by workers of the hinterland (the Maritimes and Western Canada). Thus began the regional disparities which today still account for the confrontations and conflicts in Canada, including the numerous movements toward separation in the history of Canada's hinterland. (The case of Quebec is a variation on this theme). It should be pointed out, however, that it was not simply a matter of the existence of these staples which were in popular demand in Europe, but also, the vigorous and contrived efforts by merchant groups in France, England, and Canada to encourage and promote the massive exports of these staples *for their own gain*. One of the major consequences of this was, and remains, the development of Canadian dependency – beginning with France, continuing with Great Britain, and now with the United States. A fuller explanation of the metropolis-hinterland concept is provided by Davis (1971: 6-32) and in Part One of this book (see, especially, the essay by Glenday).

This brief review of related ideological perspectives on the role of power in the structure and change of societies, as developed by some theorists and researchers in Canada, provides some idea of the considerable range in theoretical approaches. Additional approaches to the study of this topic are suggested by the other authors. Further discussion of the relationship between social science and ideology, especially as it pertains to Canadian studies, can be found in Marchak (1975), Johnson (1974), Teeple (1972), Davis (1971), and Horowitz (1966).

REFERENCES

Clark, S. D.
  1942 *The Social Development of Canada.* Toronto.
  1959 *Movements of Political Protest in Canada; 1640-1840.* Toronto.
  1968 *The Developing Canadian Community.* 2nd ed. Toronto.
Clement, Wallace
  1975 *The Canadian Corporate Elite: An Analysis of Economic Power.* Toronto.

Davis, Arthur K.
1971 "Canadian Society and History as Hinterland Versus Metropolis," in Richard J. Ossenberg, ed., *Canadian Society: Pluralism, Change, and Conflict.* Scarborough, Ontario.

Durkheim, Emile
1893 *De la division du travail social: Etude sur l'organisation des societes superieures.* Paris. (Published in English in 1933: *The Division of Labor in Society,* trans. George Simpson. New York.)
1938 *The Rules of Sociological Method,* ed. George E. G. Catlin and trans. Sarah A. Soloway. New York. (Originally published in French in 1895.)

Horowitz, Gad
1966 "Conservatism, Liberalism and Socialism in Canada," *Canadian Journal of Economics and Political Science,* XXXIII, 2 (May).

Innis, Harold A.
1956 *The Fur Trade in Canada.* Toronto. (Originally published in 1930.)

Johnson, Leo A.
1974 *Poverty in Wealth.* Toronto.

Marchak, P.
1975 *Ideological Perspectives on Canada.* Toronto.

Marx, Karl, and Friedrich Engels
1964 *The Communist Manifesto,* ed. Joseph Katz and trans. Samuel Moore. New York. (Originally published in German in 1848.)

Mosca, Gaetano
1939 *The Ruling Class,* trans. Hannah D. Kahn. New York.

Myers, Gustavus
1972 *A History of Canadian Wealth.* Toronto. (Originally published in Chicago in 1914).

Pareto, Vilfredo
1935 *The Mind and Society,* Vol. IV, ed. Arthur Livingston and trans. Andrew Bongiorno and Arthur Livingston. New York. (Reprinted in Talcott Parsons *et al.,* eds., *Theories of Society: Foundations of Modern Sociological Theory,* New York 1965.)

Porter, John

1965 *The Vertical Mosaic: An Analysis of Social Class and Power in Canada.* Toronto.

Ryerson, Stanley B.

1960 *The Founding of Canada: Beginnings to 1815.* Toronto.

1968 *Unequal Union: Roots of Conflict in the Canadas.* Toronto.

1972 "Introduction," in Gustavus Myers, *A History of Canadian Wealth.* Toronto.

Teeple, Gary, ed.

1972 *Capitalism and the National Question in Canada.* Toronto.

PART I
Political Economy:
The Dynamics of Change

EDITOR'S INTRODUCTION

The study of political economy is essentially the study of the interrelationships between political and economic structures and processes, and can be approached from the perspectives of any of the social sciences, and from any ideological position. During the pre-Marxist study of political economy, the subject was more or less considered as a "given" – the inevitably and naturally balanced and socially beneficial interdependence between the economy and the polity; indeed, a basic requirement for human survival. And, until recently, this relatively static and conservative approach has dominated studies of political economy, in spite of the Marxist critique which did not find its way into the mainstream of (Western) sociology largely because of its dominant emphasis on the perspective of order theory.

In recent years, however, there has been an important change, largely because of the recognition by some sociologists and other social scientists that "culture" and "social organization" were not in themselves satisfactory explanations for the obvious persistence of power inequalities and ongoing social-class conflicts. In a sense, then, the "causal" framework for human behaviour has been "turned-around": Social institutions, and, indeed, all aspects of social behaviour are viewed as largely a *consequence* of economic and political structures and processes. This, of course, raises the inevitable question of who controls such structures and processes.

The first step is to identify those who have the power to determine the structures and processes of political economy, and who thereby have indirect but significant power over the lives of the majority of the powerless in society. In conjunction with this endeavour, an attempt must be made to uncover the motivations of those in power in bringing about a certain form and quality of political economy. In this connection, the basic questions of "who controls?" and "for whom?" present themselves, and efforts must be made to provide some answers.

Both Glenday and Willox address these and related questions and issues in discussing the political economy of Canada – as it has been, and as it is becoming. They also discuss the sociological relevance of the control over political and economic structures by the few, and, in conclusion, consider certain recent trends in Canadian society that suggest a growing awareness among Canadians of the potential for more equitable participation and therefore greater equality in the policies and decisions affecting the political economy.

There is basic agreement between Glenday and Willox about the existence of a power-elite – essentially those who hold enormous economic power and consequent political influence. Glenday, in tracing the historical evolution of this elite, discusses some of the social consequences for Canadians in general, while Willox, although concerned about similar consequences, focuses on the evolution and contemporary status of Canada's labour movements; the reader, however, can infer from his discussion some of the related consequences for Canadians in general.

Glenday's fundamental argument is that the origin and growth of Canada's power elite must be seen in the context of this country's historical dependency status, where the *maintenance of dependency* has been beneficial to the continued survival of a power-elite. The struggle for power, according to Glenday, was the struggle for control over the extraction and export of Canada's staples and the maintenance of Canada's "hinterland" status in the context of international commercial trade. The success of the traditional commercial elite was at the expense of the development of a vital indigenous manufacturing sector, and the social consequences have been seen in the context of a consequently depressed opportunity for employment and upward social mobility for Canadians. It may be added that the alleged "conservatism" of Canadians is not so much a consequence of their values antithetical to development, but a recognition of the lack of opportunities for meaningful advancement in a society whose economic system continues, in essence, to impel Canadians to continue to be hewers of wood and drawers of water. Even though they may wear the uniforms of white-collar workers, they are basically the administrators of the exchange of our raw materials for the far more expensive imported finished products.

Glenday also discusses the historical and contemporary political-economic bases for regional inequalities in power. Confederation, according to Glenday, was not so much a victory for Canadians as a whole as it was for the entrenchment of the traditional commercial elite, who saw in the confederation of hinterland areas, including Western Canada and the Maritimes, the enormous possibilities of capital expansion for the commercial enterprises based in central Canada. But, Canada's economy was and remains dependent on the demand for and the export of raw materials (fish, forest products, wheat, minerals). Any changes in demand directly affect the political economy of the hinterlands. Thus, coal and fish in the Maritimes, while at one time holding a promise for the further enrichment of the commercial elite, declined in world demand, and the region became virtually redundant to the "metropolis-hinterland" basis of Canada's central political economy. The social costs have been enormous, as the traditional Maritime way of life has eroded and not yet been replaced by a viable economic alternative, which may have been possible had there been more interest in both manufacturing and the active promotion and modernization of the natural resources of the Maritimes. If Canada's economic elite had been less passive in responding to world market demands by neglecting fish and forest products at a time when wheat and minerals were in greater demand, the Maritimes may have sustained economic growth and, consequently, greater social vitality. But, it has been a matter of trading-off one hinterland area against another, depending on the whims of market demands. What, one could ask, happens when the demand for *all* of our staples decreases? And, why is it that we allow so few to affect so vitally our destiny, simply because dependency is vital to their survival?

Another aspect of Glenday's essay is the extent to which our political structure and processes have been influenced for foreign (predominantly American) economic domination. He suggests that there are definite indications that political parties in Canada have increasingly mirrored the political parties of the United States and that, indeed, we are rapidly advocating a republican or presidential system of "democracy." Certainly, there is little doubt that successive governments in Canada in recent decades, and especially the Liberal Party, have opted for continentalism, with its obvious political consequences for Canada's economic and political autonomy. The Conservative Party, it must be

added, has not proposed an alternative to this continentalist drift.
The analysis and evaluation made by Willox is even more
ominous. He agrees with Glenday that Canadians are in a particularly vulnerable position because of our dependency, but adds
that there has been class conflict in Canada, expressed especially
by the labour unions (beginning with Quebec). This conflict is a
potential counterbalance to the increasing monopolistic interna-
tional-corporate control over Canada's political economy.
Willox's thesis is ominous in the sense that there has been and
continues to be a *contrived* effort by the economic elite, in concert
with the political elite, to curtail the limits of democracy in Canada. As an integral part of the international capitalist market,
Canada is involved in the vicious and reciprocal cycle of
accelerating technological competition that requires accelerating
investment capital at the expense of continuing or strengthening
social services. In fact, this cycle contributes to a steadily declining standard of living. The more that capital is invested in technology, the more that tax concessions must be made to the corporations involved in technology to encourage even further
investment; the consequence is heavier taxation of individuals in
order to assure the survival of corporations which, by investing
in technology, decrease the number of labour-intensive jobs. The
net effect is increasing unemployment and heavier taxation for
the average Canadian.

In recognition of this harsh reality, according to Willox, the
labour unions are beginning to become increasingly militant.
Because efforts to co-opt them into a triumvirate corporatism
(business, labour, and government) have failed, the unions are
increasingly portrayed by the government and the media (controlled by the economic elite) as subversive and deviant in an
attempt to make them appear as the villains in the eyes of the Canadian public. The portrayal by Willox is indeed frightening,
especially his description of Canada's involvement in and support of the Trilateral Commission (North America, Japan, and
Western Europe) which, in its 1975 publication, *The Crisis of
Democracy*, advocates more controls over "excessive" democracy,
including the curtailing of the power of unions (what other
group is there to represent the powerless?), *and*, unbelievably,
the power of the mass media. Also advocated is the reduction of

education, because the educated may aspire to more than is available and in their frustration may become radical critics of the "legitimate" established order. It is in the context of Canada's involvement in the technological-competitive syndrome, in addition to the added burden of maintaining an increasingly vulnerable economy based on export of variably demanded raw materials, that attempts by government and the private media to support legitimacy for "law and order" can be understood. In spite of these attempts, as Willox suggests, the militance of unions will accelerate as members clearly see that their objective conditions are deteriorating. This will have an effect on the public at large.

CHAPTER TWO

Unity in Diversity:
The Political Economy of
Subordination in Canada*
by Daniel Glenday

This paper will be addressed to answering three related questions. First, in what economic sectors do Canadian capitalists predominate; are they in commanding positions in all areas of the national economy or does their role vary according to the historical function Canada has played within successive developments of the world economy? In order to tackle this question adequately, recourse will be made to sketching the historical development of the Canadian economic elite with the aim of uncovering their past and present function as a dominant class. Related to this, the development of the Canadian federal state will be outlined to reinforce the historical analysis by suggesting that the central political body protects indigenous capitalist "turf" only in those sectors where the economic elite predominates.

My second concern, upon identifying which of the economic sectors Canadian capitalists occupy, will be with how foreign ownership and control of selected corporations "fit" into Canadian corporate society. Third, and of equal importance, this paper will delve into some of the social and political consequences which stem from the dominant social classes in Canada.** One of my concerns here will be with the suggestion that upward

---

*I am grateful to the following people who read and commented on an earlier version of this paper: Dick Ossenberg, Laureen Snider, Gary Cake, Richard Simeon, and Hugh Thorburn.

**Certain other consequences have already been examined in Daniel Glenday, Hubert Guindon, and Allan Turowetz., eds., *Modernization and the Canadian State* (Toronto, 1978), especially in the sections entitled "The Impact of the Multinational Corporation" and "Regionalism and Community."

mobility for Canadians within economic institutions dominated by Canadian capitalists is relatively limited when compared with opportunities for career advancement in subsidiaries of corporations controlled in the United States. Finally, some attention will be given to a hypothesis that will be referred to as the continentalization of Canadian politics.

INTRODUCTION

The analytical framework of this paper contains the approach to the study of Canadian society that has been labelled "Canada's most distinctive contribution to political economy," namely, the "staple theory of economic growth" (Watkins, 1967: 49).* A "staple" is a "product with a large natural resource content . . . which does not require elaborate processing involving large quantities of labour or rare skills . . . which will bear transport charges and is in international demand" (Caves and Holton, 1959: 31). Examples of staples in Canadian history include fish, furs, timber, pulp and paper, minerals, and, of some considerable importance today, oil.

The staples theory contains the fundamental assumption that staple exports "are the leading sector of the economy and set the pace for economic growth" (Watkins 1967: 53). For example, in the analysis of the cod industry, Innis argued that the nature of the staple demanded, at best, only semi-permanent settlements, whereas the fur trade required the permanent establishment of traders, voyageurs, missionaries, the military, and various other adjunct colonial institutions. Therefore, the historical development of Canadian society can be analysed as the history of successive staple exports beginning with fish and furs and culminating today with the new staples of minerals, oil, and natural gas. A variant of this type of historical stages approach will be entertained in this paper.

*The "staples theory" is acknowledged to have been developed as a model of economic growth by the Canadian economic historian, Harold A. Innis. See, for example, his *Problems of Staple Production in Canada* (Toronto, 1933); *The Fur Trade in Canada: An Introduction to Canadian Economic History* (Toronto, 1930); and *The Cod Fisheries: The History of an International Economy* (Toronto, 1940).

Each staple in the history of Canadian society has required increasing amounts of capital before the resource could be profitably exploited. Richard Caves has added a further dimension to the staples theory which will bear on the analysis to follow. He has argued that because each new staple demands larger amounts of capital, there must be "extraregional or foreign borrowing (with no incentive for local saving), absentee ownership and no contribution to the supply of local entrepreneurial talent or profit available for local reinvestment" (1965: 433-4).

In summary, the staples theory is a theory of economic growth based on the exploitation of natural resources. It is a theory of international trade grounded on an unequal partnership between nations in which one of the partners is a passive reactor to the economic demands for raw materials of the other (e.g., the French demand for furs created the colony of New France, and the British demand for timber made Canada "Great Britain's woodyard"). The staples theory also suggests that for the host country, that is, the country where the natural resources are to be exploited, there will be little need for "large quantities of labour or rare skills." It will be a nation characterized by an "entrepreneurial gap" that will be filled by importing ever larger amounts of capital, technology, and skilled labour to exploit even further new staples for export. The deepening of this historical process would continue so long as there is international demand for the staples the host country happens to be endowed with.

A marked deficiency in the overall staples theory, at least as far as sociologists are concerned, is the initial absence of a theory of social class in the approach. Recent attempts have been made with remarkable success on including a social-class dimension to the staples approach (see Watkins, 1973; Watkins, 1976; Resnick, 1977). Still, a class and staple theory of Canadian society is not yet fully developed. For the ensuing discussion, therefore, it must be assumed that the dynamics of social class within a society represent the historical struggle for power from which one class wins out at the expense of others. The staples theory represents a framework within which the particulars of this struggle may be understood.

I THE EARLY PERIOD

The French Regime

The characteristics of the dominant economic elite in Canada have undergone numerous changes during the elite's existence of at least two hundred fifty years, 1729-1979 (Nish, 1968). Yet, internal changes took place and were consonant with external alternations in the colony or nation's leading staple exports. Fish and furs were the staple trades upon which both the French and English regimes were nurtured. During the French regime, the growth of Quebec City and later on Montreal was linked to the expansion deeper and deeper into the North American continent of the trade in beaver and other animal furs (Innis, 1970; Ouellet, 1966).

Before the Conquest in 1763, the French during the first half of the eighteenth century had over-extended themselves in the continent. Trading posts had been established as far west as the Saskatchewan River and as far south as the mouth of the Mississippi River. Even though the French fur-trading networks were remarkably efficient, the vulnerability of the system rested on the relative military weakness of France as compared to England's naval superiority and on the high transportation costs of the luxury staple which New France was dependent on. All of these factors constituted elements in the competition between the French and English empires over control of the continent. As a result, the French colonial social structure was characterized by a merging of commercial with political interests. These developments are succinctly noted by Hugh Aitken:

Military support for French traders in the interior, the construction of fortified trading posts at critical focuses of fur-trade routes, and continuous though inadequate subsidization of the colony on the St. Lawrence reflected this merging of commercial and imperial destinies. Imperial expansion in North America and effective defence against the encroachments of rival empires required an alliance of business and political resources and strategies. (1965: 499)

In addition, rivalry with England and its Atlantic seaboard colonies during the eighteenth century over the West Indies trade in sugar and rum forced France to consolidate even further its interests in North America. Attempts were made to establish a beach-head in Nova Scotia and a military presence at Louisbourg in order to compete with England's triangular trade–France, New France, and the West Indies versus England, New England, and the West Indies (Nish, 1968). The weight of her North American empire proved to be too much for France. and as a result she was unable to maintain her hold in either the North Atlantic seaboard or the St. Lawrence Basin. Consequently, England won out over France and became the sole political, economic, and military force in North America. The Conquest also meant the subordination of the former French colonial settlement to English commercial and military interests (Ryerson, 1963).

The British North American Colony

THE PROVINCIAL POLITICAL ECONOMIES

The presence of one dominant power bloc in North America (i.e., England) instead of two, coupled with England's inability to satisfy competing interests between its recently established Quebec merchants and their New England counterparts over dividing the continental fur trade (i.e., the Quebec Act), culminated in open hostilities and concluded with the political independence of the New England colonies. The outcome of an exodus from the newly created United States of America of those sympathetic to the British connection (i.e., the United Empire Loyalists) led to the establishment of agricultural settlements in parts of New Brunswick, Nova Scotia, the Eastern Townships, and Ontario. A little later, the Maritime provinces, but especially Nova Scotia, would try to compete with the newly-created Atlantic seaboard nation (i.e., the United States of America) for control over the triangular trade with England, the West Indies, and North America. And, just as the French had earlier lost out to England, the British Atlantic seaboard colonies would eventually lose out to their rival American region. The British Atlantic region during the nineteenth century, which included Newfoundland, Prince Edward Island, New Brunswick and Nova Scotia, experienced a history of increasing colonial integration with Great Britain. In the words of Harris and Warkentin: "More than anywhere else in British North America, towns with overseas connections had a vital role in opening avenues of economic opportunity, especially to the West Indies and the United States. Yet this sense of access also encouraged a colonial attachment to Britain. . . . " (1974: 169)

In addition to its historical dependence on England, the region's poor endowment in natural resources together with the colonial attachment created an unfavourable environment for the economic development of the region. Harris and Warkentin explain:

> This is a very complex region. It has no unifying configuration of physical features, and even the surrounding sea provides a matrix rather than a focus. There is no centralization of economic activity, no rich heartland. If there is any unity, it is a unity of mutual problems arising from the attempt to wrest from modest resources a standard of living roughly equivalent to that of the rest of Canada and the United States. . . . (1974: 170)

The decline in the continental demand for furs was partially compensated for by a shift to squared timber during the first quarter of the nineteenth century. The fear on Britain's part of losing her continental sources of supply, coming as it did on the heels of the Napoleonic wars, created new opportunities for growth in British North America based on a new staple export. The timber trade helped open up the frontier in New Brunswick, Quebec, and southern Ontario to lumber magnates. In addition, the cleared land in the colony gave rise to agricultural settlements whose activities ranged from subsistence to dairy farming and wheat production.

Each province by the middle of the nineteenth century was integrated into the sphere of British imperial influence, but for different reasons and with different consequences. The Atlantic region was outward looking and hoped to achieve an "entrepot" status.* Upper Canada was establishing an agricultural community and also served as a potential military presence against

---

*An entrepot, as defined by Frederick L. Nussbaum, is a "transfer point . . . in which goods arrive, not to be sold, but only to be transshipped." *A History of the Economic Institutions of Modern Europe* (New York, 1968), p. 202.

American westward expansion into British North America. The French-speaking and Catholic population of Lower Canada became an enclave within the imperial orbit and only marginally participated in the economic activities of the St. Lawrence Basin (e.g., seasonal employment in the timber trade). Innis and Easterbrook aptly characterized the contrasting political economies of the Maritime and the central provinces during the first two-thirds of the nineteenth century when they remarked that

> Different regions then turned to the exploitation of different resources. (Western Canada and the Pacific coastal strip carried on with the fur trade.) Nova Scotia concentrated on its fisheries. The financial interests of Quebec and Montreal, with their London connections, shifted to the white and red pine of the St. Lawrence area, the adjacent sections of the Canadian Shield, and New Brunswick. (1965: 442)

In summary, there was little economic integration between the various regions except perhaps at the level of the economic elite, who were all British subjects, Protestant, and lived off the profits garnered from the staple trades, at this time consisting essentially of furs, timber, and related primary industries. This was a mercantile elite, one might add, whose economic interests were dominated by such concerns as finance and transportation – two important linkages to the staple exports. Finance in the form of capital was necessary not only for the initial investment in the exploitation of the staple, but also in the construction of appropriate transportation facilities to get the staple out of the colony. Since transportation has been and remains an important industry in Canada, we must venture back, at least into the last century, to situate more properly the evolution of this industry and the relation, if any, Canada's economic elite exercised in structuring its development. Our next concern will then be with the problem of creating and locating sources of capital and the manner in which the commercial elite "solved" this problem.

TRANSPORTATION

The nineteenth century in central Canada can be roughly divided into two periods. The first half of the century concentrated on the building of canals as the means to efficiently transport Canada's staples to England and to facilitate the transportation of military personnel and equipment in the face of possible hostilities from our southern neighbour (e.g., War of 1812). The second period continued the bias in favour of transporting staples and enhancing imperial defense of British North America, but the means of effecting these goals shifted to the building of a transcontinental railroad. And, in both these periods, commercial expansion was under the direction of a mercantile elite based in Montreal. According to Hugh Aitken:

This was the expansionism of a commercial economy, whose potentialities for development were conceived as lying *not* so much *in production* as in trade. . . . Certainly in central Canada in this period few conceived of the future of the economy as lying in either manufacturing or a continued expansion of agricultural settlement. The key to the development of central Canada was thought to lie in trade. . . . in attracting down the St. Lawrence corridor the exports and imports of the American midwest. This was the final goal of Montreal's commercial ambitions. (1967: 199; italics mine)

The Rebellion of 1837-38 notwithstanding and indeed as a result of its failure, the commercial elite with its ties to London financial interests used the colonial state to further its own economic goals. The Act of Union (1840) served just those ends. It possessed all the characteristics of "a bankers' constitution." It consolidated assets, which meant that Upper Canada's large debt was merged with Lower Canada's small debt so that "the construction of the St. Lawrence waterway (could be) undertaken with purely public funds, contrary to the interests of agriculture and commerce in Canada East" (Dubuc, 1966: 118). Or, in the words of Innis and Easterbrook,

The entrepreneurial interests won out . . . and cleared away the obstacles to strong government support of transportation developments. The canal era of the 1840's reflected the faith of its promoters in the ability of the St. Lawrence system to carry to the seaboard not only the products of Canada but those of the expanding United States Middle West as well. (1965: 443)

Even though the attempt to make the St. Lawrence system the "chief continental artery of trade" failed, the reaction of the colonial commercial elite was not abandonment of expansion based on trade and a shift of priorities into promoting indigenous industrial development. Central Canada's role as an "entrepot" for transporting goods to and from the American midwest was to persist even after Confederation. Attention would then turn to the prairie provinces, which were to become central Canada's hinterland in the continued commercial expansion of the Dominion. Instead of canals, it would be with a transcontinental railroad that these hopes and aspirations of Canada's economic elite for commercial expansion could be fulfilled.

Thus, the history of Canada up until Confederation and the building of the transcontinental railroad were characterized by little in the way of economic integration between the various provinces. Each province or region specialized in particular staple exports that tied it as an enclave into Great Britain's colonial nexus. One of the integrating factors for British North America was the homogeneous character of the economic elite as evidenced by its virtual ethnic purity (i.e., Anglo-Saxon) and its predominance in commercial endeavours tied to the various staple exports. Another was the historical continuity from the French regime to Confederation of using the power of the state to assist weakly developed indigenous economic interests. In both colonial New France and British North America certain economic classes were not squeamish about using a non-market mechanism, namely the state, to advance and maintain purely market objectives.

II CONFEDERATION

Confederation represented the first step in a three-stage plan to further entrench the commercial elite in Canada. The document known as the British North America Act was as much a fiscal and commercial tract as it was a political tract. Except for the territorial expansion of the Dominion to include New Brunswick and Nova Scotia, the substance of the BNA Act did not appreciably alter the designated powers of the state established with the

Act of Union in 1840 (Stevenson, 1977: 74; Dubuc, 1966: 114). The integration of the Maritime provinces of Nova Scotia and New Brunswick was little more than an extension of the solution worked out earlier with the Act of Union: by "consolidating debts and populations, the ability to borrow [in 1867] was increased and the economy was given new life through investment in transportation" (Dubuc, 1966: 115). Although moulded to best serve the interests of a commercial elite, the BNA Act did provide certain "immediate economic advantages" for the nation as a whole, including the breaking up of each province's isolation and the creation of "a greater power with which to face the United States; it lightened the public debt burden of each [province], and increased the credit rating of the whole in the international capital market" (Dubuc, 1966: 115).

Where the activity of the commercial elite required political protection, those "functions represented by jurisdiction over railways, shipping, money and banking, the tariff and major public works were retained in Ottawa where they were already being performed prior to 1867" (Stevenson, 1977: 75). The provinces were left with jurisdiction over education, hospitals, charities, municipal government, property, civil rights, marriage, land, and natural resources. All of these provincial functions were considered, at the time, to be of minor significance to the overall interests of the indigenous commercial elite. The BNA Act placed the provinces in such a subordinate position that they did not have enough sources of revenue to meet their own expenses and therefore had to rely on the generosity of the federal government to provide them with annual subsidies. The importance of the last two areas, land and natural resources as contained in Section 109 of the BNA Act, would only acquire prominence in the twentieth century. In the words of Garth Stevenson:

In 1867, Section 109 seemed relatively unimportant. Mining was almost non-existent. . . . Forestry was important only in New Brunswick. . . . The technological developments that gave economic significance to sprucewood pulp, nickel, hydroelectric power, oil, and natural gas still lay in the future. Most of the land suitable for agriculture in the original provinces had already passed into private ownership. (1977: 76-7)

The consolidation of political power within a central but still colonial state structure was meant to increase the public finance coffers that later would be used to assist in borrowing on the London bond market. Credit extended in this manner to the Canadian state would assist in further expanding the "privileged sector" of the newly created political economy; namely, railroads. The kernel of this grand design has been aptly depicted by Alfred Dubuc:

> It was precisely the interest groups associated with the railroads which inspired Confederation. Alexander Tilloch Galt and George Etienne Cartier were at the same time administrators of the Grand Trunk Railway Company and members of the Canadian cabinet. In England, Watkin, president of the Grand Trunk, and Baring, banker to both the Grand Trunk and the Canadian government, became instrumental in working out with the Imperial government the political institutions capable of facilitating their investments. It was this same banker, Baring, who had financed the union of the two Canadas in 1840 as well as the great investments in the St. Lawrence waterway from 1842 to 1848. Confederation, like the Union, was also an answer to the problems of public finance confronting the British colonies of North America. (1966: 114-5)

Confederation, then, provided both the political and fiscal means whereby the commercial elite would be capable of maintaining their dominant position in the colonial political economy. Control of the central state and the building of a transcontinental railroad represented two of the necessary stages which would result in the entrenchment of the commercial elite. The historical fact that the construction of the Canadian Pacific Railway would be delayed for over a decade does not detract from the argument advanced above. It still remained an important pillar in the overall strategy of the commercial elite for economic development in Canada. The final cornerstone became the National Policy of 1878-79.

The National Policy
The foundation of the National Policy consisted of a series of prohibitive tariffs on imported goods. On the one hand, it was a declaration of economic independence (Underhill, 1960). It was also a "fiscal instrument designed" to raise revenue for the federal treasury (Naylor, 1975: 53). Another aim of the protective tariff was to secure jobs for Canadians by enticing foreign capital to invest in the building of factories on the other side of the protective tariff wall. Thousands upon thousands of Canadians at this time were moving south to seek employment in the expanding factories of the eastern and midwestern United States. An important problem for the Canadian federal state was how to create an economic environment favourable to industrial development and, therefore, create employment opportunities *in Canada* for those Canadians who would otherwise move south to look for work. The issue and its resolution, the National Policy, led to the establishment of branch plants of United States manufacturers on Canadian soil and thereby opened the door to the progressive expansion of American capital into Canada.* In addition to providing employment, an important influence pushing U. S. investors to build branch plants in Canada was the desire to gain access to British Empire markets that otherwise would have been closed to them. They could expand their markets by operating in Canada behind a protective tariff wall and thus could supply not only Canada with manufactured

---

*Stephen Scheinberg (1978: 85) has aptly summarized the factors which led to the promotion of United States direct investment in Canada. "The branch plants were established for several reasons. At the most general level there was the expectation of profit ... This took two important forms. First there was the protective tariff, which raised costs for some firms south of the border and led them to solve the problem by producing inside the Canadian market. A second stimulus was the Canadian patent law. The Acts of 1872 and 1903 compelled American manufacturers to establish Canadian branches, license a Canadian manufacturer, or forgo the Canadian market ... A third incentive was the British Preference, which lured some manufacturers north with the promise of competing in the empire's broad markets. As "Canadian" producers, the American corporations were entitled to the imperial tariff preferences established in 1897. Finally, Canada's magnetism emanated not only from Ottawa and the federal government. Towns and cities competed with one another in their efforts to attract American investments. Free land, tax relief and peculiar local features were the attractions held out to the American businessmen."

goods but also other countries within Great Britain's sphere of influence. Canada's special status as a member of the British Empire meant that she could act as a "launching pad" into the very large British Empire markets.

After Confederation and the National Policy, there followed the building of the transcontinental railroad and settlement of the Prairie provinces, with the establishment there during the first quarter of the twentieth century of a monocultural hinterland whose principal function was to supply an agricultural cash crop (wheat) for sale on world markets. In addition to the above, the western Canadian wheat economy was also "designed to promote industrial development within central Canada and to give central Canadian industry a preferred or monopoly position as supplier of the prairie region" (Macpherson, 1953: 7).

Tied to the National Policy, the building of the transcontinental railway, and settlement in the Canadian west were the discovery and exploitation of natural resources along the perimeter of the Canadian Shield in the wake of railroad construction through the Prairies and the Rocky Mountains (see Mackintosh, 1939: 24). These new staples of pulp and paper, oil and natural gas, and minerals became one of two economic sectors within which United States direct investment would be nurtured.* The other, as we have seen, was in the manufacturing sector, which came as a result of the National Policy and was aimed at providing jobs and supplying the Canadian and British Commonwealth markets.

One of the motives behind American direct investment in the Canadian resource industries was "the desire to secure access to raw materials that are either not available, or available only at higher real costs, in the United States" (Aitken, 1961: 85). The extent to which the National Policy, acting as a political device to

*The Report of the Task Force on the Structure of Canadian Industry entitled *Foreign Ownership and the Structure of Canadian Industry*, or, more commonly known as the Watkins Report, distinguished between direct and portfolio investment by arguing that direct investment entails "legal control of the asset ... (so that) foreign direct investment ... represents capital investment in a branch plant or subsidiary corporation abroad where the investor has voting control of the concern" (1968: 418). Portfolio investment, on the other hand, "is involved where the form of the investment (in bonds and loans) or the amount (in voting stock) *does not involve legal control of the asset*" (1968: 419).

facilitate the expansion of branch plants in Canada of U. S. manufacturing corporations and the desire on the part of U. S. capitalists "to secure access to raw materials" by investing in Canada's natural resources, can be said to have succeeded can be garnered from the statistics of foreign capital investment in Canada. Table 1 depicts both the amount and percentage of the total investment picture in Canada by nationality for the years 1913 to 1926. The year 1922 represents the turning point, after which United States investment in Canada exceeded that of the United Kingdom. Of added significance is the classification of invest-

Table 1

Foreign Capital Investment in Canada, Selected Year Ends
(millions of Canadian dollars)

	UNITED KINGDOM		UNITED STATES	
Year	Total	Percentage	Total	Percentage
1913	2,793	75	780	21
1916	2,840	66	1,307	30
1918	2,729	60	1,630	36
1920	2,577	53	2,128	44
1922	2,464	47	2,593	50
1924	2,372	42	3,094	55
1926	2,637	44	3,196	53

SOURCE: M. C. Urquhart and K. A. H. Buckley, *Historical Statistics of Canada* (Toronto, 1965), p. 169.

ment into Canada. Table 2 gives an indication of the trend away from portfolio to direct investment. The extent of direct investment as a proportion of portfolio capital becomes especially pronounced in the post-World War II period. And, since the war, if attention is given to the sectors within which foreign control predominates, accentuation of an earlier trend is in evidence with the United States making up a significant proportion of total foreign control in the manufacturing, petroleum and natural gas, and the mining and smelting industries in Canada (see Table 3).

There is little argument among Canadian historians as to the commercial character of the economic elite in the nineteenth century. A debate does exist as to whether this character persisted with only minor qualifications into the twentieth century. Tom

Table 2
Foreign Capital Invested in Canada, Selected Year Ends
1867-1974
(millions of dollars)

	1867	1900	1913	1939	1952	1960	1965	1969	1974
U.K. direct	—	65	200	366	544	1,535	2,013	2,426	3,525
portfolio	185	1,000	2,618	2,110	1,340	1,824	1,485	1,239	1,645
Total	185	1,065	2,818	2,476	1,884	3,359	3,498	3,665	5,170
U.S. direct	15	175	520	1,881	4,532	10,549	13,940	19,959	28,996
portfolio	—	30	315	2,270	3,466	6,169	9,365	11,324	15,297
Total	15	205	835	4,151	7,998	16,718	23,305	31,283	44,293
Other direct	—	—	50	49	144	788	1,255	2,039	3,716
portfolio	—	35	147	237	358	1,349	1,449	1,953	3,563
Total	—	35	197	286	502	2,137	2,704	3,992	7,279
Grand total	200	1,305	3,850	6,913	10,384	22,214	29,507	38,940	56,742
U.S. as percentage of total foreign investment	7.5	15.5	21.5	60.0	77.0	75.0	79.0	79.4	77.5
U.S. direct investment as percentage of total investment	7.5	13.4	13.5	27.2	43.6	47.4	47.2	47.9	48.1

SOURCES: Kari Levitt, *Silent Surrender* (Toronto, 1970), p. 66; Statistics Canada, *Canada's International Investment Position* (Ottawa, 1974), p. 33.

Table 3
Foreign Control as a Percentage of Selected Canadian Industries, 1926-1973

Percentage of Total controlled by all non-residents	1926	1939	1948	1963	1968	1973
Manufacturing	35	38	43	60	58	59
Petroleum & natural gas	—	—	—	74	75	76
Mining and smelting	38	42	40	59	68	56
Railways	3	3	3	2	2	2
Other utilities	20	26	24	4	5	7
Total	17	21	25	34	35	35

Percentage of Total controlled by u. s. residents						
Manufacturing	30	32	39	46	46	44
Petroleum & natural gas	—	—	—	62	61	59
Mining and smelting	32	38	37	52	58	45
Railways	3	3	3	2	2	2
Other utilities	20	26	24	4	4	4
Total	15	19	22	27	28	26

SOURCES: Levitt, *Silent Surrender*, p. 61; Statistics Canada, *Canada's International Investment Position*, p. 112.

Naylor represents the main protagonist who argues an historical continuity in the nature of Canada's dominant social class. The debate has not yet been settled but the weight of the evidence appears to point with favour in Naylor's direction. He traces the history of the economic elite beginning with the colonial merchants of the late eighteenth and nineteenth centuries who held control over the various staple exports such as fish, fur, and lumber. He suggests that later on in the nineteenth century, the same *type* of person, if not the same person, was also involved in land speculation and banking and finance.

In his latest work, *The History of Canadian Business: 1867-1914*, Naylor fits his previous analysis, with certain important modifications, into a metropolis-hinterland model. It is Canada's colonial status within the British Empire from the Treaty of Paris to the First World War that gives the dominance of Canada's mercantile class its continuity. The transition from a predominantly agricultural colony to a dependent industrial nation did not witness a reorientation of priorities toward the indigenous development of industrial capitalism as was the case in the United States after the Civil War. On the contrary, industrialization where and when it was pursued by Canadian capitalists was in just those areas that were necessary for the completion of mercantile goals: the iron and steel industry, for example, was developed primarily to meet the needs of the transcontinental railroad. The historical data Naylor marshals to support his theoretical position suggests that up until at least the First World War, Canada was primarily a colony of the British Empire dominated by a mercantile elite tied to the mother country through the export of such staple commodities as fur, timber, and wheat.

By way of a brief summary, Canadian capitalists to this day do not hold commanding positions in all sectors of the Canadian economy. Foreign capitalists, but mainly those based in the United States, are over-represented in the manufacturing, petroleum and natural gas, and mining and smelting industries. Canadian capitalists, on the other hand, are dominant in railways, utilities, and financial institutions. Furthermore, as an analysis of the British North American Act indicates, the federal state represents the political expression of the dominant Canadian capitalist class and at the same time relegates the provinces to a state of virtual subservience. It was with the exploitation of natural resources that the tables began to turn in favour of the provinces, but only to those provinces which had natural resources to exploit. Unfortunately, for example, the Maritime provinces had little to offer in the way of new staples and as a result have lost out for the most part to the economic development and political power that comes from the exploitation of natural resources. Thus, they continue to reflect the subordinate position they had been placed in within the framework of the British North America Act.

III   THE ECONOMIC "FIT"
We now must seek an explanation of the bifurcation between indigenous interests in commercial and financial activity and foreign, mainly United States, preponderance in manufacturing,

Figure 1
How Foreign Owned and Controlled Corporations
Fit into Canadian Corporate Society

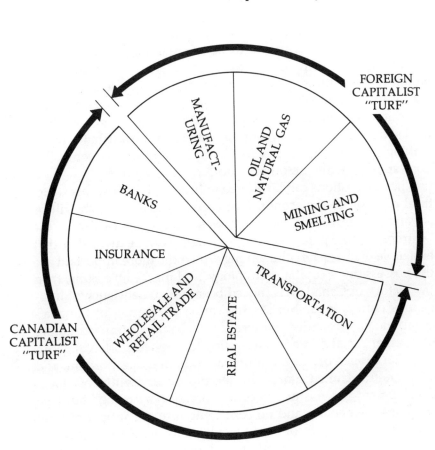

petroleum and natural gas, and mining and smelting. This duality of interests and their fit within Canadian corporate society are illustrated in Figure 1.

As Figure 1 depicts, the economic sectors where Canadian capitalists are preeminent and those where foreign capitalists play a dominant role complement each other. One without the other would not constitute a complete economy in any sense of what makes up a national economy. A nation in the modern world without a manufacturing sector could no more be defined as a total society than a nation without banks. Each contributes to the making of the whole, and in Canada's case one is controlled domestically while the other is not.

What suggestions can be offered to help explain how this structural division of the economy emerged? The one which will be advanced here centres on what was referred to earlier as the "entrepreneurial gap." If entrepreneurship can be defined as that ensemble of characteristics among which the more important are the possession of capital, technology, and marketable skills, then the history of Canada has indeed been one of deficiency of indigenous entrepreneurship. As the earlier exposition of Canada's economic elite revealed, its location in banking, transportation, utilities, and real estate has been tied to staple exports which, in turn, have relied on the metropolitan link: first Great Britain, and later on the United States. Furthermore, the nature of staple development has meant not only "foreign borrowing" but also "absentee ownership and no contribution to the supply of local entrepreneurial talent or profit available for local reinvestment" (Caves, 1965: 433-4). Put differently, this international relationship of dependence on external markets has included dependence on foreign entrepreneurship, be it British or American capital and/or expertise. But there is one very crucial difference, in historical terms, which should be accentuated and represents an important caveat to Richard Caves' contribution to the staples theory.

The existence of an entrepreneurial gap in nineteenth-century Canada was filled by British portfolio capital. Yet, portfolio capital, as earlier noted, did not include ownership of the future assets, be they canals or railroads. Neither was there any necessary concentration of technology and expertise in the metropolitan centre. On the other hand, the entrepreneurial gap in the twentieth century has been fed by direct foreign investment in manufacturing and natural resource industries, primarily from the United States. Direct investment, as earlier defined, entails "legal control of the asset." As such, neither control over the productive units nor control over technology and scarce skills would be located in Canada if foreign sources of direct investment are sought after. It is this aspect, namely, the nature of the capital imported to exploit either markets or new staples, which gives power to Professor Caves' analysis. The present-day result of this as it bears on the lack of processing natural resources in Canada has been described by Pierre L. Bourgault:

We are the world's largest producer of nickel, but we are net importers of stainless steel and manufactured nickel products . . . ; we are the world's second largest producer of aluminum, but we import it in its more sophisticated forms such as . . . precision aluminum parts for use in aircraft; we are the world's largest exporters of pulp and paper, but we import much of our fine paper and virtually all of the highly sophisticated paper, such as backing for photographic film; we are large exporters of natural gas and petroleum, but we are net importers of petrochemicals; and although we are the world's foremost exporter of raw asbestos fibres, we are net importers of manufactured asbestos products. (1972: 51)

This congruence between an indigenous economic elite historically dependent on particular forms of foreign entrepreneurship and the integration of foreign entrepreneurship into the pattern of economic development established by this elite helps to explain the contemporary continentalism of Canada's economy and its political expression in the federal state.*

*The facility of the transition from British dominance to American dominance only could have occurred with the compliance of the federal state. As Clement argues: "The fact of such extensive U.S. investment reflects political decisions to allow and encourage such a pattern of development. The system has emerged not in spite of politicians but because they have permitted it." (1977: 299)

IV   THE CONTINENTALIST DRIFT

The Canadian Economic Elite

What are some of the consequences for Canadian society as a whole which stem from an analysis of the structure of the Canadian economic elite? One, of course, is an elite made up of an indigenous component "boxed in by its own past" and a foreign sector dominated by U. S. control of manufacturing and natural resource industries. Together, these controlling factors link the Canadian economy within a continental sphere of influence. Another consequence and one bearing on our present concern, is the hypothesis raised fifteen years ago by John Porter. In 1965, he wrote that "the evidence" he had gathered on the nature of the economic elite "gives some indication that Canada is not a mobility-oriented society and has had to rely heavily on skilled and professional immigration to upgrade its labour force in periods of industrial growth" (1965: 43). In other words, reliance on foreign entrepreneurship, in this particular case "skilled and professional" labour, had the consequence of decreasing social mobility for Canadian-born citizens. The corollary of this argument would ask: why spend large amounts of money to upgrade the indigenous labour force when it is obviously cheaper to import skilled labour from abroad?

S. D. Clark has recently polemicized against Porter's analysis. Clark has no objection to the historical record, which suggests that Canadian society for most of its history had "isolated from the seats of power a large rural and working class population [because] few opportunities for advancement" were offered to them. But, he does question the evidence of the recent past. Concentrating on the post-Second World War era, Clark speculates that "what emerged after the war was a new Canadian society, one characterized by a widespread movement of people out of rural and unskilled working class levels of the population into middle-class levels" (1976: 58). Clark offers little evidence to support his contention about a middle-class Canada. What is ironic about Clark's hypothesis is that it was precisely the myth of Canada being a middle-class society, even during the post-war period, that John Porter so effectively destroyed by marshalling substantial bodies of evidence.

In a more recent study on economic power in Canada, Wallace Clement tackled much the same problem as John Porter and came up with even more dramatic conclusions. Clement begins by postulating that economic development in Canada "involves changes in the way the economy is organized and controlled; these structural changes recast opportunities available to Canadians for upward mobility and access to power" (1975: 1). Clement proceeds by analysing the issue of mobility in terms of uncovering the mechanisms that facilitate access to the economic elite, and by so doing he intends to provide an "indication of the rigidity of the entire class structure." (1975: 10).

His analysis of the banking institutions, for example, reveals that while some mobility into the ranks of the elite existed, "over the past twenty years it has become restricted with more current executives coming from upper class families, having gone to private schools and university and entered the executive ranks at a much earlier age than was previously the case" (1975: 195). On the other hand, in his investigation of the economic elite in subsidiaries of foreign-controlled corporations the picture is different. These elites, he found, are "both more middle class and more 'meritocratic' than indigenous elite members" (1975: 203).*

While the hypothesis explored above has not yet been exhaustively examined empirically, especially for the post-World War II period, the studies referred to above do point in one direction. Both Porter and Clement based their conclusion on a broad base of data. Each sought to tackle the problem of mobility in Canadian society by concentrating on who gets into the economic elite and why. While Porter did not divide the economic elite into national and foreign sectors and Clement did make such a division, they both came to similar conclusions. Mobility within economic institutions dominated by Canadian capitalists offered limited opportunities for Canadians, and in the recent past it has become even more difficult for individual Canadians to "work their way to the top." Moreover, Clement has provided an interesting twist to the argument by suggesting that the oppor-

---

*In a more recent study, where Clement analysed the nature of the Canadian and United States economic elite, he concluded that "entrance to the economic elite is easier for persons from outside the upper class in the United States than it is in Canada . . . the U.S. elite is more open, recruiting from a much broader class base than is the case in Canada. . . . Moreover, the Canadian elite is so closely knit and drawn from a narrow segment of Canadian society." (1977: 183-84)

tunities for mobility for Canadians are the greatest in the newly created economic elites that are foreign-controlled.

American Influences: Economics and Politics

In a completely different vein is the suggestion that, with the dominance of American capital coming as it did at Great Britain's expense in the early 1920's, the stage was set for the expansion of a continentalist thrust into the Canadian political process. Put differently, the major Canadian political problems began to be defined in terms of continentalist economics and policies particularly after the Second World War, and a political environment in English-speaking Canada was created within which political debate, discussion, and argument directed towards economic nationalism was not encouraged and is today in a steady decline.

It will be recalled that 1922 was the year when American capital investment began to exceed that of Great Britain. One of the early indications of increasing American political influence in Canada came at approximately this point in our history when certain alterations in the structure and practice of Canadian political parties and philosophy were introduced. Ranney and Kendell provide some interesting data on the introduction of American political practice into Canadian politics:

For no readily apparent reason, it [the party organization] has patterned itself upon American rather than British models, so that, we find the Canadians picking their party leaders at national representative party conventions. . . . The Liberal Party, the first to adopt the present system, did so with the avowed purpose of turning it over to representatives of the party's provincial organizations, which presumably could have been done without imitating such other features of the typical American convention as the keynote speech, the written platform, and nominating and seconding speeches. But the first Liberal convention (1919) imitated these features also, and departed from American precedent only by using the secret rather than the open ballot in the nominating process. The Conservatives began holding similar conventions in 1927. (1956: 106)

The point to stress is the timing of the introduction of these practices into Canadian party politics, that is, their close correlation with the encroaching dominance of American economic influence in Canada vis-a-vis the declining dominance of Great Britain. This is not meant to suggest that American influence had only just then arrived on the Canadian political scene. One need only remember Sir John A. Macdonald likening the Conservatives to a Hamiltonian party to belie that notion (Underhill, 1960: 33).

One possible explanation for this early identity with American politics can be seen in the similarities in many of the problems shared by the two countries in the latter half of the nineteenth and the early part of the twentieth centuries, such as western settlement, industrial development, and transportation. Yet, this alone is not sufficient to explain the increasing continentalization of Canadian politics in the second half of the twentieth century, especially since many Canadian political institutions and values had been transplanted from Great Britain. Why didn't these influences endure? Why have they not been cultivated in the Canadian public? The answer to these questions rests, in large measure, with the continentalization of the Canadian economy beginning roughly with the National Policy of 1879, climbing in importance during the first and second quarters of the twentieth century and accelerating in the post-war period.

The significance of the 1922 date centres on establishing some kind of a benchmark from which to gauge the increasing influence of the United States political system as a *lasting contribution* to Canadian politics.* A contemporary and probably more worthy illustration of this phenomenon is provided by Denis Smith,

*Another indication of the influence of the United States on Canadian development is witnessed by the series of academic studies on Canadian-American relations from 1933-1957. The first of these was sponsored by the Carnegie Endowment for International Peace and came under the editorship of Dr. James Shotwell. The original plan included a proposal for forty-five volumes but only twenty-six were eventually completed, in part because some later volumes in the series took a more nationalist (i.e., Canadian) emphasis instead of the continentalist orientation Dr. Shotwell had stipulated as the series' exclusive mandate. For useful discussions of this and related academic influences and manifestations, see Richard Preston (ed.), *The Influence of the United States on Canadian Development* (Durham, North Carolina, 1972), especially the essays by Preston and by Carl Berger.

who has argued that Prime Minister Pierre Elliott Trudeau encouraged the move toward a presidential style of politics in Canada. Smith has pointed out that this trend in Canadian politics predates Pierre Trudeau's tenure but that Trudeau has been the most skilful and effective in adopting this political style (Smith, 1971).*

The expanding American influence in Canadian politics roughly coincided with the demise by the end of the Second World War of Great Britain as the world's economic and political leader. As part of the British imperial nexus, Canada not only borrowed capital and expertise but also political practice and ideas. For example, the idea of "responsible government" in Canada was nonetheless tied to a British monarchy. The tradition of "cabinet solidarity" is similar to that principle in British politics. This is the tradition where all the ministers must be willing to abide by the decisions of the cabinet as a whole and are answerable to parliament for their portfolios. Also, the early recognition (Quebec Act of 1774) of the collective rights of French Canadians to retain their language and religion was legislated by the British parliament.

Further examples might include the development of radical politics in Canada, that is, the CCF and Social Credit, which owed much to the mother country. The political philosophies and many of the people who imbued the Canadian political landscape with radicalism during the 1920's and 1930's came from Great Britain. The demise of Great Britain as an economic and political force in the world, especially after World War II, has also witnessed the decline of political radicalism in Canada. To paraphrase George Grant, populist democracy belonged to the youth of Saskatchewan and Alberta of the 1920's and 1930's, not the youth of today who work for General Motors or Gulf Oil. Ex-

*A curious aside to this tendency of adopting American political practices is provided by Frank Underhill. In the *Toronto Star* (29 October 1970), Underhill remarked: "As for me, while I've wobbled somewhat in my political affiliation in Canadian politics over the last generation, I shall be voting again for Mr. Trudeau. In American politics I have never wobbled; ever since 1936 I have been voting the straight Democratic ticket, and I expect to continue doing so." This personal identification with American electoral politics reveals how far Canadian liberalism has travelled along the continentalist road, at least in terms of how it has been articulated by one of Canada's leading liberal theoreticians.

cept for the brief outburst of student radicalism during the late 1960's, which was itself more of a spillover from the United States than an indigenous criticism of Canadian society and politics, little has been advanced in either the New Democratic Party or the Social Credit Party which could be pointed to as distinctly Canadian. In other words, we cannot point to a contemporary equivalent to the League for Social Reconstruction. Politics, political debate, and questions as to what the society north of the 49th parallel should look like have been drowned in the sea of continentalist arguments and prophecies. The continentalization of politics has meant the demise of a unique brand of Canadian politics marked by Christian socialism and Christian conservatism. Furthermore, the continentalist thrust has become increasingly more legitimate as dissent has either been muzzled (e.g., Diefenbaker and the Waffle) or swamped by continentalist prophecy (e.g., Committee for an Independent Canada and the Science Council of Canada). The fate of the Waffle within the New Democratic Party and the political careers of John Diefenbaker's prairie nationalism and the Committee for an Independent Canada are three of the more outstanding examples of what has happened in English-speaking Canada when political debate around the central theme of economic nationalism has been advanced.

The former was a democratic socialist alternative for Canada within the New Democratic Party that concentrated its political platform on economic nationalism translated into such policies as selective nationalization of natural resource and manufacturing industries. Its fate was expulsion from the party.

John Diefenbaker's prairie nationalism, as George Grant has admirably shown, ran counter to the continentalist economic policies of Canada's economic elite. His fate, and the fate of the Progressive Conservative Party, has been a progressively ineffective political alternative to the Liberals.

Finally, the Committee for an Independent Canada, a loose agglomeration of disaffected businessmen and academics, has concentrated its solution on a form of economic nationalism that would benefit the weakly developed sectors of the Canadian capitalist class. The fate of this committee has been one of increasing irrelevance in the face of continentalist economics and an era when only state-owned enterprises hold out any hope for an independent Canada. Even George Grant, Canada's eminent conservative philosopher, had to admit in one of his more perceptive moments that:

> If Canada was to survive, the cornerstone of its existence was the Great Lakes region. The population in that area was rushing toward cultural and economic integration with the United States. Any hope for a Canadian nation demanded some reversal of the process, and this could only be achieved through concentrated use of Ottawa's planning and control. After 1940, nationalism had to go hand in hand with some measure of socialism. Only nationalism could provide the political incentive for planning; only planning could restrain the victory of continentalism. (1965: 15)

Economic nationalism and socialism in Canada are two sides of the same coin. If political thought entertains economic nationalism, political practice is forced to take on a degree of socialism as a solution. Only the political sectarians on the Left or the politically squeamish of the centre would contradict this simple truth.

CONCLUSION

I have argued that there exists a congruence of vested interests between the Canadian economic elite and foreign-based, but primarily United States, corporations in the natural resource and manufacturing sectors of the Canadian economy; hence, the "unity" in the "diversity" of economic functions performed by capitalists in the Canadian economy. To explain this economic division recourse was made to the historical development of the indigenous economic elite. Upon examination it was suggested that this contemporary division could be explained by postulating that foreign control of natural resource and manufacturing industries filled an "entrepreneurial gap" in the overall corporate structure of Canadian society. Canada's reliance on staple exports for economic growth throughout its history created the conditions for the emergence and persistence of this gap. During the historical period when British influence was dominant, the entrepreneurial gap was filled, for the most part, with British portfolio capital and skilled labour. This "fit" did not lead to the future control, for example, of the transportation and banking institutions by Great Britain. On the other hand, the twentieth century was marked by foreign direct investment in manufacturing, oil and natural gas, and mining and smelting, which replaced the part played by Great Britain in filling the entrepreneurial gap. The nature of direct investment, as earlier shown, does entail external control, which has created its own set of problems for Canadian society.

The two issues or consequences highlighted in this paper reflect the problems generated by the nature of the Canadian economic elite, namely, restricted opportunities for mobility within economic institutions controlled by Canadian capitalists and the continentalization of Canadian politics, which mirrors the continental integration of the Canadian economy. Alternatives to the present state of affairs could begin to be worked out by continuing, politically, to develop the theme of economic nationalism. Furthermore, it has been argued throughout this paper that one of Canada's historical legacies has been state intervention in the economy. If the economic elites, historically, were not squeamish about using the state when it suited them to further their interests, then the economically disadvantaged could use this same instrument to promote a more egalitarian and human society north of the 49th parallel.

REFERENCES

Aitken, Hugh G. J.
1961 *American Capital and Canadian Resources.* Cambridge, Mass.
1965 "Government and Business in Canada: An Interpretation," in John Deutsch, ed., *The Canadian Economy: Selected Readings.* Toronto.
1967 "Defensive Expansion: The State and Economic Growth in Canada," in W. T. Easterbrook and M. H. Watkins, eds., *Approaches to Canadian Economic History.* Toronto.
Bourgault, Pierre L.
1972 *Innovation and the Structure of Canadian Industry.* Science Council of Canada, Special Study No. 23. Ottawa.
Caves, Richard
1965 "Vent for Surplus' Models of Trade and Growth," in Jagdish N. Bhagwati *et al.,* eds., *Trade, Growth and the Balance of Payments: Essays in Honor of Gottfried Haberler.* Chicago.
Caves, Richard, and Richard Holton
1959 *The Canadian Economy: Prospect and Retrospect.* Cambridge, Mass.
Clark, S. D.
1976 *Canadian Society in Historical Perspective.* Toronto.
Clement, Wallace
1975 *The Canadian Corporate Elite.* Toronto.
1977 *Continental Corporate Power.* Toronto.
Dubuc, Alfred
1966 "The Decline of Confederation and the New Nationalism," in P. Russell, ed., *Nationalism in Canada.* Toronto.
Grant, George
1965 *Lament for a Nation.* Toronto.
Harris, R. Cole, and John Warkentin
1974 *Canada Before Confederation.* Toronto.
Innis, Harold A.
1970 *The Fur Trade in Canada.* Toronto.
Innis, Harold A., and W. T. Easterbrook
1965 "Fundamental Historical Elements," in Deutsch, ed., *The Canadian Economy: Selected Readings.* Toronto.

Mackintosh, W. A.
1939 "The Economic Background of Dominion-Provincial Relations," Appendix III to *Report of the Royal Commission on Dominion-Provincial Relations.* Ottawa.
Macpherson, C. B.
1953 *Democracy in Alberta: Social Credit and the Party System.* Toronto.
Naylor, T.
1972 "The Rise and Fall of the Third Commercial Empire of the St. Lawrence," in G. Teeple, ed., *Capitalism and the National Question in Canada.* Toronto.
1975 *The History of Canadian Business, 1867-1914,* 2 vols. Toronto.
Nish, Cameron
1968 *Les Bourgeois-Gentilshommes de la Nouvelle France: 1729-48.* Montreal.
Ouellet, Fernand
1966 *Histoire economique et sociale du Quebec.* Montreal.
Porter, John
1965 *The Vertical Mosaic.* Toronto.
Ranney, Austin, and Willmoore Kendall
1956 *Democracy and the American Party System.* New York.
Resnick, Philip
1977 *The Land of Cain.* Vancouver.
Ryerson, Stanley
1963 *The Founding of Canada.* Toronto.
Scheinberg, Stephen
1973 "Invitation to Empire: Tariffs and American Economic Expansion in Canada," in Glenn Porter and Robert Cuff, eds., *Enterprise and National Development.* Toronto.
Smith, Denis
1971 "President and Parliament: The Transformation of Parliamentary Government in Canada," in Thomas A. Hockin, ed., *Apex of Power.* Scarborough, Ontario.
Stevenson, Garth
1977 "Federalism and the Political Economy of the Canadian State," in Leo Panitch, ed., *The Canadian State: Political Economy and Political Power.* Toronto.
Underhill, Frank

1960 *In Search of Canadian Liberalism.* Toronto.
Watkins, Mel
1967 "A Staple Theory of Economic Growth," in Watkins and Easterbrook, eds., *Approaches to Canadian Economic History.* Toronto.
1973 "Resources and Underdevelopment," in Robert Laxer, ed., *Canada Ltd.: The Political Economy of Dependency.* Toronto.
1976 "Economic Development in Canada," in Immanuel Wallerstein, ed., *World Inequality: Origins and Perspectives on the World System.* Montreal.

CHAPTER THREE

Canadian Labour and the Capital Crisis: The Dynamics of Conflict
by Paul Willox*

The Canadian labour movement is facing a crisis of unparalleled magnitude and intractibility, a crisis which is part of a wider international crisis and whose resolution will decisively affect the quality and even survival of political democracy in Canada. That such a crisis is not the figment of an apocalyptic imagination but is rooted in perceptible structural realities is attested to by an emerging consensus of observers embracing a wide ideological spectrum. Described in a correspondingly wide variety of terminologies, the crisis in question is essentially related to economic dynamics but also is reflective of a complex of evolving cultural values as well as generative of profound political implications. The latter were chillingly spelt out by the Trilateral Commission in its 1975 report, *The Crisis of Democracy*. Citing former West German Chancellor Willy Brandt's prediction that "Western Europe has only 20 or 30 more years of democracy left in it; after that it will slide, engineless and rudderless, under the surrounding sea of dictatorship, and whether the dictation comes from a politburo or a junta will not make that much difference" (Crozier *et al.*, 1975: 2), the Trilateral report warned that governments throughout the Western world committed to sustaining economic expansion will need increasing increments of authority to enforce the allocation of capital, and that ultimately the very

*Paul Willox has taught at Queen's University and the University of British Columbia and is the author of a forthcoming book on Canadian political economy.

survival of democratic political institutions will hang in the balance.

I ECONOMIC DIMENSIONS

The economic roots of the crisis reside in the increasing capital-intensity of industrial production, i.e., the growing amount of capital needed per unit of production. This phenomenon stems in significant measure from the growing technological base of production – a growth continually escalated by the pressures of international competition to gain a competitive edge over one's rivals through the introduction of new technologies to secure lower unit-costs of production. Generally, each attempt to gain a competitive edge through added technology is cancelled out by the introduction of equivalent or even superior technology by rival producers, a development which then forces the initiator of a particular technology to make recourse to additional technology, in turn triggering another round of emulation by competitors. This constant upping of the technological ante can be financed only through a geometric growth of investment capital, which is of such rapidity and magnitude that neither expanded sales nor complete utilization of private sector investment resources is sufficient to cover it. Moreover, as the growing scale of technology occurs in the context of the marketplace's ultimate global limitations, industry's rising capital costs are increasingly unrecoverable even through globally expanded sales of output. In addition, the expanded production generated by widening technology accelerates the depletion of the world's natural resources and in turn feeds back upon the capital-intensity of resource-extraction (as complex new technologies are needed to tap less accessible resources) and upon the consequent costs to all industrial consumers or resources.

While debate continues over the exact dimensions of rising investment needs, there is general agreement that the amounts are astronomical. For example, in 1975 the New York Stock Exchange estimated investment capital needs for the following decade in the U.S. alone at $2.6 trillion, while the American financial publication *Business Week* projected for the same period what it called the "incredible sum" of $4.6 trillion – three times the amount used in the preceding decade (*Sun*: 23 September 1975). Similarly, in March, 1977, Donald Neelands, Chairman of Canada Permanent Trust Company, estimated that Canadian capital needs in the decade 1977-87 would be approximately $850 billion, compared to only $220 billion for the previous decade (*Globe and Mail*: 9 March 1977). Further estimating that $550 billion of the 1977-87 total would be needed by the private sector, Neelands noted that capital needs of such magnitude will necessitate a redistribution of the gross national product:

> Faced with such numbers, the obvious question is whether our economy is capable of meeting the challenge. Given that total output is unlikely to grow in direct proportion to this . . . increase in capital expenditures, it is evident that investment spending will form a larger share of GNP. (*ibid.*)

With regard to the wider implications of the capital crisis, *Business Week* warned on September 22, 1975, initially with reference to its U. S. projections but in words applicable to the entire Western industrial community, that "The obstacles of raising that kind of money . . . are formidable, perhaps insurmountable. But the social and fiscal consequences of not generating sufficient savings to provide money on that scale are not pleasant to contemplate."

The unfolding economic consequences of the emerging crisis have already proven to be momentous. In the first place, the private sector's rising capital costs force it to steadily raise the prices of its products and services, thereby generating a permanent inflation quite distinct from the cyclical inflation analyzed by Keynesian theory. A second effect is found in the growing attempts by producers to at least partially offset rising capital costs by cutting labour costs, a reaction which, along with the impact of intensifying international competition, has resulted in the phenomenon – unpredicted by orthodox economic theory – of "stagflation," i.e., simultaneous increases in unemployment through lay-offs and reduced hirings and in inflation (the unemployment being accentuated further still by the increased numbers of "second breadwinners" forced to seek jobs as a means of offsetting the rising prices of essential goods and services). Thirdly, the private sector throughout the Western world has turned increasingly to government for capital subsidies. In this connection, it is interesting to note that business rhetoric has not yet acknowledged the new realities, a point confirmed by recently retired U. S. Secretary of the Treasury William E. Simon's caustic characterization of business recipients of government aid:

> And always, such gentlemen proclaimed their devotion to free enterprise and their opposition to the arbitrary intervention into our economic life by the state. Except, of course, for their own case, which was always unique and which was justified by their immense concern for the public interest. (quoted in Galbraith, 1978: 18.)

Though their degree of enthusiasm varies, all Western governments are responding favourably with both direct and indirect reallocation of capital from the public sector to the private sector. The resultant pressures on government finances are in turn contributing to a general phenomenon described by many observers as the "fiscal crisis of the state," quite simply, the growing gap between government revenues and government expenditures.

The growing technological base of industrial production also fuels the fiscal crisis of the state through the multitudinous social costs spawned by technology. As Hazel Henderson has noted, such costs frequently are not linked to their actual source:

> We seem unwilling to come to terms with the fact that each increase in the order of magnitude of technological mastery and managerial control requires and inevitably leads to a concomitant order of magnitude of government coordination and control. . . . Because advanced industrial societies develop such unmanageable complexity, they naturally generate a bewildering increase in unanticipated social costs: in human maladjustment, community disruption, and environmental depletion. The cost of cleaning up the mess and caring for the human casualties of unplanned technology – the dropouts, the unskilled, the addicts, or those who just cannot cope with the maze of urban life or deal with Big Brother bureaucra-

cies – mounts ever higher. The proportion of GNP that must be spent in mediating conflicts, controlling crime, protecting consumers and the environment, providing ever-more comprehensive bureaucratic coordination, and generally trying to maintain "social homeostastis" begins to grow exponentially. (1978: 84)

Under the double pressures of economic-support and social-service spending, government expenditures in Canada have increased steadily: per capita federal government spending rose from $41 in 1937 to $169 in 1947 to $313 in 1957 to $515 in 1967 to $1,824 in 1977; per capita provincial government spending in the same forty-year period increased from $33 to $1,581 (Parliament of Canada: 17 April 1978). From 1965 to 1975 government expenditures at all levels grew from 26 to 35 per cent of the gross national product (*Sun*: 14 February 1978). On the economic-support side, the expanding role of government is indicated by the fact that between 1950 and 1970 government investment as a proportion of total investment in Canada increased by 20.8 per cent while the share invested by private business declined by 3.6 per cent (Deaton, 1973: 32). This investment has gone not only into such traditional infrastructural areas as transportation and utilities but also, and increasingly, directly into private corporations across the industrial spectrum in the form of subsidies, interest-free loans, and tax concessions. Between 1964 and 1972 the federal government alone gave to industry $3.5 billion in grants; in addition, federal tax concessions during the same period netted corporations nearly $7 billion (Lewis, 1972: 92, 111). This pattern, which is duplicated at the provincial level, has been expanding steadily, particularly through the device of tax concessions. As a result of the consequent decline in corporate tax revenue, Canadian governments have shifted more and more of the tax burden to the only other shoulders remaining: those of the individual citizen. Such a shift is consistent with the general Western trend: in its bi-yearly *Economic Outlook* bulletin of July, 1976, the Organization for Economic Cooperation and Development warned that investment increases of the magnitude needed by the private sector can be met, in the words of *Le Monde*'s summary of the OECD report, only through "an important modification of the internal distribution of income from the earnings of labour to the earnings of capital" (quoted in Frank, 1976: 6-7). In the case of Canada, between 1962 and 1970 alone the corporate share of federal income tax revenue decreased by 38 per cent while individuals' share (from personal income tax) rose by 23 per cent; the corresponding figures for provincial income tax show there was a 60 per cent fall in the corporate share and an 83 per cent rise in the individual share (Deaton, 1973: 39). Similarly, between 1968 and 1975 the share of revenue for all levels of government in Canada derived from direct personal taxes rose by 16.66 per cent while the share derived from direct corporate tax declined by 6.13 per cent (Wolfe, 1977: 275-6).

The general fiscal crisis facing Western governments as a whole is sharply intensified in the case of Canada as a result of the particular characteristics of the Canadian economy. The key factor in this connection is foreign, predominantly American, control of much of the Canadian economy. By the end of 1973, foreign ownership of Canadian industry amounted to 59 per cent of all manufacturing, 96 per cent of automotive manufacturing, 98 per cent of rubber production, 86 per cent of chemical production, 73 per cent of electrical-apparatus production, 76 per cent of petroleum and natural gas, and 57 per cent of mining; of Canada's 200 top industrial companies in terms of sales volume, at least 125 are under foreign control (Gordon, 1978: 30). As a result of this steadily growing satellization, economic development in Canada increasingly has reflected the priorities of external owners rather than the priorities of balanced national economic development. In particular, foreign ownership has resulted in the Canadian economy's increasing reliance on the extraction and export of natural resources and in a simultaneous erosion of Canada's manufacturing sector. As resource-extraction is characteristically more capital-intensive and less employment-generative than manufacturing, Canada's economic satellization (which, ironically, is financed increasingly by capital generated within Canada) has posed ever greater strains on the country's investment-capital and job-creation capacities. In 1977 the Science Council of Canada's committee on industrial policies warned in its report, *Uncertain Prospects*, that the cumulative impact of all these factors is ominous:

Canadian industry is chronically and gravely ill. Indeed, the country, industrially, is rapidly falling behind other nations and, by default, placing its hopes for the future on the resource sector, which . . . is inadequate to the task of raising or even maintaining the standard of living that most Canadians take for granted. . . . Canada is one of the weaker links in the global industrial system. Should the strains and stresses on that system continue for long . . . the Canadian economy will be perilously exposed. The more viable businesses will flee to the U. S. and elsewhere, while firms will decline and expire in Canada. (quoted in *Sun*: 12 October 1977)

Attempting to shore up a crumbling industrial edifice through capital injections and at the same time trying to meet the social costs of satellization and widening technology, Canada has sought to cover the growing gap between revenue and expenditure by borrowing extensively on domestic and foreign money markets. Between 1950 and 1968 the federal government increased its debt (direct and indirect) by 136 per cent, and provincial and municipal governments by 505 per cent and 511 per cent respectively (Deaton, 1973: 39). As both the general capital-crisis of the Western world and the particular pressures on the Canadian economy have continued to mount, the federal government has sought to cushion the budgetary impact of its fiscal crisis by resorting to massive expansions of the money supply – the average annual increase of 5.53 per cent in the 1960's doubled to 11.16 per cent during 1970-75 (Wolfe, 1977: 267). Borrowing has accelerated also: in 1975, largely as a result of its various levels of government seeking loans, Canada became the largest single borrower on foreign capital markets, borrowing upwards of $5 billion, or one-quarter of the year's world total (McCready, 1977: 259). In 1977 one estimate placed Canada's accumulated indebtedness at $100 billion, as compared to $175 billion for the entire Third World (*Sun*: 25 October 1977). Declining international confidence in Canada's ability to cope with the indebtedness has in turn contributed to a sharp fall in the value of the Canadian dollar abroad, a development with long-term inflationary implications for Canadians – the world's biggest importers per capita – as the dollar cost of imports rises.

II POLITICAL REACTIONS

With 1977 debt service costs for Canadian governments up 120 per cent from 1972 (*Globe and Mail*: 15 March 1977) and deficits mounting rapidly—the first 10 months of fiscal year 1977-78 brought the federal spending deficit to $6,611 million compared to $3,796 million in the preceding year (*Sun*: 2 March 1978) – Canadian political leaders in the late 1970's began joining their counterparts elsewhere in the advanced capitalist world in advocating cutbacks in governments' social expenditures as a means of easing the tax burden on an increasingly restive taxpaying public while maintaining the inflow of governmental capital into the private sector – a process some argue should be augmented by the contracting out of remaining social services to the private sector as a means of attaining greater efficiency in social expenditures as well as providing secure "social-industrial" profit-opportunities for the private sector (O'Connor, 1973). Appealing to burdened taxpayers' resentment of bureaucratic waste and benefiting from widespread voter ignorance of the relationship of the public services-private consumption trade-off to standards of living, calls for massive cuts in public sector expenditures have evoked spectacular electoral support throughout Western societies, epitomized by the victory of California's tax-slashing Proposition 13 in June, 1978. However, the "cutback" gambit is of only short-term political marketability. The magnitude of capital subsidies required by the private sector is such that, in the context of the spiralling capital-intensity generated by competition-fuelled recourse to wider technology and the simultaneous depletion of resources, only savage cuts in the most basic public services and continued tax pressures on the individual taxpayer will enable the amassing of sufficient blocks of investment capital for the private sector.

Therein lies the excruciating dilemma for politicians committed to both the survival of democratic political institutions and sustained economic expansion within a capitalist framework. How can the present economic system survive unless voters are willing to make substantial cuts in social services and, ultimately, in their overall standard of living? And yet who will support the perpetuation of a system that exacts such a human cost? The herculean dimensions of the challenge were acknowledged by *Busi-*

ness Week in 1974 (12 October):

Some people will obviously have to do with less. . . . Indeed, cities and states, the home mortgage market and small business and the consumer, will all get less than they want because the basic health of the U. S. is based on the basic health of its corporations and banks. . . . Yet it will be a hard pill for many Americans to swallow – the idea of doing with less so that big business can have more. It will be particularly hard to swallow because it is quite obvious that if big business and big banks are the most visible victims of the Debt Economy, they are also in large measure the cause of it. . . . Nothing that this nation, or any other nation, has done in modern history compares in difficulty with the selling jobs that must be done to make people accept the new reality.

The difficulty of the "selling job" is further apparent when the present social expenditures are seen to be an important factor in stabilizing the society. In this connection, a senior Ford Motor Company economist commented in 1976: "Unemployment insurance and welfare are two reasons why there isn't blood on the streets here" (quoted in Loney, 1977: 447). Similarly, Federal Minister of Consumer and Corporate Affairs Bryce Mackasey observed in May, 1976: "The stability of free enterprise depends on the welfare state. . . . As we face this capital crunch I hear businessmen saying 'Cut back on welfare and transfer payments.' But a country whose living standards are falling faces more unrest than a much poorer country whose living standards are rising" (quoted in *ibid*: 447-8). The all-encompassing scope of the state's stabilizing role is indicated by H. Armstrong's estimate that in 1971 "there were 5,853,000 Canadians directly dependent on the state as clients or workers compared to 6,298,000 Canadians who were not" (quoted in *ibid*: 449).

Politicians' efforts to secure public acquiescence to capital-raising cutbacks are reflected in increasingly blunt rhetorical assaults both on the welfare state and on expectations of rising living standards. Thus, for example, Prime Minister Pierre Trudeau declared in his 1975 New Year's interview with CTV that "we can't go back to what was before, with the same habits, the same behaviour, and the same institutions." Similarly, Trudeau stated in December, 1977, that "when the dollar falls 10 per cent in a year, it's because the world is telling us we're living beyond our means" and proceeded to warn Canadians that "if they don't discipline themselves we will discipline them." With equal bluntness, Progressive Conservative federal finance critic Sinclair Stevens declared before an audience at the University of British Columbia on February 2, 1978, that a Conservative government would impose restraints which would *decrease* the wages of the average worker (*Ubyssey*: 3 February 1978). As the Laxers have pointed out in their analysis of the "new morality" – epitomized by Trudeau's pronouncements – such attempts to reverse the public's expectations are complicated by the fact that two separate and opposed constituencies must be simultaneously mobilized:

> For business and the right, there is the message that the idea of redistribution of wealth has been pushed too far, and that this idea has led to softness among the people at large who think the world owes them a free ride. The emphasis is now on hard work, on ending the easy handouts to lazy welfare recipients, on tightening up the distribution of unemployment benefits. . . . But . . . Trudeau recognizes that belt-tightening can never be popular with those who have little room for pulling in their belts. Therefore, no simple appeal to a new code of public ethics will work. Trudeau's new morality depends on dividing those who confront him on his left flank.
> For left-liberal "public opinion" the new morality is being served up as a frothy mixture of appeals to environmentalism and physical fitness and attacks on mindless material consumption. Restraint, people are being told, is the only rational response to the realities of scarcity on this small and all-too-finite planet. . . . The new morality appeals to the desire of people to distinguish themselves from "the man on the street." "You can understand the problems of resource scarcity. . . ." the message goes. "It's too bad the masses cannot." (Laxer and Laxer, 1977: 96-7)

Though successful as a short-run political novelty item, the "environmentalist" component of the "new morality" is proving to be of diminishing political effectiveness both with regard to the environmentally conscious, who come to perceive the approach as a sham-device masking the accumulation of capital to finance industry's increasing environmental destruction, and the wider mass of workers, who, still embracing the "old morality" of maximum consumption, find the necessarily vague ecological appeals of the "new morality" an utterly inadequate response to their declining spending power. In the long term, moreover, the magnitude of cutbacks and consequent decline in living standards precipitated by the crisis of spiralling capital-intensity portend growing worker preoccupation with the more immediate concerns of unemployment and personal economic survival.

An additional complication facing Canadian politicians seeking public support for the capital priorities of an economy oriented toward international capitalism is the growing dissonance between these priorities and the dynamics of nationalism, whether Canadian or Québécois. As American, European, and Japanese corporations have reached more deeply into foreign markets and become internationally interdependent, nationalism has been gradually replaced by "multinational-corporate" internationalism as the business world's dominant political ideology. This new ideology more suitably encourages global marketing. Concomitant with this process, the continuance of nationalism in general and economic nationalism in particular has emerged as an obstacle to what former U. S. Under-Secretary of State George Ball described in May, 1967, as "the growing determination of American business to regard national boundaries as no longer fixing the horizons of their corporate activity" (quoted in Schiller, 1971: 16).

The Trudeau regime established a Foreign Investment Review Agency (FIRA) in 1974 as a concession to nationalist public opinion during its brief phase as a minority government, but by the late 1970's this government was pursuing its internationalist (or continentalist, in the Canada-U. S. context) policies with renewed vigour. In 1977, applications to FIRA by foreign investors to establish new businesses in Canada increased 74 per cent from 1976 and applications for foreign takeovers of existing businesses were up 56 per cent; while FIRA's approval rate rose from 80 per cent of applications in 1975-76 to 90 per cent in 1977-78—a situation which led *The Financial Post* (25 February 1978) to observe that "the watchdog agency has turned into something more like a lapdog." Squarely posing a challenge to Canadian labour interests through its locking of the Canadian economy into a capital-intensive, minimum job-return resource-extraction base, the satellization of the Canadian economy is firmly supported by the dominant segments of the Canadian business community. Predominantly mercantilist from its inception, the Canadian bourgeoisie has manifested a strong commitment to a middle-man role for Canadians in an internationally integrated economy under the aegis of foreign-controlled multinational corporations. It might be added that even the Parti Québécois with its state interventionism on behalf of Francophone entrepreneurs does not envisage a non-continentalist economic future; in the words of PQ cabinet strategist Claude Morin: "We may certainly expect Quebec to join any eventual North American bloc. . . . Considering the already advanced integration of the Canadian and American economies neither Canada nor Quebec really has very much room for manoeuvre in these terms" (quoted in Laxer and Laxer, 1977: 205) That the brief federal administration led by Joe Clark shared Morin's sense of continentalism's inevitability and was already willing to consider some form of closer integration with the American metropolis was intimated by Clark's Finance Minister, John Crosbie, in a June, 1979, statement to the *Toronto Star*: "If we're going to be dominated by anyone, I'd prefer it to be the Americans than anyone else. We might want to look at further auto pacts or a customs trading zone or a free trade zone."

Canada's continentalist drift has major implications for the response of the Canadian labour movement to the capital crisis. In the first place, as the Canadian bourgeoisie opts irrevocably for a continentalist future, nationalism in Canada increasingly will acquire by the process of elimination a working-class connotation and in turn will constitute a powerful mobilizing tool at the disposal of the labour movement. Labour nationalism, already manifested in growing demands by Canadian sections of international unions for more autonomy, is likely to emerge with particular force in the manufacturing sector as de-industrialization proceeds. Ultimately, as the lines of economic control and nationality tend more and more to coincide, nationalism could illuminate rather than obscure lines of class and thus encourage the emergence of a militant working-class consciousness.

It is perhaps useful in this connection to recall that tendencies toward a radicalized class-orientation would not be unprecedented for Canadian labour: it is often forgotten that before the mid-twentieth century triumph of American-style "business unionism"–first implanted in Canada in the 1890's by Samuel Gompers' craft-oriented American Federation of Labour (AFL) at the invitation of American industrialists locating branch-plants inside Macdonald's National Policy Tariff walls–a powerful tradition of radical industrial unionism existed in Canada. This was particularly the case in western Canada (and also, incidentally, in various western American states), where the mining industry's fluctuations, company-town exploitation, and owners' violent repression of unions helped produce a predominantly radical labour orientation epitomized by the Western Federation of Miners and the rise of various socialist political formations, especially in British Columbia (see McCormack, 1977). This western radicalism achieved certain legislative concessions in provincial political arenas and culminated in 1919 with the organization of a single industrial union intended for all workers, appropriately named One Big Union (OBU). Though the OBU was successfully crushed by a state-corporate-AFL alliance in a violent 1919 general-strike confrontation in Winnipeg, a significant minority of Canadian unionists continued through the 1920's and 1930's to dissent from the AFL's dominance of organized labour in Canada.

An important legacy of this radicalism was the emergent recognition by business after World War I of the futility of escalating anti-union repression, and a consequent swing toward social-welfare and other liberal-reformist policies aimed at co-opting the union movement rather than eliminating it. A prominent architect of this new policy emphasis, and its chief political beneficiary, was William Lyon Mackenzie King, who rose from Laurier's fledgling labour ministry and several years' apprenticeship as an industrial relations consultant to the Rockefellers (who hired King to chart new directions in the aftermath of the infamous 1914 massacre of miners' children by troops deployed by a strikebound Rockefeller mining company in Colorado) to become leader of the federal Liberals in 1919 and Prime Minister for all but five of the years from 1921 to 1948. Under King, the gradual expansion of the welfare state, coupled with the massive economic expansion engendered by World War II, successfully calmed Canada's first surge of labour radicalism.

That labour's post-war quiescence may prove to be a comparatively brief interregnum rather than a climactic "end of ideology" is indicated by events in Quebec, where a context of satellization, frustrated nationalism, high unemployment, deepening state fiscal crisis, deteriorating industrial relations, and government repression in the late 1960's and early 1970's generated significant labour radicalization reflected in the adoption of Marxist-oriented manifestos by the province's major union centrals in 1971-72, the Common Front general strike of 1972, and a variety of other anti-government mass actions. Originally catalyzed by policies of the provincial Liberal regime of Robert Bourassa (1970-76) and instrumental in the victory of the Parti Québécois, the energies of Quebec labour's radical activism are now gradually being turned against the PQ. Even before the 1976 provincial election, Norbert Rodrigue, president of the 160,000 member Confédération des Syndicats Nationaux (CSN), Quebec's second-largest union central, indicated labour's basic mistrust of the PQ:

> The necessity of a workers' party is no longer disputable . . . for the Parti Québécois, even though it represents a hope for a certain number of union militants . . . is a traditional, fundamentally non-labour party. It has not pronounced itself against capitalism; it has supported illusions, it has aroused deception. (Dupont and Tremblay; 1976: 102)

Since René Lévesque's victory, labour's disaffection has grown, with both the CSN and the Centrale des Enseignants du Québec (the province's Francophone teachers' federation) bitterly opposing the PQ regime's modification of 1977 labour code amendments in response to business pressure, and with the CSN's June, 1978, convention flaying the Lévesque regime for its inaction on labour grievances: "This government has yet to adopt policies which respond to the major problems of workers – inflation, unemployment, plant closures and poverty" (quoted in *Sun:* 6 June 1978). Sharing ex-president Marcel Pepin's stated fear that "if there is a big price to be paid (for separation), it won't be the national bourgeoisie who will have to pay it, it will be the mass of workers" (quoted in *Financial Post:* 26 November 1977), the 1978 CSN convention also declared its ambivalence to the PQ's independence project, declaring in its policy paper that "we've seen nothing yet" to prove it will be in workers' best interest (quoted in *Sun:* 6 June 1978). Significantly, even the 280,000 member Federation des Travailleurs de Quebec (FTQ), of Quebec's three principal labour centrals, the most supportive of the PQ, has pointedly refused to endorse separatism. Further contributing to PQ-labour estrangement is the Lévesque regime's move announced in mid-1978 to restrict certain collective bargaining rights for public sector workers under terms of Bill 50. A question of critical importance for the future is whether this estrangement process will eventually assist the forging of closer links between the Quebec and English-Canada labour movements, thereby enabling an effective bi-national coast-to-coast political labour coalition to emerge. In the short term, significant segments of the labour movement remain both pro-PQ and *indépendantiste.* Moreover, the Lévesque government's generous dispensations in its 1979 budget suggest that, notwithstanding the fiscal pressures posed by a $1.4 billion deficit, the PQ has decided to postpone any confrontations with Quebec's unions until after the referendum on independence. However, Finance Minister Parizeau's warning to public-sector unions "to curb appetites which no longer reflect reality" and an announced 2.5 per cent reduction of the civil service by April, 1980, are harbingers of a post-referendum day of reckoning.

Meanwhile, in the late 1970's a perceptible politicization of English-Canadian labour has begun to emerge: for the first time since the 1930's the union movement is demonstrating a willingness to use the strike mechanism as a political weapon against the state to force changes in national economic policies. A concrete manifestation of this new willingness was the decision by the Canadian Labour Congress (CLC) to call a Canada-wide general strike on October 14, 1976, to protest the federal government's wage-control policy. The first attempt at a national general strike in Canada's history, the CLC's "Day of Protest," though only partially successful, attracted the support of nearly one million workers and constituted a bold new departure in labour's assertiveness. The new political mood also was illustrated by the CLC's warning in 1977 that rising unemployment could produce major upheavals: "The anger and frustration resulting from continuing inaction may well lead to a degree of tension, unrest and even violent disorders seldom, if ever, witnessed before in this country" (quoted in *Star-Phoenix*: 11 May 1977).

The trend toward political militancy escalated in 1978 as moves by governments to restrict public sector union powers drew increasingly heated denunciations from labour leaders such as Grace Hartman, president of the 250,000 member Canadian Union of Public Employees, who warned her members that governments are seeking at "every bargaining table to 'gut' your agreements . . . to take away rights that we've had for longer than some of you have lived." She added that this in turn is the leading edge of general anti-labour strategy:

The whole labour movement in this country is currently the target of a large-scale propaganda attack. The refrains aren't new, but this time it's more intense, more insidious, because it's aimed at making anti-union bias politically popular. The purpose clearly is to create suspicion and fear in the minds of workers toward their unions and to inhibit unorganized workers from seeking the protection unions offer. (quoted in *Sun*: 16 June 1978)

The escalating division between labour and government is epitomized by B. C. Federation of Labour President Jim Kinnaird's warning in early 1979 of a "bloodbath" if that province's Social Credit regime implemented its proposed withdrawal of the right to strike from municipal and educational employees (*The Columbian*: 24 January 1979).

III THE AUTHORITARIAN TEMPTATION

Throughout the Western world, mounting evidence of concern in both government and corporate circles about the prospects of labour militancy in the context of the emerging capital crisis is leading to acknowledgment that authoritarian modifications of national political structures eventually may occur in order to effect the accumulations and transfers of capital deemed necessary for sustained industrial expansion within the present economic framework. Recalling the dictum that those who forget their history are condemned to relive it, it is instructive at this point to note certain disturbing political parallels between the emerging crisis of the 1980's and that of the 1930's. Describing the rise of fascism in Italy and Germany, Daniel Guerin wrote in 1936:

> When the economic crisis becomes acute . . . the bourgeoisie can see only one way to restore its profits: it empties the pockets of the people. . . . It restores to what M. Caillaux, once finance minister of France, expressively calls "the great penance": a brutal slashing of wages and social expenditures. . . .
> But such maneuvers are difficult under a democratic regime. As long as democracy survives, the masses, though thoroughly deceived and plundered, have some means of defense against the "great penance": freedom of the press, universal suffrage, the right to organize into unions and to strike, etc. Feeble defenses, it is true, but still capable of setting some limit to the insatiable demands of the money power.
> And so . . . the bourgeoisie throws its traditional democracy overboard and conjures up that "strong state" which alone can strip the masses of all means of defense, tying their hands behind their backs, the better to empty their pockets. (1973: 22-3)

Though, as Guerin duly noted, "in richer, more fortunate countries, the bourgeoisie . . . succeeded . . . in extricating itself for the time being from its difficulties resorting to expedients which at least have not required the substitution of dictatorship for democracy" (ibid.: 23), it is often forgotten that before the efficacy of such programs as Franklin Roosevelt's New Deal became apparent, fascism was openly considered as an option by significant elements of the American and Canadian business communities.

Reflecting this mood, Henry R. Luce's *Fortune* magazine editorialized in July, 1934, that "the good journalist must recognize in Fascism certain ancient virtues of the race. . . . Among these are Discipline, Duty, Courage, Glory, Sacrifice" (quoted in Seldes, 1947: 118). William Randolph Hearst hymned similar praises of fascism in a signed editorial in his national newspaper chain on November 26, 1934:

> Fascism is definitely a movement to oppose and offset Communism, and so prevent the least capable and least creditable classes from getting control of government.
>
> Fascism will come into existence in the United States when such a movement becomes really necessary for the prevention of Communism. . . .
>
> The Proletariat was the lowest order of citizenship in Rome. It was composed of the citizens without property of any kind: and the reason they had no property was because they had the lowest intelligence, the least industry and the least thrift.
>
> The Proletariat today is the body of citizenship least able to manage their own affairs and consequently least able to manage the nation's affairs. (quoted in Magil and Stevens, 1938: 162-3)

In like manner, the March, 1935, issue of *Nation's Business*, organ of the U.S. Chamber of Commerce, declared that "many thoughtful people believe that our form of government must be changed to something resembling the fascist form, without the multitude of checks or balances now prevailing" (quoted in *ibid.*: 119). Certain business elements even sought to put these ideas into action. In November, 1934, General Smedley Butler, a retired and highly popular deputy commandant of the U.S. Marine Corps, testified before a Congressional committee that he had been approached by representatives of a corporate coalition headed by Singer Sewing Machine heir Robert Sterling Clark and Wall Street broker Grayson Murphy, a director of Guaranty Trust, Anaconda Copper, and Bethlehem Steel, and asked to lead a fascist coup against President Roosevelt. According to Butler, the plotters sought to mobilize a march on Washington by 500,000 American Legion war veterans with necessary arms to be provided from certain DuPont interests through the Remington Arms Company (Seldes, 1947: 290). Though Congressman John W. McCormack, chairman of the investigation of Butler's charges, reported on February 15, 1935, that "your committee was able to verify all the pertinent statements made by General Butler" (quoted in *ibid.*: 291), formal charges were never pressed against the apparently numerous and powerful conspirators. McCormack (later Speaker of the U. S. House of Representatives) commented in a 1971 interview, ". . . it was deemed politically inadvisable" (quoted in Archer, 1973: 212). Paralleling such domestic activities was the aid given by certain industrialists to overseas fascists; most notable in this regard was the propaganda and financial support extended by Henry Ford to the Nazis during their rise to power – support rewarded with Hitler's bestowal of the Nazis' Grand Cross of the German Eagle on Ford in 1938 (Pool and Pool, 1978: 129). The flirtation with fascist methods continued to the very eve of World War II. As late as December, 1938, two hundred fifty of New York's leading industrialists cheered the remarks of Major General George Van Horn Mosely at the annual meeting of the New York Board of Trade: "Our domestic enemies should be warned . . . not to excite the wrath of patriotic America, for once these patriots go into battle they will cure the disease definitely and make those massacres now recorded in history look like peaceful church parades" (quoted in Wolfskill, 1962: 100).

Nor was Canada immune to the lure of authoritarianism, as witness the address entitled "Fascism" delivered to the prestigious Empire Club of Canada in Toronto on January 25, 1935, by Magistrate S. Alfred Jones, K. C. In his conclusion, listed in the Club minutes as receiving "hearty applause," Jones declared:

If there were a line in the fundamental principles of Fascism opposed in the slightest degree to the best ideals of the British Empire, I would not even be discussing the matter. Should Canada at any time in the future, in its wisdom, adopt Fascism, in whole or in part, it is indeed gratifying to know, gentlemen,

that the system fits so admirably into our Imperial setting. . . .
(quoted in Brown, 1973: 62)

Mirroring this mood, the January, 1937, issue of the *RCMP Quarterly*–in "Peace, War and Communism" by C. E. Edgett–cited fascism's allegedly redeeming virtues in the context of the depression:

> If Fascism had not arisen and conquered in Italy, and . . . in Germany, then today these two great countries would have been obliterated from the map in a flood-tide of Bolshevism. The typical Fascist is not perfect by any means nor very admirable from the standpoint of the normal Democrat. But at least he has applied his violence and ferocity to the enemies of traditional family life . . . to the enemies of religion . . . (quoted in *ibid.:* 82)

Even more ominously, substantial links developed in the early 1930's between the Conservative Party and Quebec fascist leader Adrien Arcand (Betcherman, 1975: 9-11, 25, 39), and there is at least limited evidence that Arcand, who later founded the Canadian Nazi Party, was offered the federal labour portfolio by Prime Minister R. B. Bennett as part of the Conservatives' (unsuccessful) re-election strategy (Milner and Milner, 1973: 123).

Given that what proved to be a viable alternative to fascism in the 1930's–the New Deal-style democratic welfare state–is itself increasingly unviable as a result of the crisis of capital-intensity, projections of growing authoritarianism in the 1980's assume particular importance. Foremost among these projections are those issued by the Trilateral Commission in its 1975 report, *The Crisis of Democracy.* Organized in 1972-73 by Chase Manhattan Bank Chairman, David Rockefeller, as a forum for influential "private citizens" from North America, Western Europe, and Japan to discuss long-term economic and political questions of mutual interest, the Trilateral Commission has evolved into an authoritative grouping of some 250 members and associates from elite corporate and political backgrounds, with only token labour representation. The Trilateral Commission's U. S. members at the time of issuance of *The Crisis of Democracy* included then ex-Governor and now President Jimmy Carter, then Senator and now Vice President Walter Mondale, then professor and now National Security advisor Zbigniew Brzezinski, then lawyer and now Secretary of State Cyrus Vance, then California Institute of Technology President and now Secretary of Defense Harold Brown, and then Bendix Corporation Chairman and later Secretary of the Treasury Michael Blumenthal, as well as an impressive assortment of other decision-makers and opinion-shapers, including David Rockefeller, Exxon Chairman J. K. Jamieson, Lehman Brothers Chairman Peter Peterson, former Under-Secretary of State George Ball, Time Editor-in-Chief Hedley Donavan, Ambassador Elliott Richardson, Coca-Cola Chairman J. Paul Austin, CBS President Arthur Taylor, Governor of Washington Daniel Evans, Bank of America President Alden W. Clausen, Sears Roebuck Chairman Arthur M. Woods, U. S. Transportation Secretary William T. Coleman, columnist and former U. S. Information Agency Director Carl Rowan, Texas Instrument Chairman Patrick Haggerty, Senator Robert Taft, Jr., and Wells Fargo Bank Chairman Ernest C. Arbuckle. European members included FIAT President Giovanni Agnelli, professor (and now Prime Minister of France) Raymond Barre, German Banking Federation President Alwin Munchmeyer, Financial Times Editor M. H. Fisher, Barclays Bank International Chairman A. F. Tuke, and Royal Dutch Shell Managing Director F. S. McFadzean. Japanese representatives included Mitsubishi Corporation Chairman Chujiro Fujiho, Bank of Tokyo Chairman Somio Haro, and SONY Corporation President Akio Morita. Participating Canadians included MacMillan Bloedel Chairman (now B. C. Hydro Chairman) Robert Bonner, Toronto-Dominion Bank Vice President Alan Hockin, Chatelaine Editor Doris Anderson, Member of Parliament (now Human Rights Commissioner) Gordon Fairweather, and former federal cabinet minister (later National Unity Task Force Co-Chairman) Jean-Luc Pépin. As such an imposing array of names makes apparent, the Trilateral Commission's reports are of particular significance in providing insights into the strategic thinking guiding the general evolution of government and corporate policies in North America, Western Europe, and Japan.

Compiled by Michael Crozier, Samuel P. Huntingdon, and Joji Watanuki, and issued under the Trilateral imprimatur with an introduction by the Commission's then-director Zbigniew Brzezinski, *The Crisis of Democracy* reviewed the growing fiscal squeeze on the state imposed by the capital crisis and concluded that political democracy rather than current economic structures constitutes the root of the problem:

> The extent of the fiscal gap, its apparent inevitability and intractableness, and its potentially destabilizing effects were sufficiently ominous for the existing system to generate a new variety of Marxist analysis of the inevitable consequence of capitalism. . . . The most recent revision, taking into consideration the Welfare Shift, identifies the expansion of the fiscal crisis of capitalism. What the Marxists mistakenly attribute to capitalist economies, however, is, in fact, a product of democratic politics. (Crozier *et al.*, 1975: 73)

Arguing that democratic politics are not adequately constrained by a sense of national economic interests, the report cited the consensus of the Trilateral Commission's Canadian Group Colloquium:

> Labour groups are not impeded . . . from making outrageous demands due to the absence of a strong public philosophy and to prevalent doubt as to whether fairness underlies the general allocation of influence and resources. . . . In the absence of a national ethos, governments are hamstrung in their efforts to cope with such prevalent difficulties as inflation and labour/management disputes. (*ibid.*: 208)

Reviewing the Trilateral region's political history, *The Crisis of Democracy* further contended that "at one time or another, threats to the viability of democratic government have come from the aristocracy, the military, the middle classes, and the working class" (*ibid.*: 6) – it is the Trilateral perspective that big business has never posed such threats – and that new strains are now arising from "an excess of democracy" (*ibid.*: 113). Citing John Adams' observation that "there never was a democracy yet that did not commit suicide," the report added that "suicide is more likely to be the product of overindulgence than of any other cause" and warned that "the arenas where democratic procedures are appropriate are, in short, limited" (*ibid.*: 115, 114). Listing various examples of the challenge facing Western government "in terms of its ability to mobilize its citizens for the achievement of social and political goals and to impose discipline and sacrifice upon its citizens in order to achieve those goals" (*ibid.*: 7), the report called for the strengthening of state authority:

> The demands on government and the needs for government have been increasing steadily in all the Trilateral societies. The cause of the current malaise is the decline in the material resources and political authority available to governments to meet these demands and needs. . . . In some measure, governability and democracy are warring concepts. An excess of democracy means a deficit in governability. . . . At the present time it appears the balance has tilted too far against governments. . . . (*ibid.*: 169, 173)

Several specific "problem" areas were singled out by the Trilateral Commission for policy recommendations. In a "reexamination of the cost and functions of higher education," for instance, the Commission worried about "the overproduction of people with university education in relation to the jobs available to them" and the "frustration and psychological hardships among university graduates who are unable to secure the types of jobs to which they believe their education entitled them" (*ibid.*: 183). Two options were seen:

> What seems needed . . . is to relate educational planning to economic and political goals. Should a college education be provided generally because of its contribution to the overall cultural level of the populace and its possible relation to the constructive discharge of the responsibilities of leadership? If this question is answered in the affirmative, a program is then necessary to lower the job expectations of those who receive a college education. If the question is answered in the negative,

then higher educational institutions should be induced to redesign their programs so as to be geared to the patterns of economic development and future job opportunities. (*ibid.*: 183-4)

The urgency of this issue in Canada is illustrated in the estimate of a June, 1978, Ontario government report that while 500,000 are expected to graduate from the province's post-secondary institutions by 1986, demand for their skills is expected to produce only 155,000 new jobs. (*Sun*: 7 June 1978)

Part of the blame for what Trilateralists perceive as the public's unreasonable political and economic expectations was assigned by the Commission's report to "adversary intellectuals":

The advanced industrial societies have spawned a stratum of value-oriented intellectuals who often devote themselves to the derogation of leadership, the challenging of authority, and the unmasking and delegitimation of established institutions. . . . In an age of widespread . . . education, the pervasiveness of the mass media, and the displacement of manual by clerical and professional employees, this development constitutes a challenge. . . . (Crozier *et al.*, 1975: 7)

Also culpable in the Trilateral perspective are the mass media, and accordingly *The Crisis of Democracy* called for "restoring a balance between government and media":

Freedom of the press is absolutely essential. . . . Like any freedom, however, it is a freedom which can be abused. Recent years have seen an immense growth in the scope and power of the media. In many countries . . . the press has taken an increasingly critical role towards government and public officials. . . . There obviously are important [media] rights to be protected, but broader interests of society and government are also at stake. . . . There is . . . the need to assure to the government the right and the ability to withhold information at the source. In addition . . . the courts should consider moving promptly to reinstate the law of libel as a necessary and appropriate check upon the abuses of power by the press. (*ibid.*: 181-2)

With reference to the content and organization of industrial work, the Commission warned that problems in this area "require a painful transformation of social relations, of cultural and authority patterns, and even modes of reasoning" (*ibid.*: 185) and that while innovative management should be encouraged, pressures for widening industrial democracy "would raise impossible problems" and must be defeated. Above all, stressed the Trilateral report, priority must be given to whatever capital-allocation decisions are required to sustain industrial expansion, and if democracy is not narrowed toward "a more balanced existence" (*ibid.*: 115) to accomplish these economic goals, more direct, authoritarian methods will be necessitated:

It is necessary here . . . to underline the extent to which the governability of democracy seems dependent upon the sustained expansion of the economy . . . . The governments in Trilateral societies have the possibility of becoming "wiser" in allocating scarce resources in the most effective way . . . . In many instances, however, political leaders have been left deficient in the institutional resources and authority necessary to achieve these goals . . . . *In the long run, the leadership vacuum will be filled one way or another, and strong institutionalized leadership is clearly preferable to personalized charismatic leadership.* (*ibid.*: 175; italics mine)

IV THE CORPORATIST DRIFT

To some observers, mention of a possible "charismatic leadership" solution by a body of the Trilateral Commission's standing is eerily evocative of the atmosphere leading to the 1934 Butler gambit in the U. S. and of the 1931 statement by then-parliamentary candidate Adolf Hitler that "an increasing number of industrialists, financiers, intellectuals and officers are now looking for a man who will at last bring some order into affairs at home, who will draw the farmers, the workers and the officials into the German community once more" (quoted in Calic, 1971:

22). While obviously only the passage of history will reveal whether parallels to such dire measures will again materialize, it is interesting to note that certain preliminary parallels are materialized in Canada in the late 1970's in the form of renewed discussions about the viability of corporatism, defined by Robert Presthus as the "conception of society in which government delegated many of its functions to private groups, which in turn provide guidance regarding the social and economic legislation required in the modern national state" (quoted in Rea and McLeod, 1976: 338) Characterizing the ideological and policy pronouncements of Pierre Trudeau as indicative of a general "drift toward corporatism" (ibid.: 333), K. J. Rea and J. T. McLeod have pointed out the obvious attraction of corporatism to those seeking to avoid class conflict in the emerging capital-intensity crisis:

Much of the motivation toward corporatism springs from the hope of discovering some method of overcoming the profound antagonisms and schisms between social classes, particularly between capital and labour. Corporatists seek a solution to the class struggle by bringing various private groups directly into the governing process as partners or agents of the state. (ibid.: 338)

On the labour scene, the corporatist drift has manifested itself in federal government attempts to secure Canadian Labour Congress participation in "tripartism," i.e., a new formal consultative mechanism wherein representatives of government, business, and organized labour would formulate binding national wage and other economic guidelines. Touted by its proponents as a device to give labour more meaningful input into economic policy-making and denounced by its critics as a two-against-one format for forcing labour cooperation with wage restraints and social service cutbacks, tripartism would in any case clearly alter organized labour's freedom of manoeuvre, for as D. V. Smiley has noted, "the present capacity of . . . labour unions – and associations of these institutions – to press their own interests within the law will be superseded by their incorporation into the apparatus of the corporatist state" (1976: 447).

Though the label "corporatist" was rejected by Pierre Elliott Trudeau, the essential arguments for a substantively corporatist response to the escalating capital crisis were presented by the Trudeau government in a series of Trilateralesque declarations in the late 1970's. With regard to the movement toward cutbacks in social expenditures, for example, Trudeau was forthright:

If we want or need to spend more in one area of the economy, we'll have to spend less in others. . . . Governments over the past 20 years have not insisted strongly enough on such a trade-off—have not insisted that if people demand and receive benefits like higher pensions and medical insurance, for example, we must all pay the cost by accepting either a lower level of services in other areas, or alternatively, a slower rate of increase in our standard of living. (Trudeau, 1976: 452)

. . . It is both possible and desirable to seek a substantial reduction in the rate of government expenditure and direct government intervention and to search for alternative strategies—less expenditure-oriented—to serve the legitimate social concerns of government, and in fact to better serve society. (quoted in Radwanski, 1978: 307)

As to the critical question of how to secure public, especially labour, acquiescence to the coming capital reallocations and their impact on living standards, Trudeau's response combined calls for a reduction of the public's expectation levels with warnings that government authority must be augmented. He stressed consistently that the public's "unreasonable" demands and attitudes are the principal barrier to resolving the emerging economic crisis and that society will accordingly have to be restructured substantially:

A very high priority for this country must be to find a way to settle labour-management disputes with justice, while at the same time avoiding the enormous loss of productivity which strikes are now causing. . . . I believe all Canadians want their governments to have an adequate strength and power to protect the public interest; and that therefore the legislative and regulatory aspects of government might well have to increase in the future. . . . Our greatest hope lies . . . in the capacity of each of us to adopt different social and economic values in response to the new reality of our times. (Trudeau, 1976: 452-3)

A year before his government fell from power, Trudeau warned:

We have fostered expectations of higher incomes that, in turn, have become an important part of the inflationary process. . . . Once again the directions are evident. Governments must . . . be careful in their social policy pursuits not to damage incentive. They must . . . arrive at responsible and non-inflationary wage bargains. Where power exists to realize excessive expectations, that power must be constrained. (Trudeau, 1978)

The mistaken apprehension by a still significant segment of the Canadian business community that Trudeau's call for increased government power portended a move to socialism (a misapprehension paralleling the initial fears of many American businessmen in the 1930's that Franklin Roosevelt's New Deal was some sort of bolshevik plot) politically benefited Joe Clark and the Progressive Conservative Party in the May, 1979, election. Yet Clark's Conservatives are themselves committed to major public-to-private capital transfers and cutbacks in social expenditures: " . . . we must make major cuts in spending first by removing the principle of universality from family allowance, unemployment insurance and some other programs, and second by imposing strict spending limitations on each department of government" (Clark, quoted in Laxer and Laxer, 1977: 114). Accordingly, the Clark government faced the same stark options which again confront Trudeau vis-a-vis securing labour assent to the new division of national income: a hands-off, minimum-regulation, "free market" approach would provoke spiralling management-labour confrontations; on the other hand, the government must attempt to co-opt organized labour through corporatist consensus-building and reallocation-legitimizing techniques a la tripartism.

Given what would be the disastrous impact of escalating labour-management strife on Canada's foreign capital markets as well as its domestic destabilizing effects, the attractiveness of the corporatist approach is self-evident. It is therefore not surprising that Progressive Conservative federal labour critic John Fraser (later chosen as a member of Clark's inner cabinet) responded sympathetically to the opening debate on tripartism, arguing that "we must bring labour, management and government together and create a climate of understanding," that labour wants "to be both respectable and responsible," and that problems will continue "until you get representatives of these three organizations to talk about the state of the economy, the course of the economy and the relative shares that each can take out of the economy" (quoted in *Queen's Journal*: 26 November 1976).

The late 1970's have seen steadily intensifying pressures for corporatism spawned by Canada's economic deterioration, a decline summarized by the country's May, 1978, "discomfort index" reading of 17.6 per cent (the combination of unemployment and inflation rates) as compared to a 1965 index of only slightly over 6 per cent. The response of organized labour to these pressures and to tripartism in particular was initially favourable; indeed, the tripartite notion was welcomed in the Canadian Labour Congress's Manifesto for Canada issued in May, 1976. More recently, however, CLC support has tempered to ambivalence as labour leaders have begun to express certain apprehensions about the incompatibility of corporatism's long-term implications with organized labour's freedom and ultimately with the very survival of political democracy. Asked in 1977 to clarify the type of tripartism acceptable to labour, Canadian United Auto Workers director – now CLC president – Denis McDermott emphasized labour's determination to avoid previous corporatist entrapments:

A lot of people are agonizing over the mechanics of the tripartite system. . . . But if we can get the concept of serious, legitimate input into the decision-making process, not as an alternative to the parliamentary system but as an addition to it – now that's what we seek . . . It looked . . . to a number of other people that we were setting aside the parliamentary system.

We would be the last people to do that, because whenever the parliamentary system is substituted by something else we [organized labour] are the first ones to go. We found that out in Hitler's and Mussolini's days . . . . (*Maclean's*: 21 March 1977)

The current debate inevitably has renewed examination of corporatism's historical record, in particular the linkage between corporatism and fascism. In both pre-1922 Italy and pre-1933 Germany, for example, variants of tripartism were offered by fascist parties to crisis-weary electorates as a means of producing labour-management peace and national social harmony that would supersede the parliamentary framework of liberal democracy. Thus, in 1919 Mussolini declared to the constituent assembly of Italian fascists: "Present political representation cannot suffice. . . . We want direct representation of all interests"—to which the assembly responded with a call for the "creation of national technical councils of labour, industry, transportation, etc., elected by the entire profession or trade" (quoted in Guerin, 1973: 92) Similarly, the Nazi party in 1920 promised the restoration of social harmony through a consultative economic Chamber consisting of elected regional economic councils representing management and labour. That such an arrangement would in turn be conducive to labour's containment and forced submission to national economic policies was emphasized by parliamentary candidate Adolf Hitler in a confidential interview with newspaper editor Richard Breiting on May 4, 1931:

On the right is the nationally-minded bourgeoisie. . . . On the left is the working class . . . which, unfortunately, has become completely divorced from any thought of the nation through the influence of Marx. It is the business of the NSDAP [Nazis] to create a common platform upon which those now incited to revolt can find their place. . . . There is only one form to extremism and that is communism. . . . As long as we do not succeed in committing the German proletariat to the aims of the national State, the State will have no justification for existence. . . .

Naturally an end must be put to trade union policy in its

present form. The trade union policy has ruined us. Between 1925 and 1928 the budget increased by 18 milliard marks as a result of the trade union policy on wages, social security, unemployment insurance, etc. The two milliard annual reparations payments are nothing compared to this. If today we had no more reparations to pay, social democracy, in other words trade union policy, would immediately demand wage increases to absorb the two milliard saved. . . .

The elite, whether inside or outside our Party, senses that only a dictatorship can create order. The interests of the various social classes will be protected by a corporative institution, not by the Reichstag. (quoted in Calic, 1971: 21, 24, 35, 39, 41)

While no one is suggesting that Trudeau's tripartism proposals of the 1970's reflected even a particle of sympathy for fascism, a lively debate has emerged as to whether Canada's present corporatist tendencies will lead, in the 1980's and 1990's, to an authoritarian outcome similar to that of the European corporatism of previous decades. K. J. Rea and J. T. McLeod, for instance, argue that while fascism is not an inevitable consequence of corporatism, the general prospects for Canada are not bright: "As we witness the drift, or rush, toward corporatism, we have grave doubts about the prospects of individual liberty in a democratic society" (1976: 344). Even more pessimistic is D. V. Smiley, who argues that the current drift has overtones of incipient fascism:

More than a generation ago Sinclair Lewis asserted that if fascism came to the United States it would do so in the name of anti-fascism. The Canadian euphemism is to be "co-determination" or perhaps in more Orwellian language "Liberalism". A very few years ago Mr. Trudeau's spear-carriers in the intellectual and journalistic communities conferred on him an exaggerated reputation for philosophical acuteness on the basis of his reiteration of the trite but true proposition that a free society required autonomous sources of countervailing power. But where are the Trudeauvian "counterweights" in the new regime for which we are being ideologically conditioned? (1976: 448)

A supreme irony of the present Canadian situation is that of the various analyses of corporatism available to the Canadian Labour Congress as it weighs the long-term implications of tripartism, among the most cogent is the assessment of an earlier corporatism in Quebec by then freelance commentator Pierre Elliott Trudeau:

. . . Objective political economy and sociology have not yet shown how a legal superstructure, which changes nothing essential in capitalist institutions, could reconcile the opposed interests of capital and labour, except for short durations in localized sectors; monopoly tendencies (social and economic) inherent in these agreements would likely create conflicts of interest (cartel against cartel, cartel against consumers, etc.) which would be resolved only by oligarchy or removed only by dictatorship. (Trudeau, 1956: 37; my translation)

British economist E. J. Mishan warned in 1977 that "an instinct for survival is impelling the Western democracies along the road to the totalitarian state" (1977: 265). It is sobering indeed to realize that the ultimate response to capital-transfer corporatism by organized labour – the major countervailing power to state and business power – will determine to a significant degree whether Canada travels that road.

REFERENCES

Archer, Jules
  1973 *The Plot to Seize the White House.* New York and Scarborough, Ontario.
Betcherman, Lita-Rose
  1975 *The Swastika and the Maple Leaf: Fascist Movements in Canada in the Thirties.* Toronto.
Brown, Lorne and Caroline
  1973 *An Unauthorized History of the RCMP.* Toronto.
Business Week

1974   12 October
1975   22 September
Calic, Edward
   1971 *Unmasked: Two Confidential Interviews with Hitler in 1931.*
   London.
Columbian, The (New Westminster, B. C.)
   1979   24 January
Crozier, Michael, Samuel P. Huntingdon, and Joji Watanuki
   1975 *The Crisis of Democracy: Report on the Governability of Democracies to the Trilateral Commission.* New York.
Deaton, Rick
   1973 "The Fiscal Crisis on the State," in Dimitrios I.
   Roussopoulos, ed., *The Political Economy of the State.*
   Montreal.
Dupont, Pierre, and Gisele Tremblay
   1976 *Les Sundicats en Crise.* Montreal.
Financial Post, The
   1977   29 October, 26 November
   1978   25 February
Frank, Andre Gunder
   1976 "World Crisis and Underdevelopment," paper delivered
   at Tilburg, Netherlands, 26 October.
Galbraith, John Kenneth
   1978 Review of William E. Simon, *A Time for Truth,* in *The
   Guardian* (June 4): 18.
Globe and Mail, The
   1977   9, 15 March
Gordon, Walter
   1978 *What is Happening to Canada.* Toronto.
Guerin, Daniel
   1973 *Fascism and Big Business,* 2nd U.S. edition. New York.
   (Originally published in French in 1936.)
Henderson, Hazel
   1978 *Creating Alternative Futures: The End of Economics.* New
   York.
Laxer, James, and Robert Laxer
   1977 *The Liberal Idea of Canada: Pierre Trudeau and the Question
   of Canada's Survival.* Toronto.
Lewis, David

1972 *Louder Voices: the Corporate Welfare Bums.* Toronto.

Loney, Martin

1977 "A Political Economy of Citizen Participation," in Leo Panitch, ed., *The Canadian State: Political Economy and Political Power.* Toronto.

Maclean's

1977   21 March

Magil, A. B., and Henry Stevens

1938 *The Peril of Fascism: The Crisis of American Democracy.* New York.

McCormack, A. Ross

1977 *Reformers, Rebels, and Revolutionaries: The Western Canadian Radical Movements.* Toronto.

McCready, Gerald B.

1977 *Profile Canada: Social and Economic Projections.* Georgetown, Ontario.

Milner, Sheilagh Hodgins, and Henry Milner

1973 *The Decolonization of Quebec: An Analysis of Left-Wing Nationalism.* Toronto.

Mishan, E. J.

1977 *The Economic Growth Debate: An Assessment.* London.

O'Connor, James

1973 *The Fiscal Crisis of the State.* New York.

Parliament of Canada

1978   17 April

Pool, James, and Suzanne Pool

1978 *Who Financed Hitler: The Secret Funding of Hitler's Rise to Power 1919-1933.* New York.

Queen's Journal, The (Queen's University)

1976   26 November

Radwanski, George

1978 *Trudeau.* Toronto.

Rea, K. J., and J. T. McLeod, eds.

1976 *Business and Government in Canada: Selected Readings,* 2nd ed. Toronto.

Schiller, Herbert I.

1971 *Mass Communications and American Empire.* Boston.

Seldes, George

1947 *One Thousand Americans.* New York.

Smiley, D. V.
1976 "The Non-Economics of Anti-Inflation," in Rea and McLeod, eds. *Business and Government in Canada: Selected Readings.* Toronto. (Originally in *The Canadian Forum,* March, 1976.)

Star-Phoenix, The (Saskatoon)
1977   11 May

Sun, The (Vancouver)
1975   23 September
1977   12, 25 October
1978   14 February, 2 March, 6-7 and 16 June

Trudeau, Pierre Elliott
1956 *La Grève de l'amiante: une étape de la révolution industrielle au Québec.* Montreal.
1976 "Reflections on the Economy," in Rea and McLeod, eds., *Business and Government in Canada: Selected Readings.* Toronto.
1978 Text of address to the Economic Club of New York, 22 March – published in *The Sun,* Vancouver, 23 March: A14.

Ubyssey, The (University of British Columbia)
1978   3 February

Wolfe, David
1977 "The State and Economic Policy in Canada, 1968-75," in Panitch, ed., *The Canadian State: Political Economy and Political Power.* Toronto.

Wolfskill, George
1962 *The Revolt of the Conservatives: A History of the American Liberty League.* Boston.

PART II

Class, Culture, and Legitimation

EDITOR'S INTRODUCTION

In this section, the authors discuss topics which seem only remotely related to power in the sense that it was viewed in the first section. It would appear that the educational system and engagement in sports and leisure are "givens," which, even if "public," involve matters of individual choice and achievement. Of these areas of social life, education, discussed by Pike, is the basic institution most obviously considered essential in any society. Everyone participates in the educational process but the power aspect is obvious only insofar as people in urban-industrial societies are "compelled" to attend school until a certain minimum age. But, as will be seen, there are numerous political dimensions to the educational institution and process, including not simply the question of the extent and quality of education in a particular society, but the ways in which education either perpetuates the inequality of social classes and minority groups or utilizes its potential for transforming society. Thus, for groups in power, the education system is a vital agency of socialization in transmitting either supportive or transformative cultural values. The potential of formal education in doing this is particularly great in urban-industrial societies where religion and the family, the traditional "socializing" institutions, appear to play a decreasing role in the development of values and personality.

Sports or games (the engagement in spontaneous "non-work" activities), as Gruneau suggests, appear to transcend the mundane aspects of social life, releasing individuals from the everyday constraints imposed by the more utilitarian aspects of the world of work and other aspects of society which are rational or contrived. It would thus appear that sports offer a "time-out," a temporary escape from the more inhibiting aspects of social life.

But sports and play, while having the potential for social transformation and the actual effect of providing psychological and physical pleasure and gratification, are also areas that reflect the power relations in society. In the context of their spontaneous or potentially creative nature, however, sports and play may be viewed as a threat to the established order. Therefore, according to Gruneau, they are controlled to a much greater extent than most people might be willing to acknowledge.

Each of the authors, then, in different ways, discusses how these basic social institutions, which have the potential for enhancement and emancipation, are "used" by people in power, wittingly, or simply as the uncontemplative expression and influence of their status, toward making decisions that complement what they believe to be the proper norms for social order.

Education, more than sport, has been an important subject of sociological study, and the relationship between education and social-class structure has long been recognized. What has been less emphasized is the study of the role of *power* in inhibiting or encouraging changes in the class structure. This is basically the issue Pike addresses, and in doing so he provides a useful synthesis of the work done in the area. What is of even greater value in Pike's essay, in the context of the focal concern of this volume, is the comprehensive review and evaluation of both conflict (Marxist, or neo-Marxist) and order (functionalist or liberal) approaches to the study of education. The reader is fully exposed to the basic logic of these fundamentally antithetical ideological interpretations and is also presented with the empirical evidence. In this endeavour, Pike has provided discussions and evaluations of both order and conflict theories which should be of considerable aid in distinguishing the two approaches as they may apply to any topic of study, including the essays at hand.

Drawing on extensive historical data and contemporary studies, Pike points to a relationship between power and education but denies that either theoretical approach can provide a satisfactory explanation of this relationship. He cites cases where there have been contrived efforts to limit access to higher education to those who already enjoy privileged positions in the class structure, but also shows how both government policy and public opinion have caused an ever-increasing universality of access with the result of a gradual (albeit, not yet significant) narrowing of the wide gap between individuals of different social classes in educational and vocational opportunities. Pike finds merit in "neo-Marxist" or "radical-revisionist" interpretations of education in the sense that the general pattern in Canada, as in other predominantly capitalist societies, has been the reproduction of the class structure through education which, in effect, socializes individuals to accept their class position and, at the same time, legitimizes this structure of inequality. On the other hand, Pike clearly expresses his dissatisfaction with neo-Marxist "conspiracy" theories which hold that the inequalities in education, as expressed in social-class differences, are the consequence of an intentional scheme on the part of the powerful to solidify their own status and authority and to exercise social control over the potentially revolutionary powerless individuals and groups. Pike does see some merit in these approaches if they are considered in the context of specific instances, but not as a general and continuous process. With this caveat in mind, Pike concludes that there is yet potential in the existing liberal philosophy of education to bring about reforms that will provide the basis for equality of access for all.

Gruneau, in his discussion of "Power and Play in Canadian Society," employs a basic conflict perspective. His extensive historical review of sports and play points to variations in these activities as related to variations in the political economy of Canada, wherein sports, whether "amateur" or "professional," "organized" or "spontaneous," both reflect and legitimate the interests of the dominant economic elite. He shows, for example, how, in spite of the massive transition from a basically agrarian to an urban-industrial society, class differences remain in terms of both the forms of sports engaged in and the power and control over sports and play. Of the many fundamental points made by Gruneau, one of particular note is that sports have become rationalized and utilized in the arena of consumerism. Much the same might be said of other areas of popular culture, such as art and literature. They have not only served as legitimizers of the status quo, but, in their "mass production," have served as additional sources of capital revenue for the power-elite.

Both Pike and Gruneau, in this section, show how power relates to social class, culture, and the legitimation and manipulation of education and leisure. Their analysis could well apply to many other institutional areas.

CHAPTER FOUR

Education, Class, and Power in Canada
by Robert M. Pike
Queen's University

The main task of this paper is to examine the interlinkages which have existed between the educational systems and the systems of social stratification and power in Canadian society during the century and a quarter since the inception of mass public education. The paper is divided into three related parts. The first part is devoted to a brief theoretical review of the basic tenets of functionalist and conflict perspectives on education, class, and power. The second part explores the development of public education in Canada from the 1850's to the 1950's with particular reference to recent historical research within the conflict school of thought. Finally, the third part of the paper explores a number of issues and problems of schooling and inequality in Canada that have characterized educational development policies over the past twenty-five years.

I THEORETICAL CONSIDERATIONS OF EDUCATION, CLASS, AND POWER

Functionalist and Conflict Perspectives on Education

In recent years, the controversy between conflict theorists of a Marxist orientation and functionalist theorists has become "sufficiently intense to have created something of a crisis in educational research" (Karabel and Halsey, 1977: 4). The characteristics of these two approaches to the study of education have recently been examined in detail by Canadian sociologists (Murphy and Denis, 1979; Martin and Macdonell, 1978: 4), so there is no need to reiterate them in detail here. Suffice it to say that it is a

general feature of functionalist theory to view society as consisting of a relatively stable and persistent structure of elements in
which each element has a function, i.e., contributes to the maintenance of the society as a whole. Given this characteristic, it is not
surprising that functionalist writers have tended to concentrate
upon the task of describing the perceived functions of the educational system in the society, and of outlining the relationships between the educational system and other institutions such as the
family and the media (Karabel and Halsey, 1977: 35).

The functionalist approach does have the strength of clearly establishing the relationship of education to other aspects of the
social structure, but in recent times its emphasis on social integration, cohesion, solidarity, and shared norms at the expense of
such features of social life as conflict, coercion, and the struggle
for scarce resources has brought it into some disrepute as an
approach to the study of education. Conflict theory, on the other
hand, does lay emphasis upon these latter aspects of social life,
for example, on the role of education as a means of maintaining
class inequalities rather than of reducing them, and for this
reason is growing in popularity among members of the sociological fraternity. In their examination of various sociological
approaches to the study of educational institutions and processes,
Karabel and Halsey distinguished between two major kinds of
conflict orientation. One, which they described as "neo-
Weberian," is linked to Max Weber's perception of the existence
of various status groups in society which compete, partly
through the educational system, for wealth, power, and prestige
(1977: 29-30). The other, described as "neo-Marxist," takes a
number of forms, but its main thrust lies in the argument that the
role of education in capitalist society is to assist in the
intergenerational reproduction of the social division of labour associated with the capitalist economy. Among the more notable of
the neo-Marxist educational writers, American political economists Samuel Bowles and Herbert Gintis have elaborated the
interrelationship between schooling and the social relations of
production through the development of "the correspondence
principle" (1976: 131-41). In essence, this principle asserts that
non-cognitive personality traits linked to social class – for example, middle-class willingness to work hard and consistently with-

out supervision as opposed to working-class emphasis on rule-following and conformity to external authority – are reinforced through differential treatment of children of different class origins at school, and are actually more important than mental ability in allocating young people to various positions in the class structure. The correspondence between schooling and workplace is said to occur because the school reinforces the children of the privileged classes in those very traits deemed the necessary characteristics of individuals occupying positions at the upper levels of the occupational (and hence, the class) structure of capitalist society. Similarly, lower-class children tend to be reinforced in those personality traits which confirm their original class position.

Because, from the neo-Marxist perspective, the social functions of schooling are so closely tied to the overall structure of capitalism, it is evident that neo-Marxism is not only opposed to traditional functionalism, but also to the dominant liberal ideology of North America, which tends to place a good deal of faith in the opportunities offered by the institutions of free-enterprise society and which believes that reforms can be made to improve the functioning of these institutions without the need for radical social change (see Marchak, 1975). For the same reason, neo-Marxist writers on education would have little truck with the greater part of Canadian historical writing in the educational field, for here, too, with the exception of a small network of English-Canadian historians, dubbed "radical revisionists" (Sutherland, 1975: xiii-xiv), the prevailing tone has been a liberal one. However, recent studies generally have been far more critical of Canadian education than the writings of earlier historians, which tended to portray the spread of education in the nineteenth and early twentieth centuries, quite uncritically, as evidence of continuous "progress." However, like the neo-Marxists, the radical revisionists (particularly historian Michael Katz and his disciples) are worthy of special attention because they appear to accept many of the conclusions of neo-Marxist research on the history of North American education, although not necessarily all of the ideological baggage that has tended to accompany it. In particular, their critique of the tenet of liberal ideology which interprets the development of mass education in Canada since the

mid-nineteenth century as offering growing "parity of competition," and hence substantial equality of opportunity, to children
from various social strata in the population, is succinctly summarized by historian Neil Sutherland:

> North American society [radical revisionists argue] has not
> and does not offer equality along these or any other lines
> [proposed by the liberal ideology]. Even the fruits of
> industrialisation, in which the promise of abundance and con-
> sequently equality for all could most likely be realised, did not
> bring about any more egalitarian a society than the
> agricultural and commercial one that preceded it. Schools have
> not and do not offer "parity of competition." On the contrary,
> mass education has ensured – some say deliberately – that the
> old divisions of power and resources were maintained and
> extended into nineteenth and twentieth century urban and
> industrial society. Family and other factors determine what
> use youngsters will make of the school. Thus the passive
> liberal version of educational equality is merely a device to
> permit those who already have the advantage to use for their
> own benefit a system that the rhetoric says is designed for all.
> (1975: xvii-xviii)

Whereas functionalism and liberal ideology have tended to
perceive the advent and expansion of mass public education as a
positive response to the occupational and technical needs of an
increasingly complex society, we have in radical revisionism a
conflict interpretation of the development of mass public education that stresses the role of the educational system in replicating,
strengthening, and legitimizing the inequalities of the existing
social order, and thereby serving the interests of dominant social
strata. It follows from this conflict interpretation, to quote Sutherland again, that "reformers cannot hope to change schools in any
significant way without first changing the total system" (1975:
xviii). In other words, whereas supporters of liberal ideology
believe in the possibility of useful educational reform without
radical social change, this possibility tends to be rejected or
pessimistically viewed by radical revisionist historians, as it is by
many neo-Marxist sociological theorists.

II CANADIAN EDUCATIONAL DEVELOPMENT
BETWEEN THE 1850'S AND 1950'S

I want to turn now to a brief review and analysis of the development of mass public education in Canada during the hundred years from the 1850's to the 1950's: that is, from the beginnings of the movement for mass elementary education through to the eve of the post-secondary expansion of the 1960's. My purpose is to explore recent radical perspectives on educational development and change during this period in the light of more traditional historical interpretations. Inevitably, of course, the attempt to compress a century of educational history in nine disparate educational jurisdictions into the space of a few pages means that much of importance must either be ignored or given short shrift. On the other hand, the tendency to concentrate rather heavily on education in Ontario and Quebec should not be taken as yet another example of central Canadian chauvinism, but rather as a reflection of the fact that most radical sociologists and social historians have focused their attention on central Canada, and particularly upon Ontario.

Traditional Interpretation of Educational Development
The traditional historical interpretation of the development and spread of public education across the country, often in the face of regional, climatic, and sectarian obstacles, is that it could be perceived as "progress" and hence the course of the development could be traced, usually uncritically, as evidence of the successful activities of school promoters and reformers (Sutherland, 1973: xii-xiii). According to this interpretation, after a long period of instability, conflict, and change respecting the form and structure of education in the Canadian provinces prior to the 1840's there was a gradual extension of the provisions for public elementary schooling in the English-Canadian provinces (the Maritimes and Upper Canada) over the next few decades, with a possible high point being achieved in the attainment of free, compulsory, and universal education at the elementary level in Ontario in 1871. Similarly, over the following forty-year period, from Manitoba's initial Education Act, also in 1871, to the creation of public school systems in the Northwest Territories (later Alberta and Saskatchewan) around the turn of the century, the provision of

tax-supported elementary schooling was extended to the great majority of children in the western provinces. This elementary schooling was followed relatively swiftly by the development of public secondary education which, in the words of one historian, was beginning by 1914 to replace elementary schooling as "the university of the people" (Stamp, 1970: 325). By the 1930's, according to another historian, high school students were no longer a select group, but "every man's son and daughter," so that these institutions were obliged to broaden their previously narrow academic and professional curricula (Johnson, 1968: 144).

Proponents of this particular view of educational history do not generally suggest that the "progress of education" was without some setbacks – one of the nastiest of which was the trampling upon minority rights to tax-supported separate schools by the Manitoba government in the 1890's. However, these bad spots en route to mass public education for English-Canadian youth are somewhat easier to obscure in a rosy haze of optimism than is the history of education in the province of Quebec. In that province, after some initial hopeful moves in the direction of mass public schooling in the 1850's and 1860's, the School Act of 1875 granted the Protestant minority of the province almost complete autonomy in the running of their own educational system, thereby ensuring that there would be little chance for the exchange of ideas and cooperation between the two entirely distinct cultural communities, English and French-Canadian (see Quebec, *Report of the Royal Commission*, I, 1963: 12-13). The Quebec School Act of 1875 also dramatically increased the power of the Catholic Church hierarchy over educational policy within the Catholic school system. The consequence of this latter development, according to French-Canadian historian Louis-Philippe Audet, was to bring together a coalition of conservative, traditionalist, and ultramontanist Catholic influences which successfully denied the provincial government any important role in the field of education in Quebec for many long decades to come (Audet, 1970: 338). Indeed, it was the ideology of "anti-statism" associated with this coalition which many educational historians believe can account for the repeated defeat of attempts to pass legislation imposing compulsory education prior to the final success of a compulsory education bill in 1943. Furthermore, while the effective exclusion of the provincial government from educational matters did not unduly hinder the relatively wealthy Protestant (and predominantly English-Canadian) community from building up a well-articulated series of levels of schooling from elementary through secondary to university, French-Canadian youth who wished to proceed beyond the primary level in Quebec could do so only through attendance at one of a number of fee-paying classical colleges which constituted an effective barrier to all but children of the privileged few (Audet, 1970: 344-55). Despite some attempts to expand educational opportunities for French-Canadian youth during the 1920's and 1930's (mainly through the introduction of "superior" elementary schools offering some limited secondary instruction), public secondary schooling, that is, free, tax-supported secondary schooling, was not made fully available to French-Canadians in Quebec until 1956 (Johnson, 1968: 151).

Radical Interpretations of Educational Development

THE CASE OF PUBLIC ELEMENTARY EDUCATION

The above paragraphs clearly constitute a very brief version of the growth of public education in Canada. Also, it must be admitted that the comments on the fate of public education in Quebec possibly could be seen as constituting evidence of an uncritical acceptance of the merits of mass public education, which radical historians and conflict theorists so frequently question. Nonetheless, while the popular line of many French-Canadian historians, that the Catholic Church and its lay supporters were a monolithic and reactionary first cause of the backwardness of Quebec education, has recently been questioned by Terry Copp (1974), it is certainly a blow to common knowledge to be told, in Stephen Schecter's recent Marxist-oriented historical study of class and educational reform in Canada, that Quebec had the highest daily attendance rate of all the provinces *before* the passing of the compulsory attendance bill (1977: 383). The actual significance and meaning of this observation is open to some debate,* but it fits

---

*As shown in the Census of Canada returns for 1921 and 1931, Quebec had a

well with Schecter's more general argument that the early Canadian proponents of mass public schooling, in the first half of the nineteenth century, anticipated a time when the social misery and class conflict associated with the rise of laissez-faire capitalism in Europe and the United States would come to their own less-industrialized country. Hence, Schecter argues, they fought against the obscurantism of those conservative vested interests that opposed the spread of mass education, because they believed that education could be utilized to ensure the formation and maintenance of a self-disciplined and quiescent population and labour force. Ultimately, although the lack of compulsory education did not mean the lack of schooling (as the Quebec case indicates), the compulsory attendance laws became utilized, in Schecter's view, as one more weapon in the arsenal of the ruling class. Yet – and the point is important – "proponents of public education could . . . delude themselves that what they were doing was really in the best interests of the working class; and the arguments invoked [for compulsory education] became new elements in the legitimizing myths of schools" (1977: 384).

Schecter is imputing a variety of states of mind to the early school promoters: they were clear-sighted enough to see that class conflict was on its way, but could later delude themselves that they were working in the best interests of the working class. This point, of course, raises a whole set of questions about the motives of the school promoters and reformers in Canada during the nineteenth and early twentieth centuries, as well as about the consequences of their action for children from the various social strata of the society. Since both liberal and radical scholars agree that the development of mass public education in English Canada

---

somewhat smaller proportion of its population in the 7-14 age group "at school for any period" than any other province with the exception of New Brunswick in 1921 (Census of Canada, 1931, vol. I, Table 69). Again, in 1931, 67 per cent of 14 year olds in Quebec were reported as being "at school for any period" compared with 90 per cent of 14 year olds in Ontario (ibid., Table 70). Clearly, therefore, while it is possible that those children who did attend school in Quebec did so more regularly than those children attending school in other provinces, it is dubious logic to utilize high daily school attendance rates in the province as an indication that compulsory education laws were unnecessary. However, while this appears to be what Schecter is implying, the point is not made quite clear in his paper.

between about 1850 and 1930 was largely the work of middle-class men and women who lived in the growing urban centres of the province (see Sutherland, 1976: 14-15), it is well to inquire into their motives and actions through a more detailed analysis of the kind of society they wanted to see maintained and strengthened, and the challenges within their social environ-ments to which mass public schooling seemed an appropriate response.

We may start this inquiry with a look at the challenges by which the school reformers saw themselves confronted. The most notable of these challenges (common, incidentally, to Quebec and to English Canada alike) were the perceived threats to social stability and to the virtues seen to be inherent in the old, pre-dominantly agricultural way of life, of the growth of the towns and cities. The spread of urbanization in Canada, which turned the society from a largely rural and local one in the 1850's and 1860's to one in which, by 1891, over a quarter of the population lived in cities of 100,000 or more inhabitants, was fed by long-term migration of people from the countryside to the towns as well as by successive waves of foreign migrants, many of whom settled in or gravitated to the urban areas. In turn, many of these new city dwellers became members of a growing urban proletariat which included not only "respectable" tradesmen and craftsmen but also large numbers of impoverished children and adults who constituted an underclass beyond the pale of respec-table society. The urbanization process started early in central Canada, and its impact upon the middle-class "school pro-moters" is excellently documented in a recent study by Alison Prentice of the relationship between education and social class in Ontario around the mid-nineteenth century (Prentice, 1977). As she notes there, the middle-class school promoters looked askance at an urban society, of which they were themselves mainly the products but which they saw as increasingly domi-nated by crass materialism, ignorance, and an increase in juvenile crime (ibid.: 50). They viewed, similarly, the large numbers of impoverished and wretched immigrants, notably from Ireland, who poured into North America in the late 1840's and 1850's as a potential threat to public order and to the principles of industry and hard endeavour (ibid.: 56). Finally, in Prentice's words, the school promoters "became more and more concerned about the potential for conflict between the two great classes of society. What was to prevent the poor from robbing or murdering the rich? Was there a real likelihood of class war and, if so, could it be contained?" (*ibid.*: 67) The answer to this latter question for the middle classes was, in Prentice's view, to create a network of free elementary schools which would provide the industrious and intelligent youth of the province with the opportunity to set out on the road to wealth and power, while concurrently ensuring that those members of the lower classes who failed to better themselves would be taught, through the schools, to become disciplined, productive, and safe members of the society (*ibid.*: 115).

Since those who plan, establish, and administer an educational system are hardly likely to approve of its utilization in ways which might undermine (as opposed to maintain or augment) the power of the social groups or classes to which they belong, it is hardly exceptional to discover that the school promoters of mid- and late-nineteenth century Ontario hoped that the new public educational system would enhance the prospects for social stability and good order upon which the power of the middle classes rested. On the other hand, if the recent radical revisionist studies of schooling in Hamilton and Toronto in the 1850's can be taken reasonably to represent educational developments elsewhere in the province (see particularly Katz, 1975; Davey, 1975), there is a certain irony in their discovery that children from well-to-do families took at least as much and possibly more advantage of the new public schools than did the children of the poor. If correct, this finding would indicate that the new school facilities did not confer particular opportunities for upward mobility upon the able children of the lower classes, but rather, by increasing the general levels of schooling in the population, obliged the poor, as Michael Katz puts it, "to run harder than ever just to keep from falling behind" (Katz, 1975: 284). The radical revisionist view is that the move towards universal and compulsory elementary education in Ontario between the 1840's and the 1870's, accompanied as it was by the increased centralization and bureaucratization of the system of public education as the reformers attempted to bring the frequently recalcitrant lower classes into the schools, reinforced rather than mitigated class inequalities. While compulsory education entrapped the lower classes in the coils of bureaucracy, it did little to improve their educational position relative to the privileged position of the wealthy.

At this point, one must ask an important question: that is, can the fact that mass public elementary education may not have lived up to the promises that its proponents made for it be taken as an indication that the school promoters of the nineteenth century were wittingly engaged in a form of subterfuge? In other words, did they utilize mass education in their own interests as a tool of class domination and legitimation while being aware that it would not "deliver the goods" of upward mobility for the lower classes? The answer to this question clearly cannot be known for certain, but much of the available evidence does, in fact, suggest that the reformers believed what they preached. For example, the doyen of them all, Chief Superintendent of Schools Egerton Ryerson, combined fears about the dangers of social disorder with what appears to have been a genuine concern for the education of the poor and a genuine concern that "arbitrary" class distinctions of an inherited nature should play no part in the educative process (Prentice, 1977: 123). We do not appear to be looking at a case of conspiracy, sugar-coated by hypocritical protestations of liberalism, on the part of the Ontario school promoters. Rather, what we seem to have here is a case of the impact of a "dominant value system" which these promoters themselves believed and propagated, and which most of the lower classes either passively acquiesced to, or actively supported. Therefore, although radical revisionist historical research on education at later historical periods remains in its infancy, it seems reasonable to assume that a dominant-value perspective is generally a far more useful framework for analysis over time and geographical space than the frequently naive conspiracy viewpoint.

However, a caveat is in order here, because one is obliged to admit that there are numerous examples in Canadian educational history between the 1850's and 1930's where the political and educational representatives of the dominant Anglo-Canadian (or, in the case of the Indians, the dominant European) majority group instituted policies designed either to restrict drastically the educational opportunities of racial and immigrant minorities or to assimilate them forcibly into the culture and language of the majority. This may be called either "conspiracy" or "coercion" by a dominant group, but in any event it evoked far more bitterness and more opposition than is apparent in the response of the Anglo-Canadian working class to the establishment and expansion of mass public education. But then, of course, most racial and immigrant minorities combined the double stigma of being both lower-class and linguistically and culturally distinctive (see, for example, Sutherland 1976: 201-15).

SECONDARY EDUCATION IN ENGLISH CANADA:1880-1950

The revisionist perspective on the expansion of public elementary education clearly stresses the interrelationship between this expansion and the social control function of schooling – that is, the elementary schools to a large extent were established and expanded in the late nineteenth century because the elites needed subtle mechanisms of control to enable them to promote an acceptance of the existing social order among the mass of the population (and, the neo-Marxists would add, to train an acquiescent work force for the capitalist labour market). Similarly, while revisionist study of the expansion of Canadian public secondary schooling in the late nineteenth and early twentieth centuries is limited mainly to a section of the paper by Schecter, his neo-Marxist explanation for this expansion again is mainly in terms of social control. For example, he argues that the developments in technical education during the early decades of the century "were important not for the skills they provided but for the character formation they permitted. . . . The education the working mechanic and foreman received would ensure that they possessed the dispositions and attitudes necessary, from capital's viewpoint, to hold subordinate but supervisory positions in the new occupational hierarchy emerging within capitalist production" (Schecter, 1977: 388). Again, on the social control theme, the development of testing and tracking functions within the expanding secondary schools was carried out by educators in the name of child development, but, in Schecter's view, "functioned so as to bring the working-class child to acquiesce in his own subordination" (ibid.: 390). Similar perspectives on the rise of the comprehensive high school in the United States are offered by Bowles and Gintis.

One can accept that the above neo-Marxist views on the expansion of secondary education have some explanatory value without thereby being committed to the crude notion that the only significant reason for the expansion of schooling in capitalist societies – whether at the elementary, secondary, or post-secondary levels – has been the desire of elites for more sophisticated mechanisms of social control. This point needs to be stated because, while elite theory and dominant value theory are certainly elements necessary to a full understanding of the processes of educational reform, there are also a number of other reasons why schooling has expanded in North America, and in many economically advanced countries elsewhere, during the last one hundred years. For example, the traditional functionalist position that this expansion may be linked to the necessity to provide the more sophisticated cognitive skills required in occupational life in industrial, as compared to predominantly agricultural, societies presumably has some validity, irrespective of whether we are looking at education in a capitalist or state socialist country. Again, it is difficult to deny that, both in English Canada and in the United States, the increasing momentum of the growth in popular demands for more education played an important part in the expansion of elementary and secondary schooling, just as it has, in more recent times, in the growth of post-secondary education. It might conceivably be argued by radical historians that these popular demands were initially stimulated by ultimately unfulfilled promises of upward mobility and equality of opportunity (and hence by the dominant ideology of liberalism), but there is little doubt, nevertheless, that such demands were instrumental in developing more support for the expansion that was partly independent of the interests of particular elite groups (see Hurn, 1978: 72).

In short, explanations for the expansion of mass education at any level need to be multi-causal; but what does remain a problem is whether the growth of public secondary education in English Canada during the first half of this century provided more opportunities for "the common people" than, if the revisionist histories of education in nineteenth century Ontario are to be believed, did the prior expansion of the public elementary schools. In the absence of detailed socio-historical research on the expansion of public secondary schooling, it is much easier to raise the question outlined above than it is to answer it with any great degree of confidence. However, one can make some informed suggestions about the probable impact of the expansion of secondary education on educational opportunity, and certainly they are not as sanguine as the observations of the two educational historians cited above who noted that, by 1914, secondary education in English Canada was becoming "the university of the people" and that, by the 1930's, high school students were no longer a select group but "every man's son and daughter."

These observations are valid to the extent that they imply that the new secondary schools did not cater exclusively to one privileged social segment of the population. On the other hand, insofar as they appear to be claiming that the schools were catering to a broadly representative social cross-section of the population, they are in conflict with much of the available evidence that suggests the public secondary schools of English Canada retained a relatively high degree of both academic and social selectivity until well into the fourth and fifth decades of this century. For example, at the time of the Census of 1951, the social selectivity of secondary schooling was shown in the fact that the proportions of young people then aged 14-24 years in school who were living at home ranged from 71 per cent of the sons and daughters of professional people down to about 35 per cent of the children of unskilled manual workers (Porter, 1965: 180). Again, in their written submission to a review of educational policies in Canada undertaken by the Organization for Economic Cooperation and Development in 1975, the Ministers of Education of the four western provinces observed that prior to the 1950's, secondary education in the west existed mainly in the larger urban centres and tended "by reason of its strong academic emphasis, to eliminate all but the intellectual elite, those whose native abilities, motivations and opportunities warranted or permitted pursuits in higher education in the universities" (OECD, 1975: 42). Since, as John Porter has shown in The Vertical Mosaic (1965: 87), the children of well-paid professional and managerial workers made up almost one half of the relatively small proportion of the 18-24 age group who reached university in Canada during the 1950's (an estimated 46 per cent in 1956, although the children in these classes constituted only 11.5 per cent of children in the total population), the evidence is that the "intellectual elite" referred to by the western ministers was, in fair measure, also the social elite.

If we add to the above data an awareness of the social exclusivity of many of the fee-paying private secondary schools of both English Canada and Quebec, which were the alma maters of close to one-third of the members of Canada's economic and political elites in the 1950's, although they catered to only 6 per cent of boys in secondary schools in English Canada in 1951 (Porter, 1965: 284), then we are led to suggest, in line with the revisionist perspective on the growth of compulsory elementary education, that the expansion of public secondary education probably did not lead to any major equalization of previously existing class differentials in educational opportunity. More specifically, what this suggestion implies is that, although larger percentages of children from all social class backgrounds were receiving some secondary education in 1950 than in 1930 or 1900, the children of the more privileged classes had apparently succeeded in maintaining all or most of their *relative* advantage within the educational system compared with those from lower-class homes. The maintenance of this relative advantage does not mean, as simplistic neo-Marxist interpretations sometimes seem to suggest, that lower-class youth were entirely excluded from levels of education which gave them access to the top positions of prestige and power in the society. On the contrary – and certainly an indication that the neo-Marxist "correspondence principle" is hardly inviolable – even during the 1950's a substantial minority of Canadian university students were the children of ordinary white-collar and skilled manual workers for whom access to higher levels of education provided the main mode of upward mobility. Thus, the correspondence between class and schooling, although strong, was far from absolute; this fact, when viewed from a liberal perspective might, despite the glaring inequalities, have given hopes that further educational reforms would prove an effective means of achieving a meritocratic system of educational selection unencumbered by the influence of family and home environment.

THE CASE OF EDUCATION IN QUEBEC

The main issue held to be at point in the province of Quebec is whether radical arguments, applied mainly to Ontario (and, by implication, to the rest of English Canada), are appropriate to an analysis of the development of public education in the distinctive social and religious context of Quebec society. The late establishment of compulsory schooling in that province has already been noted, as has the tendency for French-Canadian historians to blame the poor elementary and secondary educational facilities made available to French-Canadian youth, in particular, upon the reactionary attitudes of the Catholic Church. However, it is the opinion of Terry Copp (1974) that the blame placed upon the admittedly conservative role of the Church in educational affairs tends to obscure the very real problems imposed upon the Catholic educational system of the province by lack of adequate financial resources. More particularly, in Montreal finances for the support of education were obtained mainly from property taxes. Since the Catholic community of the city was far less well-endowed with affluent members than the relatively prosperous Protestant community, the Catholic school system suffered from grievous financial hardships as a result of a limited tax base. For example, the Catholic population of Montreal constituted more than three-quarters of the population of the city between 1897-1910, yet in those years the Catholic School Board received roughly the same amount of municipal school tax as the Protestant Board, which catered to the remaining quarter of the population. As a result, the latter Board was able to provide better educational facilities and hire better teachers than were available to the Catholic Board, and hence to the French-Canadian majority of the city (Copp, 1974: 62-3). For Copp, this factor, rather than the role of the Church, helps to explain the delay in providing public secondary education for Catholics in Montreal (and presumably in other parts of Quebec) and also the low retention rates among Catholic school children.

To continue Copp's argument, the differences in quality and quantity of public education in Montreal for Protestants and Catholics were a product of the unequal division of the school tax, and this undoubtedly reflected the greater political and economic power of the Anglo-Protestant minority. He points out, however, the necessity of going beyond this rather obvious point to stress that, since the Protestant Board was hardly excessively funded, an equal division of the tax would have resulted in two impoverished school systems (*ibid.*: 69). The really interesting question for Copp is why the French-Canadian elite exerted so little pressure to fund an adequate public school system while the Anglo-Protestant leaders in Montreal proved to be very active in public school affairs. The answer to the question, he believes, lies in the fact that the Catholic upper classes did not send their children to public schools but rather to subsidized private schools and classical colleges, whereas the Protestant public school system catered both to the Anglo-Canadian upper class as well as to the Jewish and Protestant working class. Hence, the Catholic (and mainly French-Canadian) elite lacked any concrete reason for major interest in the provision of adequate public education for the Catholic (and mainly French-Canadian) working class; the Protestant elite, by contrast, had good reason to be concerned with the condition of the schools which catered to their children (Copp, 1974).

The educational situation in Quebec during this period and Copp's analysis of education in Montreal raise some interesting questions for an understanding of Canadian educational development. For example, the radical interpretation of the development of public elementary and secondary education in English Canada places much emphasis on the role of compulsory attendance as an elite mechanism for the avoidance of class conflict and as a mode of class domination; but how is it that the Quebec elites delayed so long before instituting the same effective means of social control? In a province with a relatively strong tradition of elite dominance, did the prospect of a proletarian uprising seem more unlikely to the elites of Quebec than it did, say, in Toronto or Halifax? Or were the elites perhaps content in the knowledge that the government and the Catholic Church in the province were endeavouring to ensure that the French-Canadian working class remained quiescent and humble in the face of exploitation by one of the most unbridled free enterprise systems in North America? At present, we do not have answers to these, and similar, questions, but research into them would certainly introduce an interesting comparative element into radical interpretations of

Canadian educational development.

The gloomy financial picture Copp paints of Catholic education in Montreal persisted, in some measure, until the 1950's; and it undoubtedly was replicated in many other parts of the province. This being so, one might well hypothesize that, if the Catholic elite of Quebec had shown as much concern for the financing of public education as their Protestant counterparts, or as the middle-class school promoters of English Canada, then the predominantly French-Canadian working class would have been among the beneficiaries. Further, whether this elite concern had been motivated by "enlightened self-interest" or liberal zeal, its impact would have varied little. As it was, however, the full force of the social inequalities of the wider society were given free play within the Quebec educational system, so that, as late as 1949-50, only 21 per cent of Catholic boys in Quebec were still at school in Grade IX compared with 50 per cent of Protestant boys and girls in the province and 53 per cent of boys and girls in Ontario (Tremblay, 1955: 36). Such an hypothesis does, of course, tend to make a case in favour of the activities of the school promoters of Canada during the long period under review. Admittedly, few of them showed much interest in the possibility of a direct attack on the major inequalities in the distribution of income, power, and prestige that were an integral part of the society in which they lived, and for this reason, they tend to stand condemned by radical authors. However, such a condemnation appears to be based upon the assumption that the school reformers should have been much more enlightened than the rest of their educated contemporaries. It also tends to ignore the very real benefits to all social strata of such liberal measures as the major expansion of health care services for children through the schools, which occurred between the 1890's and 1930's, and the emphasis on increasing rates of functional literacy. In saying this, we are not, of course, casting aside the abundant evidence that many of the benefits of educational expansion and reform were distributed in a manner which favoured the continued dominance of those who already had, rather than in favour of the have-nots. The real issue, both then and now, is whether a socially and economically unequal society can ever achieve a fair distribution of educational opportunities and whether, indeed, radical egalitarian policies within the wider society do, or do not, constitute the only viable solution to the problem of educational inequality.

III   CONTEMPORARY DIRECTIONS AND ISSUES IN EDUCATION

The Education Expansion

In the twenty years immediately following the Second World War, many scholars believed that the systems of public education in Canada were ill-fitted and unprepared to meet the occupational demands of advanced industrialization. Thus, in 1965, John Porter wrote that the country had created an illusion of educational adequacy through the importation of much of its skilled manpower, but that "it can scarcely be said in a country where in 1951 only two-fifths of those between fifteen and nineteen years of age were still in school and where less than one in twelve of the college age group were in college, that the demands of an industrial society were being met" (Porter, 1965: 166). Such a view may, of course, appear ironic from the vantage point of the late 1970's when one of the major educational issues is the under-employment of skilled and educated manpower rather than its shortage, but the contrast over time is indicative of the great expansion in public education which occurred from the late 1950's through to the early 1970's. Although not alone among the nations, Canadian governments and people were caught up in a wave of education worship which was without parallel in the nation's history.

A few statistical trends serve to tell the tale of the great expansion during the sixties. Between 1961 and 1969, the proportion of Gross National Product which was devoted to education rose from 4.3 per cent to 7.6 per cent; in 1961, education had accounted for 14 per cent of all major expenditures at all levels of government; in 1971-72, it accounted for 22 per cent of such expenditures. School retention rates rose sharply, too, with the percentage of seventeen-year-old males still in school standing at 66 per cent in 1972-73 compared to 51 per cent just eleven years earlier (the increased retention rate among girls was even greater, being 63 per cent in 1972-73 compared with 42 per cent in 1961-

62).* In turn, this increased retention in school was linked to the enhanced opportunities for admission to post-secondary institutions, which included not just the universities but also the new colleges for post-secondary technical and vocational education established in most provinces during the decade. As a result of both demographic influences and increased school retention, full-time enrolments at the post-secondary level rose from the equivalent of 10.6 per cent of the 18-24 age-group in 1961-62 to 18.4 per cent in 1972-73.

In 1976, the external examiners who reviewed educational policies in Canada for the Organization for Economic Cooperation and Development summarized the changes thus: "until the late 1940's, Canada could be counted as one of the less developed (educationally) of the great democracies. Today, it is numbered clearly amongst the educational leaders, certainly so far as quantitative development is concerned" (OECD, 1976: 22). Indeed, in at least one province, Quebec, where one of the cornerstones of the so-called "quiet revolution" of the 1960's was the modernization of the systems of public education, the changes which took place in the space of a very short period—only eight or nine years—were quite profound. A Quebec Ministry of Education was finally established as the central organization for the administration of education for both Catholic and Protestant communities, and the Church lost much of its hitherto direct involvement in educational affairs. By the late 1960's, both Catholic and Protestant youth in Quebec had access to a fairly wide range of educational programs and levels, which stretched from kindergarten to the newly-formed colleges (CEGEP's) and the rapidly expanding universities. The traditional framework of education in the province, geared as it was to rural society, had finally fallen before the pressure of urbanization and industrialization.

Having outlined some of the major features of the expansion, our task now is to explore the nature of the benefits which governments and people perceived as accruing to more education, and which motivated them to devote a seemingly ever-

*All these statistical data are taken from the statistical appendix to the report of the Organization for Economic Cooperation and Development on Educational Policies in Canada (1976).

increasing proportion of national and individual financial assets to the pursuit of educational growth.

Human Capital and Rates of Return

Throughout the 1960's, American and Canadian economists advocated the expansion of higher education because it constituted an investment in "human capital." In essence, human capital theory was based upon the belief that, once a high level of physical capital accumulation and advanced industrial organization had been achieved, further economic growth depended mainly on technical innovation; and, in turn, technical innovation was seen as a product of highly skilled and qualified "brain-power." Hence, more educated people meant more productivity. In Canada, the appeal of the theory was particularly great because higher productivity in the United States and a generally better-educated labour force, including more university graduates, was often interpreted by Canadian policy-makers as an indication that the attainment of American educational levels also would result in the attainment of American productivity levels (Pike, 1970: 13).

If this was the view of human capital at a macro-social level, at the level of family and individual the theory showed its impact through the increased willingness of Canadian parents and their children to invest more time and money in education. Most of them did so because such an investment was assumed to pay substantial dividends in the form of better occupations and higher incomes. The message of "investment in self" was an integral part of human capital-productivity theory, and well-attuned to the traditional ideology of the "open society" with its wide opportunities for upward social mobility. However, the post-secondary institution rather than the primary or secondary school became the goal of ambitious Canadian youth.

The evidence is that human capital theory, both in its linkage to national productivity and to individual achievement, played a substantial role in fostering the educational expansion of the 1950's and 1960's. Nonetheless, one may doubt that the impact of the theory would have been nearly as great as it actually was, had the materialistic message it purveyed not melded very neatly with the moral tenets of the liberal notion of equality of educational opportunity. At the roots of this notion lies the belief that all young people should be provided with an opportunity commensurate with their abilities irrespective of their origins, locality, sex, or race. From a human capital perspective, as well as a moral one, such a belief is attractive, since the failure to eliminate barriers to educational achievement that arise from the inequalities of the wider social environment can be seen as an inefficient utilization of human resources. This failure, then, would reduce the potential for growth in Gross National Product. Not unnaturally, too, since many functionalist writers argue that social stratification attracts the most talented and ambitious persons to the highest occupational positions in the society, they could whole-heartedly support an economic doctrine which, in alliance with a moral concept, presented the notion of an ideal "fit" between top jobs and top talents as a sound social and economic goal.

In retrospect, this merging of economic theory, liberal doctrine, and functionalism can be seen as having created an almost irresistible set of arguments in favour of educational expansion and reform. Thus, educational policies could be proposed by politicians and administrators on the grounds that they would be socially egalitarian, with an added impetus to reform being offered by the perceived economic benefits it offered to individuals and to society. Certainly, the outcome was a wide range of educational measures instituted between the mid-1950's and the early 1970's. Some of these measures – for example, the establishment of large-scale public financial aid programs for post-secondary students, the consolidation of small school districts, and the abandonment of many small schools in favour of the busing of rural children to large central schools offering more comprehensive facilities – fitted, like many earlier reforms, into the ideological framework of the "passive" liberal version of educational equality, insofar as their main purpose was to make educational facilities and services more equally available to all students who were intellectually capable and desirous of making use of them. However, other measures – notably those associated with a growing range of counselling, vocational, and testing services and with the provision of remedial education and special programs for disadvantaged and immigrant youth – were based upon a more "active" definition of the concept, insofar as they were linked to the assumption that the educational system could be utilized as an active agent of social equalization.

In their report, the OECD examiners refer to the educational efforts linked to the passive version of the principle of educational quality as being the first, and earliest, of a succession of educational equalization policies, while those linked to the view of the educational system as participating actively in social equalization constitute a more advanced, and recent, second phase (OECD, 1976: 38-9). Not fitting neatly into either phase, but certainly relevant to equalization policies, is the substantial emphasis on child-centred learning which emerged during the 1960's, and which was accompanied by the relaxation of hitherto rigid patterns of streaming and grade promotion in favour of much more flexible curricula choice and promotion on an individual subject basis. These child-centred reforms were intended to be of benefit to all children. In theory at least, they might have been expected to be of most advantage to those lower-class and minority group students who all too frequently had been trapped in holding programs at the elementary school or junior secondary school levels.

Educational Reform and Educational Opportunity in Contemporary Canada

What were the effects of the educational expansion of the 1950's and 1960's, and of the educational reforms which accompanied it, on the established links between social inequality and differentiated educational opportunities in Canadian society? At earlier stages of this paper, we asked similar questions about the growth of mass elementary education in the nineteenth century and of mass secondary education during the first half of the twentieth century. In both instances, we were led somewhat pessimistically to doubt whether, on the basis of available evidence, the earlier expansions had been accompanied by any significant decline in differences in educational opportunity related to class. Here, we shall be concerned mainly with the social impact of the expansion of post-secondary education, although with due recognition of the fact that the particular social characteristics of the post-secondary student population largely result from the patterns of social selection which occur in the secondary schools.

Thus, given the above, it is well to commence the discussion with a glance at the process of social selection in the secondary schools. Here we may note that the many educational reforms of the period did not succeed in overcoming the impact of social inequality on educational opportunity. As the OECD examiners expressed it in their review of the impact of phase-two equalization policies, "even the most comprehensive program of in-school efforts has not alone sufficed to eliminate the many-sided forms of disadvantage and inequality of opportunity that children experience" (*ibid.*: 39). Indeed, we do not have to seek very far in the research data on educational opportunity in Canada to prove this point; it is well enough known not to require extensive elaboration. As just one example, the detailed survey of Ontario high school students by Marion Porter, John Porter, and Bernard Blishen showed, among many manifestations of social inequality, that lower-class high school students in the top third of the measured ability range were far more likely to enroll in the four-year academic and vocational program terminating at Grade XII, and giving immediate access to the Ontario Colleges of Applied Arts and Technology but not to the provincial universities, than were middle-class students in the same range of mental ability. These latter were much more likely to opt for the five-year program terminating at Grade XIII and, where successfully completed, qualifying for entrance to university. Furthermore, while entrance to the four-year program was found by the authors to have a depressing effect upon students' educational aspirations, it was also the case that, irrespective of the course in which they were enrolled, bright lower-class students experienced a far greater gap between their educational aspirations and their educational expectations than bright middle-class students: that is, a substantially smaller proportion of bright lower-class students than of bright middle-class students who aspired to go to university actually expected to do so (M. Porter *et al.*, 1975: chapter 3). The authors believed that this patent manifestation of educational inequality had, at root, an economic basis.

To the above evidence of the continuing interconnection between social selection and academic selection *within* the high schools, we must, of course, add the continued role of the more exclusive private schools which, since they concentrate heavily on university preparatory study and still play a major part in the transfer of upper-class and elite status from one generation to the next, help to form a pattern of academic and social stratification *between* schools (see Clement, 1975; Maxwell and Maxwell, 1971 and 1975). Not surprisingly, of course, in view of these various patterns of class-based educational selection at the secondary school level, recent surveys of the socio-economic characteristics of full-time post-secondary students continue to show that, as in the 1950's, they still tend to be drawn from the upper socio-economic strata of Canadian society. For example, the data in Table 1

Table 1
Educational Attainment of Fathers
of
Full-Time Post-Secondary Students: Canada, 1974-75

Fathers' Educational Attainment	(1) Terminal	(2) Transfer	(3) Undergraduate	(4) Educational Attainment of the 45 to 64 Male Population (1975)
Elementary	31.9	23.9	19.8	37.4
Some High School	29.0	21.7	23.8	25.3
Completed High School	14.5	14.9	15.1	13.5
Total Elementary and Secondary	75.4	60.5	58.7	76.2
Post-Secondary Non-University	13.0	15.3	12.5	12.7*
Some University	3.9	7.0	7.1	3.6
University Degree(s)	7.7	17.2	21.7	7.6
Total Post-Secondary	24.6	39.5	41.3	23.9
Grand total	100.0	100.0	100.0	100.0
Numbers	93,195	59,437	189,275	2,113,003

*This percentage includes males with "other education or training" not necessarily of post-secondary standing.
SOURCES: Department of the Secretary of State, *Post-Secondary Student Survey 1974-75*, Ottawa, 1976; and M. von Zur-Muehlen, *The Educational Background of Parents of Post-Secondary Students in Canada*, Statistics Canada, Finance Statistics Branch, 1978 (unpublished). The level of educational attendance of the 45-64 male population in 1975 is based upon the Statistics Canada *Labour Force Survey* of 1975.

show the educational level of the fathers of those post-secondary students who responded to the nation-wide Post-Secondary Student Survey carried out by the federal government in 1974-75.

The full-time students in the table have been divided into three categories: community-college terminal students (i.e., those whose courses terminate at community college level); community college transfer students (i.e., those whose courses lead on to university studies); and university undergraduate students. The educational levels attained by the fathers of students in each of these categories are taken to constitute a reasonable indication of overall socio-economic status, and hence are compared with the educational levels attained by men aged 45 to 64 years in the general population in 1975 (column 4). The comparison reveals quite clearly that both community college transfer students and undergraduate students are between two and three times as likely to be drawn from the upper socio-economic strata (that is, where the father has some university education or a university degree) as their numbers in the total population would appear to warrant. On the other hand, students whose fathers had only an elementary education (and who are likely to be lower status in origin) are substantially under-represented among both transfer and undergraduate groups. However, in contrast to this evidence of the continued social selectivity of university-related studies, it is interesting to note that the community college students in terminal programs appear to be reasonably representative of all socio-economic categories in the Canadian population.

Of course, one limitation of the above data is that while they provide some indication of current levels of class-related inequality of access to university or university-related studies, they do not show whether class differences have lessened, or indeed widened, since John Porter carried out his pioneering research on the social origins of Canadian students at university in the 1950's (Porter, 1965). Another limitation, although less obvious, is that the table excludes part-time post-secondary students, and evidence both from the Post-Secondary Student Survey and my own research on the Ontario part-time undergraduate population (Pike, 1978) suggests that a relatively substantial proportion of the increasing numbers of older students who enrolled in part-time university studies during the 1960's and early 1970's were of lower- and lower middle-class origins. However, we have problems enough if we restrict ourselves just to the first of the above limitations, because substantial methodological difficulties must be faced in comparing levels of accessibility to university education for various social strata over time. Perhaps the most that can be said is that, while university expansion of the 1960's and early 1970's clearly provided access to degree-level studies for higher proportions of students from all social strata of the society, most of the available evidence does not indicate there was more than a small increase in the participation levels of students of lower-class origins relative to the participation of students from the more privileged classes. This evidence is based upon research of Pike (1970) and Harvey (1974; 1977a; 1977b), and should be balanced against the substantial opportunities for access to post-secondary technical and vocational studies which were created with the establishment of the community colleges.

*The Case for Greater Equality of Condition**
If we relate the above conclusions to our overall historical discussion of the impact of educational change and educational reform in Canada, there is a strong sense of *plus ça change, plus c'est la même chose*—that is, educational reforms are made and educational facilities expanded, but the students of relatively privileged backgrounds are still highly over-represented in the universities which traditionally have provided the qualifications to the most prestigious and well-paid occupations in the society (even though, as we shall see, the close relationship between educational attainment and extrinsic returns has weakened in recent years). By the same token, lower-status youth still seem to face substantial barriers to the full realization of their potential in the schools, and they are relatively more likely, when they continue their education beyond high school, to enroll in the terminal programs of the community colleges that lead to "middle-range" white-collar technical and semi-professional employment. Of course, these facts nicely fit the arguments of some radical historians and conflict theorists that educational expansion

*Some of the material contained in this section, and in the final section of the paper, is taken from the author's "Equality of Educational Opportunity: Dilemmas and Policy Options," *Interchange*, 9, 2 (1978-79), 30-9.

and reform in Canada – whether taking place during the 1850's or during the 1960's and 1970's – cannot have much impact upon those major inequalities of opportunity which arise from a socially and economically unequal society. They can, indeed, buttress their arguments by the additional evidence that although women are in the process of overcoming their traditional under-representation in post-secondary studies (albeit sharing with lower-class students the common characteristic of achieving their highest levels of participation in the terminal programs of the community colleges), class-related factors appear to be no less important in influencing their educational opportunities than in the case with men.* Again, while there is evidence that the educational reforms in Quebec have helped virtually to eliminate the under-representation of Francophones in post-secondary education in that province (Harvey, 1977b), there is again little evidence that this trend has been accompanied by any substantial socio-economic democratization in class patterns of participation.

It is true that the increasing participation of women and Francophones in the universities and colleges may certainly be counted as progress toward achieving a more equitable participation of social minorities at the post-secondary level. However, since progress in these directions does not appear to be closely tied in with any substantial socio-economic democratization of advanced levels of education, we must still examine the conflict argument that the impact of educational reform upon differences in educational opportunity between children of different socio-economic backgrounds is inevitably limited in the context of a

*The participation of women in university studies rose from 24 per cent of the full-time university population of Canada in 1960-61 to 40 per cent and 48 per cent of the full-time and part-time university populations, respectively, in 1975-76 (Statistics Canada, *Advance Statistics of Education*, Ottawa, 1977: Table I). However, among the full-time undergraduate students responding to the 1974-75 Post-Secondary School Survey, 31 per cent of the women students compared with 29 per cent of the men students came from homes where fathers had attended university; and at the other end of the status spectrum, 17 per cent of the women students and 20 per cent of the male students had fathers who had obtained an elementary education only. Again, in full-time community college terminal programs, the class characteristics of both sexes are very similar (see M. von Zur-Muehlen, "The Educational Background of Post-Secondary Students in Canada," Ottawa, Statistics Canada, 1978 [unpublished], Table 14, p. 38; Table 19, p. 49.)

socially and economically unequal society. Before so doing, it is necessary to reiterate that much of the social selection for post-secondary education actually occurs through processes of selection which occur long before, in the elementary and secondary schools. Accordingly, in assessing the validity of this argument, we will once more direct our attention primarily toward the elementary and secondary school settings.

In my opinion, the above conflict view of educational reform is essentially correct. The school can only take children for a few hours each day, and to suppose that policy measures like remedial education can compensate for disadvantaged environments that continue to exert a far more powerful influence on the child than the school itself is able to do, is manifestly absurd (see Carnoy and Levin, 1976: 1-20; Karabel and Halsey, 1977: 230, 241). Furthermore, it is well to note the comment of Christopher Jencks, that even within the school setting, reformers have very little control over those aspects of school life that really affect children. In his words, "reallocating resources, reassigning pupils, and rewriting the curriculum seldom change the way teachers and students actually treat each other minute by minute" (Jencks, 1973: 255); that is, the intimate classroom relationships between students and teachers play a major part in determining whether lower-class and disadvantaged children are likely to take advantage of learning situations. The implication of this argument is that any educational reforms designed to enhance educational opportunities for lower-class students are not likely to be effective unless they take the nature of these classroom relationships into account and also are accompanied by policies designed to provide greater equality of condition (i.e., equality of income and general living conditions) than currently prevails in the society. After all, it is reasonable to suggest that if a country does not make major efforts to foster a greater equality of income and living conditions, but attempts rather to remove educational inequalities solely through the resources of the school, then the policy-makers stand to be branded as hypocrites for their unwillingness to seek to remedy the economic determinants of educational inequalities at the source. They are bound to fail in their school-related measures because of the primacy of family and neighbourhood in the process of socialization.

In the light of these observations, therefore, it would appear that one factor likely to be important in determining whether we have more socio-economic equality in our schools and colleges is whether or not we succeed in creating a more equal society: and indeed, it is a manifestation of the limitations of dominant liberal ideology that educational jurisdictions in North America have been willing to utilize the schools as instruments of social equalization in the hope that they will provide the opportunities for a greater degree of upward social mobility for lower-class and minority-group youth without, at the same time, making serious efforts to confront directly the touchy political issues associated with the extremes of poverty and wealth which lie beneath. We are not suggesting here that a greater degree of economic equality will do away with all class differences in educational opportunity, only that it will help, because studies of Eastern European countries which are state socialist, and in which the political elites have made strenuous efforts to enhance the educational chances of manual workers and peasants, have shown that children from the non-manual social strata are still considerably more likely than those from manual backgrounds to gain access to post-secondary institutions. According to David Lane, who has reviewed many of these studies in *The Socialist Industrial State*, the main explanation for this phenomenon is not purely economic but also cultural: in his words, "the unequal initial distribution of cultural resources in the home puts the children of manual workers at a great disadvantage when in competition with children from a non-manual background" (Lane, 1976: 189). Accordingly, one may assume that various cultural differences, including those between various racial and ethnic groups, would still influence educational behaviour, attitudes, and opportunities in a more economically egalitarian society.

Limitations of the Neo-Marxist Perspective on Educational Development and Reform

Do radical egalitarian policies within the wider society constitute the only viable solution to the problems of educational inequality? This issue was raised, but not resolved, in the conclusion of our analysis of education in Quebec. However, in the light of the "equality of condition" arguments just enunciated, it would appear that I am committed to answering the question with a partial affirmative: the "partial" qualification resulting mainly from my belief that there is still some hope for the creation of a more equitable educational order in a society which, although it remains wedded to a predominantly free enterprise economic system, is prepared to combine effective educational reform measures with a substantially greater emphasis on equality of condition than now exists in most western industrial countries. Shortly I will flesh out the bare bones of this "qualified affirmation of liberalism" with some suggestion for necessary educational reforms, and with an elaboration of some hopeful ongoing educational trends. A necessary prior task is to point out some of the weaknesses of much neo-Marxist theorizing on educational reform, because, as we have seen, the prevailing tendency has been for many sociologists to view conflict theory and especially neo-Marxism as providing a far more effective framework for the analysis of educational systems and processes than the traditional functionalist and liberal perspectives.

There have been a number of significant critiques of neo-Marxist theories of education (see, especially, Hurn, 1978; Rosenblum, 1978), and it certainly is not possible for us to deal with more than a few of the more salient of those criticisms. In particular, the main weakness of the neo-Marxist viewpoint on education appears to be that it commits its proponents to an almost paralyzingly negative view of the processes of educational reform in western industrial societies: that is, apart possibly from some "revolutionary actions" within the schools which may help in the general process of restructuring the socio-political order of the society, there is seen to be little point in attempting to formulate educational measures which might – just *might* – improve the lot of disadvantaged youth, because the schools and colleges are, after all, the mirrors of the capitalist order. Furthermore, insofar as "the correspondence principle" enunciated by some neo-Marxists appears to show an almost perfect fit between family, school, and workplace in the process of transmitting inequalities from one generation to the next, there is a danger that neo-Marxist analyses of educational systems will degenerate into a type of left-wing functionalism which offers no better theoretical framework than traditional functionalism for the explanation of the various imperfections that exist (Karabel and Halsey, 1977: 40-41). For example, we are entitled to wonder (ironically, of course) how it is that the Canadian bourgeoisie have been so unsuccessful in their efforts to link the socialization functions of the schools to the changing requirements of the capitalist marketplace; how it is that they have permitted a growing number of increasingly frustrated university and college graduates (many of them of middle-class origins) to bring their unrealistic hopes and ambitions onto a glutted labour market. This is a potentially disruptive social scenario, if ever there was one.

Because of its importance, this last point is worth pursuing a little further. We recognize now that the emphasis upon human capital theory which occurred during the 1960's had, as one of its effects, the quite excessive tying-in of the Canadian educational systems, and especially of the post-secondary institutions, to the market demand for highly educated and skilled manpower. Consequently, when the Canadian economy stubbornly failed to respond with a major economic upswing to the expanding output of university and college graduates (i.e., of human capital), and the demand for highly qualified manpower proved to be insufficient to provide many graduates with the well-paid and compatible careers they had come to expect, it was as if a mutual contract had been broken between youth and society, with the post-secondary systems in the role of institutional whipping boy: they had failed to deliver the goods to either side and were bound to pay through cutbacks in public financial support and a growth slowdown and, in some cases, an actual decline in student enrolments. Thus, we are presently in the midst of a general retreat from the worship of the "god of Extrinsic Returns": a retreat so swift that the point is rarely made that the chances of a Canadian youth being unemployed (underemployed is another matter) are still highly correlated with the level of education which he or she has obtained.*

But where do the above observations fit into the general criti-

---

*A recent study from Statistics Canada by Z. Zsigmond et al., Out of School – Into the Labour Force (Ottawa, 1978), shows that during the 1974-77 period the unemployment rate for 15-24 year olds was 23 per cent for those with only an elementary education, 13.5 per cent for those with secondary school education, and 5.4 per cent for degree holders.

que of neo-Marxism? The answer to this question lies, as American sociologist Christopher Hurn has recently intimated, in the evidence that current imbalances between the demands of the economy and the output of the educational system provide for the existence of a strong irrational element underlying patterns of educational expansion and contraction. This irrational element tends to belie the rationality and intentionality neo-Marxists often perceive as a feature of the relationship between schooling and society (Hurn, 1978: 75). Indeed, while Hurn does not deny the relevance of both functionalist and neo-Marxist explanations of educational expansion during the past one hundred years, he does suggest that an important cause of much expansion has been "status competition": that is, the higher status groups have constantly "bid up" the demand for education in an effort to prevent a narrowing of the educational gap between themselves and the members of lower-status groups. Had this narrowing occurred, Hurn suggests, it would have threatened the disproportionate command of people of higher-status origins over top-level occupational positions (ibid.: 72-5). However, because this status competition is based upon a general societal confidence in schooling as a means of mobility (and also because it may create a demand for education not necessarily closely tied in with labour-force needs), we may well witness the kind of so-called "irrational" phenomena which have been occurring in recent years in Canadian post-secondary education: that is, an apparent over-supply of graduates in many disciplines leading to some decline in the individual economic returns to higher education, and thence to a diminution of confidence in higher learning as a means of mobility. Of course, once the confidence in higher education is undermined, the tendency for status competition to lead to educational expansion can presumably go into reverse. As may well now be the case in some parts of the country, numbers of high school graduates decide to stay out of university or college because they are no longer convinced that post-secondary studies are the route to high-status jobs.

The above criticisms and comments should not lead us to ignore the undoubted merits of neo-Marxist theory, but they do suggest a necessity for critical awareness of its limitations. In the last resort, one is bound to recognize that the acceptance or rejection of the possibility of meaningful educational reform under capitalism constitutes an "act of faith" which depends upon one's interpretation of the meaning of a particular body of data. Indeed, since the same data may be utilized both in order to support the principle of interventionist liberal educational reform and to condemn it as being yet another example of the machinations of capitalism, we are really dealing here with issues of ideology which go beyond the realms of logical discussion. Take, for example, the social impact of the establishment and expansion of the community colleges during the past fifteen years. On the one hand, as we have seen, the colleges can be regarded as a step toward the democratization of higher education because they cater to a more representative socio-economic cross-section of the population than do the universities. On the other hand, because students in the terminal courses of the colleges are more likely to be of lower-class origins than students in university and university-related courses, and because such terminal courses are seen to prepare students for levels of the occupational hierarchy somewhat less prestigious than those occupational levels traditionally open to university degree-holders (in the current education-jobs crisis, this point is debatable), the establishment and expansion of the colleges can be interpreted by neo-Marxists such as Bowles and Gintis in the United States and Escande writing of the CEGEP's in Quebec, as providing just one more mechanism for ensuring the intergenerational transmission of inequality and for meeting the evolving demands of the capitalist labour market (see also Murphy and Denis, 1979: 122-35).

Alternative Policy Options: The Prospects for Future Educational Reform
In suggesting at the beginning of the preceding section that educational reform measures might be combined with the measures designed to provide a greater degree of equality of condition, in order to bring a more equitable educational system, we have clearly been left with the task of suggesting what form some of these reforms might take. We might well consider taking steps to initiate reforms in two major directions. First, we must attempt to reverse the trend toward large-scale impersonal bureaucracy and centralized decision-making, which has become a major

threat to the maintenance of a sense of community and of student participation in educational affairs. Second, we should seek to accelerate recent moves toward "life-long learning" and "recurrent education." The first of these directions is certainly important, but we have insufficient space to explore it here. Accordingly, the following discussion will be limited to an examination of the prospects which life-long and recurrent education hold out for educational equalization in Canadian society.

Earlier I noted the observation in the OECD report on Educational Policies in Canada that measures designed to promote equality of educational opportunity have occurred in a series of successive phases, with the first phase being based upon a desire to make educational facilities more equally available to all children, and the second phase involving a perception of the school as a positive agent for social reform. Both of these phases have been aimed at children and adolescents and both, as we have seen, have met with but limited success. Partly because of this limited success, and partly because of a redefinition of what constitutes equality of educational opportunity, some countries, including Canada, have moved on to a third phase which, though it does not involve the abandonment of the policies of the first two phases, is characterized by "the recognition that the right to equality of educational opportunity should not remain confined to the short period of childhood and youth, but should be a lifelong, recurrent principle, aimed at catching up on lost chances, and at opening up new opportunities" (OECD, 1976: 39). In other words, while we undoubtedly will continue to combat the impact of environmental inequalities upon the educational opportunities of young people and adolescents, the field of battle is now being extended to the provision of new educational opportunities to adults of all ages.

The educational ideas and concepts behind this third phase of the pursuit of equality of educational opportunity appear to be particularly attractive. What the principles of recurrent or life-long education stress is the elimination of institutions and programs which are dead-ends, and which block further educational progress of students. What they encourage is the belief that education is a life-long process, so that although a student may drop out of the educational system at the age of 16, he or she is not thereby permanently labelled and stigmatized as a drop-out, but rather as someone who may wish, and hence, be provided with the opportunity, to drop back into the system at the age of 20 or 30 or in later life, on a part-time or full-time basis. The particular attraction of many recurrent and life-long educational policies – evident, for example, in the establishment of adult high schools in Denmark and in the wide provisions for correspondence education for adults in many countries – is that not only do they facilitate the re-entry to the educational process of numbers of people who were denied educational opportunities in their youth; but also that, by de-emphasizing the traditional attitude that education is something that happens between the ages of 4 and 24 (and mostly between the ages of 6 and 16), such policies help to take some of the burden of combatting the external causes of educational inequality off the beleaguered institutional shoulders of the existing primary and secondary schools.

As already mentioned, Canada has embarked upon this third phase of policies for educational opportunity. What then is the way ahead? From this writer's perspective, it lies along the route outlined in the reports of two provincial education commissions which were published during 1972 and which have been described, by a non-Canadian educationalist, as offering "two instances from 'advanced' democratically-based societies of detailed proposals for educational systems based on patterns of recurrent learning" (Molyneux, 1974: 119). These Commissions – the Commission on Post Secondary Education in Ontario and the Commission on Educational Planning in Alberta – were concerned with far broader policy issues than those linked directly to educational opportunity, but in Molyneux's words ". . . the time has come to invest [the individual student] with a considerable choice in deciding when, where and how he will seek to learn. Such choice has long been a hall-mark of the elite in various societies. Alberta and Ontario are significant in seriously proposing to make the traditional privilege a universal opportunity and in regarding it as a social necessity" (ibid.). These are brave words, and it is more than a little disillusioning to recognize that the practical impact of the reports on educational policy-making in this country appears, so far at least, to have been very limited. However, there can be little doubt that the substantial increase in the variety of modes and channels of learning which these reports propose would, if instituted, facilitate in the task of educational equalization. Yet, to stress a point made earlier, only the most idealistic or the most naive would believe that educational reform, unless accompanied by greater equality of condition, can successfully achieve its desired goals.

IV   A CONCLUDING COMMENT

In brief, the view of the interrelationships between education, class, and power which has been presented in this paper constitutes a "modified conflict interpretation" of their links in Canadian society. It is a conflict approach insofar as it does not deny the necessity of equalizing conditions in a socially and economically unequal society. Nor does it deny that the values of a dominant group or class may become the dominant values of the society, even when these values may not necessarily be in the interests of the majority of that society. On the other hand, it is "modified" because, with certain exceptions, it rejects conspiracy interpretations of class relations. And at the same time, it accepts the possibility that further educational reforms may have beneficial effects in equalizing educational opportunities if these reforms are combined with measures designed to create a greater equality of income and living conditions. By no means, of course, should such a view be interpreted as inimical to all major existing strands of conflict theory. On the contrary, radical and neo-Marxist studies which deal with the unintended consequences of structural change, which are not wedded to revolutionary political strategies as the only real bases for educational reform, and which, finally, do not take for granted that a particular consequence of the functioning of an educational institution denotes a witting "purpose" or "goal" of that institution, undoubtedly offer fruitful avenues for further analysis of education, class, and power in Canada.

REFERENCES

Audet, L. P.
1970 "Educational Development in French Canada After

1875," in J. D. Wilson, R. M. Stamp, and L. P. Audet, eds., *Canadian Education: A History.* Scarborough, Ontario.
Alberta, Province of
1972 *A Choice of Futures.* Report of the Commission on Educational Planning. Edmonton.
Bowles, S., and H. Gintis
1976 *Schooling in Capitalist America.* New York.
Carnoy, M., and H. Levin, eds.
1976 *The Limits of Educational Reform.* New York.
Clement, W.
1975 *The Canadian Corporate Elite.* Toronto.
Copp, T.
1974 *The Anatomy of Poverty: The Condition of the Working Class of Montreal, 1897-1929.* Toronto.
Davey, I.
1975 "School Reform and School Attendance," in M. Katz and P. Mattingly, eds., *Education and Social Change.* New York.
Escande, C.
1973 *Les Classes Sociales Au CEGEP.* Montreal.
Harvey, E.
1974 *Educational Systems and the Labour Market.* Toronto.
1977a "Accessibility to Post-Secondary Education – Some Gains, Some Losses," *University Affairs,* October.
1977b *Opportunity and Choice: Changes in the Canadian Post-Secondary Student Population 1969-1975* (unpublished).
Hurn, C. J.
1978 *The Limits and Possibilities of Schooling.* Boston.
Jencks, C.
1973 *Inequality: A Reassessment of the Effect of Family and Schooling in America.* New York.
Johnson, F. H.
1968 *A Brief History of Canadian Education.* Toronto.
Karabel, J., and A. H. Halsey
1977 "Educational Research: A Review and an Interpretation," in Karabel and Halsey, eds., *Power and Ideology in Education.* New York.
Katz, M. B. , and P. H. Mattingly, eds.
1975 *Education and Social Change: Themes from Ontario's Past.* New York.

Katz, M.
1975 "Who Went to School? in Katz and Mattingly, eds., *Education and Social Change*. New York.
Lane, D.
1976 *The Socialist Industrial State*. London.
Marchak, M. P.
1975 *Ideological Perspectives on Canada*. Toronto.
Martin, W. B. W. , and A. J. Macdonell
1978 *Canadian Education: A Sociological Analysis*. Scarborough, Ontario.
Maxwell, M. P. , and J. D. Maxwell
1971 "Boarding School: Social Control, Space and Identity," in D. I. Davies and K. Herman, eds., *Social Space: Canadian Perspectives*. Toronto.
1975 "Women, Religion and Achievement Aspirations: A Study of Private School Females," in R. Pike and E. Zureik, *Socialization and Values in Canadian Society*, Vol. II. Toronto.
Molyneux, F.
1974 "International Perspectives," in V. Houghton and F. Richardson, eds., *Recurrent Education*. London.
Murphy, R., and A. Denis
1979 *Sociological Theories of Education*. Toronto.
Ontario, Province of
1972 *The Learning Society*. Report of the Commission on Post-Secondary Education in Ontario. Toronto.
Organization for Economic Cooperation and Development
1975 *Submission of the Ministers of Education for the Provinces of British Columbia, Alberta, Saskatchewan and Manitoba to the Review of Educational Policies in Canada*. Paris.
1976 *Review of National Policies for Education: Canada*. Paris
Pike, R.
1970 *Who Doesn't Get to University . . . and Why*. Ottawa.
1978 "Part-time Undergraduate Studies in Ontario," in R. Pike et al., *Innovation in Access to Higher Education*. New York.
Porter, J.
1965 *The Vertical Mosaic*. Toronto
Porter, M., J. Porter, and B. Blishen
1975 *Does Money Matter?* Toronto.
Prentice, A. L.

1977 *The School Promoters.* Toronto.

Quebec, Province of

1963 *Report of the Royal Commission of Enquiry on Education in the Province of Quebec* (Parent Commission), 2 vols. Quebec.

Rosenblum, S.

1978 "The Marxist Theory of Education: A Sympathetic Critique," revised version of paper presented to annual meetings of Canadian Sociology and Anthropology Association.

Schecter, S.

1977 "Capitalism, Class and Educational Reform in Canada," in L. Panitch, ed., *The Canadian State: Political Economy and Political Power.* Toronto.

Stamp, R. M.

1970 "Evolving Patterns of Education: English Canada from the 1870's to 1914," in Wilson, Stamp, and Audet, eds., *Canadian Education: A History.* Scarborough, Ontario.

Sutherland, N.

1975 "Introduction: Toward a History of English-Canadian Youngsters," in Katz and Mattingly, eds., *Education and Social Change: Themes From Ontario's Past.* New York.

1976 *Children in English-Canadian Society: Framing the Twentieth Century Consensus.* Toronto.

Tremblay, A.

1955 "Contribution à L'Etude des Problèmes et des Besoins de L'Enseignment dans la Province de Quebec." Report to the Royal Commission of Inquiry on Constitutional Problems. Quebec.

CHAPTER FIVE

Power and Play in Canadian Society*
by Richard S. Gruneau
Queen's University

INTRODUCTION

There is a sense in which human play has always appeared separate from the practical affairs of everyday life. The creative autonomy, drama, and sheer "unreality" of play often combine in such a way as to suggest a universal form of human activity that stands outside of space and time. Play absorbs us in the sometimes serious pursuit of the inconsequential and, to the extent that this occurs, we are prone to celebrate its joyful freedom and expressive autonomy.

Yet, in another sense, play involves much more than expressive freedom, peak experiences, or simple fantasy. The social world of play may have its immediate dramatic shape, its sense of transcendent *form*, but it is more significantly an important symbolic commentary on social arrangements and social processes. As Christopher Lasch has noted, play consciously retains an "organic connection with community life by virtue of its capacity to dramatize reality and offer a convincing representation of the community's values" (1977: 30). These "representa-

*Much of this essay is a condensed summary statement of the argument put forward in Chapters 4-7 of my dissertation, *Class, Sports and Social Development in Canadian Society* (University of Massachusetts, 1980). Individuals wishing a more detailed analysis of the themes discussed here should refer to this larger project. In the case of the essay at hand I am grateful to Rob Beamish, Hart Cantelon, Kay Herman, Dave Neice, Dick Ossenberg, Charles Page, Don Swainson, and Lee Wetherall for their comments and criticisms on an earlier draft. A somewhat longer version of this essay was published as a *Working Paper* in the winter of 1979 by the Sport Studies Research Group at Queen's University and I want to thank the members of the Research Group for allowing me to include most of the material in this earlier article here.

tions" not only tell us something about the nature of community life, its basic organizing principles and essential conflicts, they also help us to understand our own place in the social order. Thus, it can be argued that one of the major characteristics of human play is its *interpretive* character. We might say, as Gregory Stone emphasizes, that our play tends to be "responsible" rather than merely "responsive." Humans have always imbued their play with "meaning and affect" and have "stylized" it in historically and culturally specific ways (1973: 66).

It is important to understand, however, that these different "styles" of play are not simply the collective result of freely associating individuals who play in the absence of constraint. All humans play, but they do not always play in a fashion of their own making. For example, the organizational structures, traditions, and values associated with the so-called "play" of games and sports are primarily shaped by the social and cultural forces characteristic of given societies at different moments in history.* We "play" games according to rules that are created for the expressed purpose of insulating our play from the "outside" world, but this very act of rule construction embeds play deeply in the prevailing logic of social organization and diminishes play's autonomy. As a result, the dramatizations of social life that are provided by games and sports are far from innocent individual and collective experiences; rather they represent a powerful affirmation of the legitimacy of existing social conditions and thereby tend to reinforce these conditions.

Acceptance of this last point is necessary if we are to move the study of play, games, and sports out of the realm of idealist philosophy and into the realm of social analysis. Attempts by idealist philosophers to celebrate the "perfect order" and "playful spirit" of modern games and sports are limited because they tend to ignore the extent to which the boundaries and contents of games and sports are contoured by their social surroundings. The assumption that play itself actually exists outside of history as

---

*I do not have the space to define play, games, and sports at length. Useful discussions on the distinctions that can be made between play and games, different types of games, and sports can be found in A. Guttman, *From Ritual to Record: The Nature of Modern Sports* (New York, 1978); and in J. Loy, "The Cultural System of Sport," *Quest*, 29 (1978).

some vaguely autonomous expressive *form*, and that this form is realized in our popular recreation, community games, and competitive athletics, makes moving theology (see, for example, Michael Novak's *The Joy of Sports*) but it is bad sociology. In actuality, once we go beyond the simplicity of free play, most of our so-called "play" activities seldom represent anything more than the promise of a contest between equals or the opportunity for creative self-expression that is reasonably free from restraint. What these activities actually deliver is an approximation of this promise that is limited and shaped by existing social conditions. By dramatizing these conditions these activities carry with them the importance of all of those aspects of culture that offer interpretive statements about the moral and political-economic order of society.

My purpose in this essay is to elaborate on this importance by linking the study of play and those activities that are supposedly "played" (notably, games and sports) to an understanding of power and change in Canadian social life. This involves a two-part discussion. In the first part of the essay I outline some theoretical relationships between power, play, games, and sports, and then review a number of perspectives that are commonly associated with the study (and the lack of study) of power and "play" in sociological and historical writing. Building upon this discussion, the second part of the essay is devoted to a more concrete analysis of the relationships between games and sports and the changing features of power in Canadian social development. In this analysis I have *not* sought to provide a detailed historical discussion of changes in the social organization and meanings of game and sporting activities at different moments in history; my intention has been only to identify patterns of development that may aid in understanding the current nature and significance of such activities in Canadian society.

I   THE REPRODUCTIVE AND TRANSFORMATIVE FEATURES OF PLAY, GAMES, AND SPORTS

Perspectives on Reproduction and Transformation

In *Economy and Society* (vol. III) Max Weber emphasizes how the ritualized game forms of European and Japanese feudalism were far more than expressive fantasies. Rather they were important cultural features in their own right that tended to support the logic of traditional domination. The pomp, ceremony, and status-symbolizing that surrounded martial games and the feudal tournament helped to reinforce a collective commitment to traditional beliefs in hierarchy, church, and state that militated against the spread of rational thinking that might challenge the social and ideological foundation upon which traditional power rested. In other words, what Weber tells us about the significance of certain play and game activities in feudal societies is that they tended to aid in the *reproduction* of power relations.

How does this process of reproducing the main features of power in social life occur?* One answer might proceed as follows. First, let us assume that the essence of power in societies lies in the ability of a person or group to mobilize resources in order to achieve some desired end even in the face of opposition from others.** By this definition power differentials potentially lie in all forms of human interaction. However, at the societal level, specific types of power relations under given historical circumstances tend to become structured into forms of domination. These forms are based on a comparative advantage in the mobilization and deployment of resources that one group is able to achieve and they are given a material and symbolic substance in the institutional and cultural orders that develop in social life. These symbolic features take on a character that essentially

---

*No society "reproduces" itself completely; hence, my use here of the word "reproduce" tends to overstate the forces of social persistence in societal development. Nonetheless, notable and persisting tendencies for social and cultural reproduction exist in all societies. For useful discussions, see L. Althusser, *Lenin and Philosophy and Other Essays* (London, 1971); and P. Bourdieu and J. C. Passeron, *Reproduction: In Education, Society and Culture* (London, 1977).

**This definition of power is loosely derived from Max Weber's view that power is "the chance of a man or of a number of men to realize their own will . . . even against the resistance of others. . . . " (H. Gerth and C. W. Mills, *From Max Weber: Essays in Sociology* [New York, 1958], p. 180.) One problem with this Weberian view lies in its tendency to identify "power" too closely with "coercion." To alleviate this tendency I have tried to adapt the Weberian definition to include a broader view of power as the use of resources, of whatever kind, to secure outcomes, as discussed in A. Giddens, *Studies in Social and Political Theory* (New York, 1977), p. 347.

legitimizes the institutionally supported allocation of resources at a given point in time and they are passed on to children through agencies of socialization that define appropriate behaviours and reinforce a belief in the organizing principles of the established order. Since children's play and "established" game forms appear to figure centrally in socialization (see Loy and Ingham, 1973) they may act as sources of potential legitimation and help to minimize the necessity for the implementation of coercive measures by those in power.

All of this seems straightforward enough, but viewed in its extremes this line of reasoning can easily become extremely mechanistic. By emphasizing the homogeneity of dominant values and ruling interests it is possible to deny any creative role in the development of cultural forms. For example, a view which sees play as nothing more than a simple validation of social roles associated with the dominant institutional structure does not satisfactorily grasp the complexity of meanings associated with play and related game activities. Moreover, as Stanley Aronowitz emphasizes, if established patterns of domination and hierarchy are seen to be completely integrated into the "self-system" of individuals then any evidence of "rebellion against the essential structure of social hierarchy and authority" can only be seen as an aberration or as a form of "deviance" which can never "congeal" into an "alternative consciousness or structure of social action" (1973: 39).

This problem can be avoided by recognizing that the moral order of highly stratified societies is extremely complex and fragmented and that domination may still occur even though a complete consensus on values is not evident. Michael Mann (1970) has even suggested that it is actually a "lack of consensus" among subordinate groups in a society that keeps them compliant. Members of subordinate classes may not necessarily agree with certain standards even though they are guided by them. Their actions, however, are often products of capitulation rather than acceptance. At the same time, subordinate groups in a society develop their own characteristic forms of cultural expression that dramatize the contradictory nature of their experiences. These forms often suggest a paradoxical collage of antagonism, acceptance, and compliance to the conventional morality of the institutional order but, viewed in the context of this morality, they do *not* always have reproductive consequences. Weber was not suggesting, for example, that ritualized "play" forms can be seen universally as pillars of the status quo. Rather he was arguing that the capacity of these forms to aid in the reproduction of established patterns of domination is dependent upon specific historical circumstances. Feudal society is, after all, a somewhat special case where there is a reasonably complete domination of all of the forms of civil society by church and state. In different circumstances this latter relationship may be considerably altered. When a subordinate group is in a position to challenge a dominant group as a result of some change in historical circumstances there is a tendency for the forms of cultural expression of the subordinates to take on a transformative rather than a reproductive character. *In the case of games and sports the system of rules and cultural traditions that can be identified with a contending interest group often becomes a symbolic feature of the realization of that group's collective interest.*

Yet, all of this discussion still leaves unanswered some important questions about the degree to which the self-generated, expressive features of play may also contain transformative potential. It is true that the nominal freedom of early children's play almost immediately becomes subject to the "contents" of culture and the logic of social structure. But it also seems true that human playfulness continues as a kind of "nostalgia and periodic resistance" to authoritarianism that is never quite purged in later life even though it is accorded an inferior status and trivialized (Aronowitz, 1973). Play does much more in socialization than merely serve as a non-reflexive arena for assimilating existing structures and accommodating ourselves to our surroundings. As John Shotter (1973) points out, play is an assertive expressive act through which individuals attempt to expand their personal "powers" and exercise a degree of control over their immediate environments. It is an essential statement of our human capacities, not only to transform ourselves in interaction with our surroundings, but also to exert an influence on these surroundings. Similarly, Richard Sennett (1978) has argued that the essence of play lies in its capacity to dramatize the plasticity of the social world and give us the energy for public expression necessary to transform the world when it blocks and represses human potential. This energy, however, is often enervated by certain patterns of social and political arrangements and our *transformative capacities* as historical actors often go unrealized.

Play as the Creator of Culture

It is possible that Max Weber might have elaborated on the issues described above if he had ever sought to write an extended analysis of the social significance of play and games. But Weber was far less interested in the study of play and games in themselves than in their association with different types of social action. Nonetheless Weber did pay considerably more attention to play and game activities than the majority of his contemporaries. The legacy of eighteenth and nineteenth century European political economy contained an emphasis on the importance of labour in the organizational logic of social life that relegated play to the level of a residual consideration. Play came to be seen either as a simple antithesis to labour, or else as an area of life whose sole purpose was to perform certain biological and psychological functions in human growth and development.

This view continues to be popular, but it has been challenged brilliantly by the Dutch historian, Johan Huizinga, in a classic study of the play element in western civilization. Huizinga argued in *Homo Ludens* (1938) that play is actually a primary element of social existence that has great importance in cultural development. We labour and produce out of necessity, but we play for fun and it is this non-purposive spirit in human life that underlies our creative impulses, our ritualized forms of behaviour, and, ultimately, our humanity. The fundamental spirit of the contest, and of a detached playfulness, Huizinga noted, can be seen to infuse all areas of cultural life including law, statecraft, and even war, so that it may be argued that culture itself moves and develops both in and through play.

However, Huizinga was not satisfied to argue simply that the spirit of playfulness provides the driving force in the advancement of western civilization. He also sought to graft this argument to an interpretation and evaluation of the present and future course of human development. Huizinga believed that such an evaluation could be drawn by first recognizing the fundamental difference between the unrestrained and innovative character of the play spirit as the *creator* of culture and the structured, more regulated character of those derivations of play that represent *creations* of culture (e.g., sports and games). By assessing the degree to which those creations of culture, nominally known as play, measure up to the standard of creativity and innovation that is embodied in the spirit of play in the purest form, Huizinga believed that one could evaluate the quality of life in different historical periods. Following this logic, he went on to create a sweeping theoretical appraisal of the relationships between play, human nature, ritual, and social development which opposes the secularization of the play element in modern times and its subjugation to the rational and calculating logic of industrial life. When Europe "donned the boiler suit," Huizinga concluded, the play element in all of the basic forms of cultural expression, such as law or politics, was weakened and, as a result, people no longer maintained any creative attachment to them; instead, they began to seek diversion in the surrogate play of modern sports and the excesses of the spectacle.

It is not my intention in this brief summary to provide a detailed accounting and assessment of Huizinga's theory. It will suffice, perhaps, simply to note the most problematic issue that his discussion raises for the argument that I shall develop in the paper at hand. Feudal society, Huizinga suggested, was "brimful of play" and in it the higher forms of "recognized play" were filled with ritual and the spirit of public festivity. By contrast modern sports have lost their play character through the rationalization of play activities and the subordination of the contest to the "seriousness" of science and technological development. Huizinga saw this transformation as part of a movement from the *sacred* to the *profane* and thus demonstrates a somewhat romanticized attachment to the "traditional" order of feudal life. Play's ritual significance and ubiquity in feudal society apparently suggest a richer, more fulfilling, and happier age than our own.

Now if we are to view the "spirit" of festival and the contest in feudal societies as a condition of mind that is fundamentally culture-creating and not blocked or repressed in any way then it is easy to see how Huizinga arrived at this view. With its many ritual holidays and festivals and with its reasonably "ordered" features of social organization, feudal society seems rather idyllic compared to the long working hours, intolerable conditions, and ideological turmoil of early industrial capitalism. On the other hand, if one were to interpret play and game activities in feudal societies as products of existing social structural and cultural conditions then something of the glamour of feudal life is lost. As Max Weber (1968) saw so clearly, the ascriptive order of feudal life was not so much the festive system of mutual obligation that Huizinga implies as it was a system pervaded by brutally exploitative relationships that were given their symbolic expression in traditional cultural forms. Thus, it might be concluded that play's "ideal state" was no more realized in feudal societies than it has been in capitalist or socialist industrial societies. To borrow Weber's terminology, the degree to which play can be seen to be any more liberating or culture-creating in societies characterized by "traditional" action than in societies characterized by "rational-legal" action is questionable at best. What occurs is simply that one type of domination replaces another. By committing the study of play to its "unreal" features of spirit rather than to its relationships to social structure and patterns of domination, Huizinga's legacy has been to emphasize the significance of play while simultaneously downplaying its relations to social conditions.

Games and Sports as Creatures of Culture and Production
   I have argued above that *Homo Ludens* is a flawed but remarkable book. Its insight and sense of imagination rescues the study of play from mechanical discussions of biological and social-psychological "functions" and challenges scholars in general to embark on critical analyses of the role of play, games, and sports in *social* development. This challenge, however, has largely gone unrecognized. For example, most contemporary sociologists, if interested at all in such things, continue to ignore the historical developmental factors and social significance of play, games, and sports in favour of social-psychological assessments of the significance of such activities in role learning and childhood socialization. At best, where macrosociological studies of these activities have been conducted, sociologists have limited the focus

of their analyses to the area of social necessity – usually in research about changing recreational and leisure patterns in the modern industrial societies. Historians, with few exceptions, have been even less sensitive to the social importance of play, games, and sports. Indeed, it might be argued (and one senses at least one dimension of Huizinga's legacy in this) that historians have been so impressed with the idea of "play" as non-utilitarian fantasy that they have tended to ignore it altogether.

Arguing along similar lines, S.F. Wise (1974) has recently chided Canadian historians for their tendency to overlook the significant role "played" by game and sporting activities in the social development of Canadian society. Wise points out that the elevation of an ostensibly "non-serious" and trivial area of life to a level of scholarly concern evidently runs contrary to the "higher earnestness of the historian's professional calling" especially when compared to those political and economic events commonly seen to be of "real significance." In his own case, Wise goes on to note how the eminent Canadian historian, Arthur Lower, gently criticized him on numerous occasions for "wasting valuable time" indulging his interest in the history of sports and games in Canadian society.

But if such attitudes from Lower and others have led to a dearth of sociological and historical studies about the relationships between play, games, and sports and social development, there has been no shortage of authoritative pronouncements about such things. As Wise notes, Lower himself argues in *Canadians in the Making* that the growing emphasis placed on games and sports in Canada during the twentieth century is indicative of a generalized descent into barbarism. Implicit in this statement are a number of assumptions not only about the significance of games and sports in certain circumstances, but also about the "ideal state" of human play and the quality of life in late nineteenth century Canadian society.

What are some of these assumptions? Perhaps the most significant of them stems from Lower's well-known belief both in the inherently democratic character of frontier life and in the moral values associated with an austere existence dedicated to hard work and self-reliance (see Lower, 1930; Careless, 1967). Under conditions of pastoral simplicity, play might well be ennobling as long as it was not associated in any way with idleness or trivial amusements. In fact, for Lower, play appears to take on its highest form in its relationship either to simple recreation or to productive activities themselves. By this standard, the barn raisings and quilting bees of the nineteenth century Canadian rural community could be seen as playful, but more significantly, they could be interpreted as an affirmation of the determined collective spirit of a democratic people. Yet no sooner had such values become established, Lower argues, than they became contaminated by the spread of urban values and commercialized forms of cheap entertainment which transformed the traditionally simple and pure forms of playful expression into a corrupting social force.

This version of the debasement of play has a familiar ring to it. It resonates well with the anguished cries of modern cultural critics who see a retrograde fascination with display accompanying the rise of big-time commercial sports and it is somewhat reminiscent of Huizinga's condemnation of the rationalistic tendencies of modern sports and games. However, Lower differs from Huizinga in his belief that play, in its desirable form, should maintain some kind of moral use-value. Huizinga would have rejected the idea of associating play with some desired end and would have seen such ideas as an infringement on play's necessary lack of restraint. Yet, while these positions differ in their interpretations of play's "ideal" characteristics they are similar in their conservatism. Each maintains an implicit recognition that the solution to the degradation of culture that can be seen through the apparent corruption of play lies in a return to some romanticized state in the past. For Huizinga that state lay in the supposedly unfettered spirit of play that he saw associated with the basic fabric of feudal life. For Lower it lay in the moral devotion, hard work, and "wholesome" recreation of late Victorian Canadian society.

The views of Lower and Huizinga do not exhaust the kinds of criticisms that are commonly leveled at modern games and sports. Marxists and cultural radicals, for example, have identified their own versions of the debasement of play by arguing that most of what passes for play in capitalist society merely symbolizes the logic of competitive capitalism (see Rigauer, 1969;

Hoch, 1972; Brohm, 1978). Modern sports in particular, the argument runs, reflect bourgeois ideology and help to maintain the hegemony of middle-class values by glorifying meritocratic standards of hierarchy and success based on skill, celebrating rampant commercialism, and accepting a false belief in "progress" through the continued assault on the record books. In other words, to refer back to the distinctions that I developed earlier, Marxist and cultural radicals have tended to focus on and criticize the *reproductive* character of modern games and sports. A somewhat different version of this argument attacks the notion of the "unreality" of games and suggests that games and sports in the twentieth century have become what organized religion was to the nineteeth century–"the sigh of the oppressed creature, the heart of a heartless world . . . the opium of the people" (Marx and Engels, 1975, III: 75). Sport and other forms of supposedly "playful" expression have become a false avenue of escape or a substitute for alienating work in a repressive polity and thereby serve to undermine the revolutionary project of social transformation.

It is easy to be sympathetic to at least some of these arguments. Games and sports certainly provide the illusion of an escape from alienating social conditions because they offer the promise of play–drama and excitement and a flowering of the imagination that provides the kind of autonomous expression of self that one might ideally find in creative work. But, at the same time, we must recognize the degree to which the continuing promises of such things under present conditions become alternatives to their realization. There is considerable merit in arguing that institutionally established sports and forms of popular recreation sometimes do substitute for an intense involvement in other areas of social life–perhaps even to the exclusion of regular participation in the political process. At the same time, one might question the degree to which the national passion for games has become caught up in the ethos of labour. Where Canadians might "play" at their work, in the craftsman-like sense that Huizinga saw to be so important, we seem increasingly to be labouring at our play. This work ethos is linked to a complex cycle of production and consumption and to our slavish commitment to science and technology. Amateur sports, at their highest level, have become monuments to such new sciences as biomechanics, exercise physiology, and sport psychology where rationality is expressed in a mechanical quest for efficiency in human performance that is indentured to state and commercial sponsorhip. Professional sports, meanwhile, have essentially reduced the playful freedom and self-expression of the contest to a dramatization of simple commodity relations.

Yet to argue, as Paul Hoch (1972) has, that modern institutionally established games and sports effectively socialize their participants with reactionary elitist, racist, sexist, and consumerist attitudes, and thereby function directly as instruments of class rule, does more to mystify the relationship between power and play in modern times than explain it. Such an argument rests on a number of highly questionable assumptions. In the first place, it falls prey to the mechanistic reasoning that I have described earlier wherein all contemporary games and sports are seen as straightforward reproductions of exploitative relationships rather than meaningful dramatizations of reality. Secondly, there is the two-fold assumption that members of the dominant class in capitalist societies actually manage successfully to mobilize culture in the defence of class interests and that cultural "representations" are interpreted in a consistent fashion by subordinates. Added to this, as Ralph Miliband points out, are the highly questionable assumptions that working-class participants in mass culture are largely unreflective dupes, or else that a deep interest in the fortunes of local teams is incompatible with militant trade unionism and the pursuit of class struggle. Of these final two assumptions, the first is as elitist as the ideology that it seeks to replace and the second completely overlooks the transformative potential of games and sports. For the Marxist critic of modern sports, Miliband concludes, there is much to do and "to murmur 'bread and circuses' is no substitute for serious thinking upon the matter" (1977: 52).

Miliband's point about the necessity for Marxists to engage in some "serious thinking" about modern sports is certainly well-taken. Yet, in actuality, Marxists and Marxist-inspired cultural radicals have tended to think more seriously about these things than most. Furthermore, while such critiques may have been only of limited applicability, they are infinitely preferable to liberal apologetics that avoid encounters with critical evaluation altogether. In most of these apologetics the shape of "play" forms in the industrial societies is seen to be part and parcel of a general movement toward an increasingly welfare-oriented and technocratic world order. The "progress" made in the organization of human "play" (state-run programs, etc.) and the great improvements of human performances in sporting activities are seen to celebrate rather than condemn the basic social organization of industrial life. The reasoning which underlies such arguments focuses on the degree to which the structured forms of play-related activities in Canada and other western industrial societies have developed from ascriptively-based folk and elite recreational activities to a democratized component of mass culture and mass entertainment. Participation in organized or semi-organized sports has become the new standard by which to gauge our capacities for play and, along these lines, it is assumed that participation itself has evolved from a *privilege* of class and status in the nineteenth century to a *right* (and, perhaps, even an obligation) of citizenship in the twentieth. All of this has been supposedly brought on by the general transformation and opening-up of the Canadian class and power structures.

Since I have criticized these views at some length in other work (Gruneau, 1975, 1976, 1978) I do not intend to devote a great deal of space to them here except to point out that they contain an emphasis on the achievement of a consensus in Canadian life that is neither theoretically adequate nor consonant with our historical experience. Additionally, the view of expanding opportunities for participation in organized sport or recreational activities as an index of "social improvement" completely overlooks questions about the "meaning" of these activities and their relationships to either the reproduction of existing social structural conditions or their transformation. Problems of power and play are ignored or else taken to be resolved and the result is a view of play, games, and sports that does little more than devolve into an ideological defence of the basic organizing principles of modern life and thereby become yet another substitute for systematic study.

II POWER, PLAY, AND CANADIAN SOCIAL DEVELOPMENT

Power and Traditional Play

One might begin discussing the changing relationships between power and play in Canadian society by attempting to relate the organization of "play" at different moments in history to the unique pattern of Canadian colonial development. An understanding of this pattern, as it is outlined in much of the recent work in Canadian social history and political economy, focuses on the recognition of two basic issues: (1) the importance of social class as an analytic category for understanding conflicts over scarce resources in Canadian society; and (2) the idea that class structures and patterns of social development are greatly influenced by the relations of domination and dependency that occur between a metropole (or centre) and a hinterland (or periphery). Power is seen to inhere in the metropole and this leads to an underdevelopment of certain features of the hinterland.

The application of such an analysis to the understanding of early patterns of class and power in Canada is quite straightforward. The initial shape of Canada's class and power structure emerged out of the cultural traditions of French and British colonial empires and the set of colonial institutions that these empires generated. Particularly dominant in Canada were the implementation of ascriptive colonial policies of land allocation, and the institutionalization of a mercantile system heavily funded by foreign portfolio investment and designed to extract staples from the Canadian hinterland in the service of European markets. The initial effects of these patterns of social, economic, and political organization in late eighteenth and early nineteeth century Canada can be measured primarily in three areas.

First, as Naylor (1975) has recently argued, by gearing to the international movement of staples rather than the development of secondary processing in domestic markets (especially following the "Conquest"), an emphasis on industry and manufacturing in Canada was retarded and financial institutions became over-developed. Second, a conscious attempt to maintain traditional European patterns of landed power combined with over-development of financial institutions to allow for the strengthening of a strong merchant class in the fledgling Canadian urban areas which eventually grew to share power with the remains of the colonial ruling class of the Conquest era, the Church, and the Empire Loyalist elite. Finally, the close connection under colonial rule between the merchant class and the state generally opposed in principle both the laissez-faire political-economic philosophy commonly associated with industrial capitalism and the rational utilitarian ethics that were later to become the cornerstone of liberal-democratic sentiment in industrial Britain.

These developmental patterns provide an important background to an understanding of the meaning of early forms of play and games in Canadian society. Most significantly they suggest some important limitations to the vision of democratic frontier recreation that is alluded to by Arthur Lower and celebrated in the writings of Canada's few self-proclaimed sport historians (see Howell and Howell, 1969: 54-6; Roxborough, 1966). The fun and spontaneity of colonial games may be readily documented, but it is extremely important to recognize the extent to which the symbolic meaning of frontier games and popular recreation was mediated by the effects of a conservative political economy and a semi-feudal class structure.

Consider some of these effects. To begin, it can be argued that few of the settlers on Canada's "hard frontier" participated regularly in any type of organized games or sports (Wise and Fisher, 1974: 8). When organized games or sports did occur, however, they tended to affirm the logic of a pattern of domination that, if not really feudal, was nonetheless highly traditional and paternalistic in nature. This affirmation was likely more true of the activities of the colonial elites than of those of small farmers or independent artisans, but the basic rituals of play are invariably defined by imported colonial traditions. For example, a large fragment of the dominant class, many of whom viewed the aristocracy and gentry of late eighteenth century Britain as a reference group, stressed in play anti-utilitarian attitudes toward consumption and toward life itself that reinforced the ascriptive character of the class structure through the exclusion of all forms of utilitarian rationality. In particular, the values of manly character and conspicuous leisure that had characterized the ritual games and field sports of European life were indicative of much more than the mere "spontaneous enjoyment of life"–such values also served as means of self-assertion and as weapons in the endorsement of a cultural legacy which stressed hierarchy, deference, and class distance.*

These traditions continued in Canadian life after the turn of the nineteeth century but, given a marked increase in immigration and the gradual "filling in" of the frontier, the strengthening of petit bourgeois and middle-class reform interests, and the growing mechanization of production and trade, they became increasingly modified. For one thing, by the 1820's and 30's there was a notable shift in attitudes about the lower classes as a "problem" and as a threat to established traditions. As Michael Cross (1974) has noted, in a vast and comparatively empty frontier, tolerance to the occasionally "uncivilized" behaviours of the underclasses could be justified as an unfortunate but understandable part of colonial life. Members of the dominant class saw their subordinates as "curious but harmless beings," were often sympathetic to their forms of recreation, and largely sought to maintain a measure of traditional tory disinterest in their affairs. However, the growing contact with the expanding and increasingly less docile "lower orders" led to an advocacy and acceptance of mechanisms for controlling the potentially "unruly" impulses of lower-class groups. An apparent manifestation of these impulses was seen to lie in the steady growth of taverns in the colony and in the proliferation of gambling and other "idle" activities that might serve to encourage the "degeneration" of physical activity into "amusements" and "moral levity."

Several writers have commented on the movements for moral reform that swept through the colony in the late 1820's and 1830's (see Burnet, 1961), and it has been common to interpret such concerns as an indication of the growing significance of middle-class Methodist religious sentiment as a social force (Moir, 1967). This is undoubtedly true, but at the same time one must not lose sight of the fact that the erosion of tory sympathy

*It is no accident, for example, that the military played an important role in the early organization of Canadian sport. See P. Lindsay, "A History of Sport in Canada: 1807-1867," Ph.D. dissertation, University of Alberta, 1969, for a discussion of the significance of the British military garrisons on this point.

or disinterest and the rise of Methodist moral concerns to a level of public policy was only one dimension of a growing concern over the "problem" of the poor. Both Lasch and Bailey have suggested, for example, how the attempt to police the underclasses in the early stages of capitalist development in Britain and the United States led directly to an obsession with social control. Drinking and merrymaking among an urban working class were seen to disrupt the daily routine of businessmen, disorient people from their work, encourage extravagance and insubordination, and stimulate debauchery (Lasch, 1977: 26). Thus, the dominant class of the 1820's and 30's began to seek the elimination of the spirit of playfulness from all areas of life, especially from the work place (Bailey, 1975: 22).

Of course, the implementation of such policies did not always go unchallenged. Overt gestures of control may have helped to spur the tensions between rulers and ruled and, at the same time, the regulatory thrust of moral reform was occasionally contested by the more aristocratic fragments of the dominant class. In Canada many of the colony's self-styled aristocrats tended to support the notion that the pastimes of the people ought to be left unregulated since they remotely retained an attachment to the traditional rural order of frontier life, an order which their own conspicuous participation in hunting, fishing, and horse racing symbolically affirmed. However, such defences of traditional recreations in Canada's development were less entrenched than similar defences in Britain, and they quickly eroded in the face of the political threat posed by activities that seemed to be largely out of control. As the social organization of Canadian society became less traditional and more rationalized, as cities grew, and as production began to change in response to technological advances and new ideas, the elements of pretence and fantasy inherent in traditional play were freed from their ritualist contribution to social solidarity. Unfettered by tradition, and grounded in changing social conditions, the festival spirit of pretence, mimicry, and make-believe could very easily have developed transformative rather than reproductive consequences.

But, the fact is that such activities were effectively regulated. The apparent infusion of such middle-class values as sobriety and piety into the Canadian dominant class of the 1820's and 30's is no indication of any real loss of power by this class. In a manner somewhat similar to Britain, the moral reform movements merely bonded emerging middle-class asceticism and commercial concerns onto the political fears of the powerful. E. P. Thompson has argued that the opposition of church and state to primarily underclass forms of recreation in Britain (traditional elite pastimes were of less concern apparently) simply combined the "ethos of Methodism with the unction of the establishment" (1968: 442). Moral control was not a dictum that developed solely as a theological ideal free from practical considerations, nor did it symbolize completely the end of an aristocratic era and the rise of bourgeois power. Reformist concerns merely gave legitimacy to an expedient strategy of political control. The "grand law of subordination" laid down by Pitt's moral lieutenant Wilberforce was a response to the belief that moral levity among the underclasses (and the large gatherings often associated with popular amusements) led readily to political sedition.

Thompson suggests that in late eighteenth century England such policies can be interpreted as part of a broader response to the perceived threat of Jacobinism, and, as Hearn (1976) has pointed out, one may make a strong case for the argument that the eighteenth century movements for emancipation from the fetters of traditional domination often took on a festival and playful character. The attempt to tame this festival spirit and transform people's play from "brute riot" to "decorum" was in large measure a response to a chaotic and rapidly changing socio-economic situation. Given the growing class tensions in early nineteenth century Canada and the constant threat of liberal-democratic values imported from the United States, members of the dominant class in Canada increasingly feared large underclass gatherings and the political implications of "immoral" behaviour. They responded not so much with welfare as with control, and introduced regulatory statutes designed to exorcise the lower orders from areas where they were not appreciated. This led naturally to rigid rules about *where* and *when* one might play. To cite but one example, Donald Guay (1973) has shown quite clearly how the regulations of horse racing in Lower Canada in the 1830's were essentially a response to the perceived threat posed by the swelling numbers of Francophone workers at previously elite events.

Regulation of a different sort was also occurring within the confines of other elite pastimes. The focus for this new emphasis on regulation, and ultimately the new focus for much of the recognized play of the upper class in Canadian society, was the private school generally modelled after Britain's reformed public school system. Recently, Dunning (1976) has argued that the British public school reform movement represented an important break from traditional anti-utilitarian attitudes toward playful activity. The emphasis on discipline, religion, and "civilized" team sports that emerged as a part of Dr. Thomas Arnold's program of "muscular Christianity" at Rugby School ostensibly represented a "mid-Victorian compromise" and "mutual accommodation" between growing industrial bourgeois and declining aristocratic interests. Dunning notes how this process helped to transform chaotic play into more organized games by stimulating the development of codified rules designed to "civilize" play activities by "equalizing" the participants.

Dunning's reasoning is masterful on this issue, but his entire analysis overstates, I believe, the degree to which the reformed public school was a concession to middle-class criticism of the aristocratic style of life. For example, Rupert Wilkinson (1964) and Walter Arnstein (1973) have each pointed out that, rather than becoming increasingly middle-class, the reformed public schools merely captured middle-class talent in the promotion of gentry-class power. By indoctrinating the sons of the bourgeoisie as gentlemen, the public schools really acted as a safety valve in the social system. They helped to avert class conflict, not by instilling the values of self-help and the entrepreneurial ethos into the sons of aristocrats, but rather, by educating the young bourgeois in a sense of gentlemanly propriety that would subvert their individualistic tendencies and integrate them into a broader, more organic commitment to the collectivity. Arnstein concedes that the reformed public schools rejected undisciplined chivalric and aristocratic attitudes, but he argues that they continued to emphasize the non-utilitarian virtues of a classical education, the values of continuity and tradition more than those of utilitarian rationalism, and the belief in hierarchy rather than social equality (Arnstein, 1973: 236).

These conclusions are especially applicable to an understanding of the Canadian scene in the early 1830's, where the private school was designed to solidify a fragmented Canadian ruling class that could model itself after the British gentry and thereby provide leadership and stability in the "new society." Hodgins points out, for example, how Sir John Colborne hoped that Upper Canada College might keep alive "a love of the old manly British Field Sports" and stimulate among the boys the disciplined and "self-reliant spirit" that he saw necessary for coping with the "difficult problems incidental to the development of a new country" (1910: 198). The subsequent development of team games in most Canadian private schools emphasized these sentiments, especially in the case of the early importance of cricket. Cricket not only provided an excellent and enjoyable forum for learning discipline, civility, and the principles of "fair play" but its traditions and rules also dramatized the traditional power of the colonial metropolis and the class interests that were associated with it. As the Toronto *Patriot* editorialized on July 13, 1836: "British feelings cannot flow into the breasts of our Canadian boys through a more delightful or untainted channel than that of British sports. A cricketer, as a matter of course, detests democracy and is staunch in his allegiance to his King."

Amateurism and the Conflicts with Commercial Sports
It is probable that the conscious attempt to establish semi-aristocratic traditions and institutions in early nineteenth century Canada only intensified growing pressures of class antagonism. This antagonism erupted into open conflict in the rebellions of 1837-38, and, while the rebels were easily controlled, the rebellions themselves clearly revealed the strength of liberal sentiments in Canada and the rise of the interests of labourers and independent commodity producers as a new social force (Ryerson, 1973: 133). Less aristocratically minded governments soon followed and the repeal of the British Corn Laws in 1846 provided the material conditions necessary for the ascendency of an indigenous "liberal-tory" component to the Canadian upper class by ending the direct colonial-mercantile domination of the

"first commercial empire of the St. Lawrence" (see Creighton, 1956). It should not be assumed, however, that utilitarian ethics and democratic political principles were generally ushered into Canadian life as a result of such changes. Conditions became more favourable for Canada's petit bourgeois to develop as an indigenous capitalist class, and "responsible government" free from direct British control was achieved. Nonetheless, Canada remained a conservative, staple-producing economy with a close association between the accumulative interests of dominant class and the state (cf., Clement, 1975; Panitch, 1977).

Again, changes in political-economic relationships in Canada received a cultural expression in the organization of play. The regulative tendencies begun in earlier decades, rather than easing with the apparent infusion of middle-class ethics into social and political life, continued to intensify. The rebellions themselves had reinforced the fear of population with "time on its hands," and as the frontier began to "fill in" even more with massive immigration during the 1840's and 50's, the view of the lower orders hardened accordingly (see Cross, 1974). Concerned over the possible spread of disease from an impoverished lower class, more thoroughly committed to reformist ideals which sought to replace traditional class obligations with state policies of control, and not quite so secure in their socio-political dominance, members of Canada's commercial-political ruling class of the pre-confederation era continued to design regulations which would maintain order, discipline, and health among the working population and promote the interests of liberal civility.

One area where such programs were established after lengthy controversy between reformists and traditionalists was in the tax-supported free school system. Susan Houston has noted that in Ontario, Egerton Ryerson and his followers deeply feared the unfettered forces of urbanism and industrialization, and saw the "spirit" of underclass "insubordination" abroad threatening the "honest independence of the working and labouring classes, particularly servants" (1972: 251). Based on such attitudes, and on a concern for the necessity for a "fit" population for industrial production and military service, play activities in the schools emphasized discipline and regimentation through the teaching of military drill and gymnastic exercise (see Cosentino and Howell,

1971). By contrast, the private schools continued to emphasize the values of leadership, fair play, and the disciplined but spontaneous enjoyment of games.

A more significant dimension of major changes in the social development of play, games, and sports during the 1840's and 50's was the growth of the urban sports club. Field sports flourished among a landed and agrarian upper class, but they were less suited to the recreational aspirations of a bourgeois class that needed to locate close to urban markets and transportation centres. In conjunction with "incipient industrialization" in Canada and the growth of new indigenous commercial (primarily banking and retailing) activities, the recreational sports club developed as a new organizational form for the social expression of the play impulse. At first, as Alan Metcalfe (1976) has pointed out in his ground-breaking study of sport and social stratification in nineteenth century Montreal, the leadership of these clubs was limited to the professional, commercial, and military elite in the community, and their focus was clearly social rather than competitive. The club leaders, while representatives of Canada's ruling bourgeois class, had an approach to games and recreation tempered by strong tory biases: a belief in the spirit of sociability in fair play and an acceptance of the legacy of anti-utilitarian sentiments about the role of games in life.

Metcalfe has emphasized how actual membership in the elite clubs of the 1840's and 50's was clearly limited by ascriptive criteria. Nonetheless, a few of the clubs did sponsor "open" competitions. Open competitions featured contact between social classes in athletic contests and demanded the formulation of universal rules that "equalized" all participants. However, even in such open competition, where lawyers competed against Indians and working-men, class distinctions were implicitly recognized by the provision of trophies for "gentlemen" and cash prizes for others (Metcalfe, 1976: 80-84; Metcalfe, 1978). A measure of commercialism invested in the contest was tolerated, but only within the context of limits defined by the dominant class.

Still, the incipient industrialization of Canadian production had altered class and power relationships by the late 1860's to the extent that the entire organizational development of play, game, and sporting activities was affected. In a *material sense*, this industrialization allowed for an expansion of the middle class; it created the necessary conditions for the wider production of manufactured goods; it allowed for the all-important "rationalization" of working time (see Thompson, 1967); and it allowed for the technological developments in transportation and communication which were necessary for certain types of play activities to grow beyond their localized character (see Jobling, 1976). In an *ideological sense*, industrial development stimulated the growth of a more "pure" type of bourgeois values in the Canadian business community: rational utilitarian and, frequently, Darwinist values that were generally "unsullied" by the direct contact with ascriptive gentry class attitudes or the "gentlemanly" ethos of professionals and administrators (Cross, 1974). These new values differed from the "liberal-toryism" that had evolved into the dominant ideology in Canada by the 1860's and they created the normative environment for the development of more highly structured achievement-based competitive sports as an addition to the more loosely structured social and recreational activities that had hitherto served as the prime outlet for people's desires for play. The focus for this new emphasis in play activities occurred primarily in the urban sports club.

By the mid-1860's, the urban club movement had begun to democratize, not on the basis of the elimination of discriminatory patterns of membership selection and recruitment, but rather through the proliferation of the clubs themselves. Yet, the democratization of clubs through proliferation merely reinforced existing class distinctions and shaped them into new organizational forms. These forms continued to dramatize the hierarchical arrangement of social groups and the crystalization of new forms of domination based on personal worth equated to position in the market place. An example of the conflicts which developed along these lines can be found in the debate over "amateurism" and "professionalism."

During the 1840's and 50's, as noted previously, elite sporting clubs occasionally sponsored open competitions where upper-class individuals would compete against working men. Upper-class "trend setters," as Dunning and Sheard (1976) have called similar groups in England, were relatively secure in their positions and competed in sport for fun. Their identities and statuses were not at stake in a race or other athletic contest and it is unlikely that they would have been very concerned about losing to "inferiors." Losing was likely non-problematic since it did not affect the established order in any way. Moreover, professionalism was not seen as a problem since it was assumed that it could always be controlled (see Dunning and Sheard, 1976). Metcalfe (1976) reminds us that such occasional cross-class athletic contact should not be interpreted as a utopian view of friendly competition; competitions were not that frequent and class distinctions were still evident. But the point is that open competitions sponsored by elite clubs did exist on occasion and facilitated contact between classes in the pursuit of games and sport.

There is some evidence, however, that from the 1850's and 60's on there were fewer of these elite-sponsored open competitions (see Metcalfe, 1976: 81). Open competitions, often associated with church or company annual picnics, did become popular after the 1860's but these were not events usually sponsored by members of Canada's dominant class. We may theorize, perhaps, that as the Canadian class structure began to elaborate, and as meritocratic liberal values began to develop widespread support, members of the dominant class apparently became unable to tolerate the possibility of defeat at the hands of groups which they defined as their social inferiors. They also presumably became progressively more alarmed at the prospect that commercialism in sport could very easily get out of hand under such conditions and vulgarize "the nobility of play." There were two possible responses to such developments: (1) withdraw completely from the world of competitive sports and establish social clubs which could be easily defended against the forces of democratization, or (2) set up formal organizations designed to provide particular standards for ensuring that the nobility of play would remain uncontaminated by either crass commercialism or unrestricted meritocratic principle (see Gruneau, 1975: 130-1). Members of different strata within the dominant class tended to pursue one or the other of these strategies: many of the traditional tory establishment withdrew to the socially-oriented hunt and tandem clubs and vigorously defended entry against the "lower status" bourgeoisie (for example, entry by the smaller indigenous industrial fragment of the bourgeoisie). The other component of the upper class consolidated their "Victorian legacy" through the cult of the "amateur" (see Mallea, 1975). Thus, as Dunning and Sheard (1976) have pointed out in the case of the English Rugby Football, the concept of amateurism seems to have evolved as conscious strategy of exclusion in class relations.

By the mid-1880's the key organizational structures in the world of games and sports were dominated by amateur agencies. Central among these were the early national sporting associations (e.g., the National Amateur Lacrosse Association), the newly formed Amateur Athletic Union of Canada, and the powerful Montreal Amateur Athletic Association. The executives of these agencies were not recruited entirely from the top stratum of Canada's dominant class; rather, the major amateur agencies were governed by a loose coalition of younger and less established members of this class whose origins lay in the business, professional, and military communities of the major urban centres (see Wise, 1974; Metcalfe, 1976; Gruneau, 1978). Of these three communities the business community dominated the executive positions of amateur agencies. As Wise has emphasized (1974), the club movement and the standards of amateurism it embraced were intimately connected to the concerns for order and sobriety that were so much a part of the dominant commercial ideology of the period.

It is instructive to note what parts of the Canadian urban business community many of these executives came from. Given that the 1880's in Canada represented what Acheson (1972) has called the halcyon days of Canadian industrial development, one might hypothesize that many of the executives of the amateur agencies would come from the dynamic industrial sector of Canadian business. But this was not the case. Individuals like W. K. McNaught, who combined his role as an executive member of the National Amateur Lacrosse Association with the Presidency of the Canadian Manufacturers' Association, were the exception rather than the rule, and the major concentration of occupations for those executives in amateur agencies involved in business lay primarily in the areas of finance and retail or wholesale trade.

Given the political-economic framework that I have outlined, the under-representation of the industrial sector of the economy in the occupations of the organizers of amateur organizations of the 1880's should not be surprising. I say this for two reasons. First, while the major amateur organizations did not generally recruit their leadership from the highest stratum of the Canadian upper class, this leadership was nonetheless unabashedly Victorian in focus and organization and rooted to an ascriptive liberal-tory conception of play, social organization, and hierarchy. The laissez-faire and rational utilitarian standards of industrial interests were not generally compatible with such traditions and views. Secondly, and because of the historical dominance of finance capital in Canada, the indigenous Canadian industrial bourgeois had never been in a position to develop as a full-fledged component of the Canadian upper class. Acheson (1972) has noted that while few of the 1885 industrial elite were men of humble origins, industrialists generally considered themselves as the proletariat of the Canadian business community. Moreover, despite the economic nationalism of the National Policy (1879) period, the domination of Canadian industrial production by Americans that had been stimulated by the Reciprocity Act of 1854 continued to act as a serious limiting factor to the development of indigenous and independent industrial power.

But, to note that the industrial development of Canada was retarded by the branch-plant character of production and that progressive industrial bourgeois interests were rarely reflected in the games and sports of the dominant class in Canada is not to argue that industrialization as a social force should be trivialized. Similarly, the fact that the small manufacturer or skilled artisan was not generally a part of the creation of an amateur orientation to organized games and sports should not be taken as an indication that these individuals were unimportant in the increasing organization and re-orientation of play in late nineteenth century Canada. Undoubtedly, many upwardly mobile industrialists and skilled labourers utilized the dominant class as a reference group and became closely attached to the values of sobriety, fairness, and moral development in games. However, for some middle-class shopowners, and certainly for most labourers, the ideal of the true gentleman-amateur was only remotely attainable, and the pious concern with temperance and morality associated with it was not always ideologically appealing. An alternative arena for cultural expression was provided, however, in the development and expansion of commercial forms of games and popular recreation.

Dunning and Sheard (1976) have noted how the presence of the ascendent industrial component of the bourgeoisie in England stimulated an open, more meritocratic and commercial approach to games and sports. The small-scale industrialists were often self-made men who kept in direct touch with the manufacturing process from a small office attached to the workshop. Close contact with employees and a feeling of commonality in production were conducive to a low degree of status-exclusiveness and class distance and hence formed the foundation for open Rugby clubs, often associated with the plant. Similar patterns in Canada are easily identified in some of the sports clubs of the 1870's and 80's, and it is frequently within these clubs that the emphasis on skill and winning begins to rival the amateur ideal of fair play as a legitimate standard for gauging the quality of the play experience.

This last point must be accompanied by a caveat, however. Much of the production in Canada was based on an impersonal type of industrial organization and, given the long hours and lingering policies against sabbath-breaking and amusements, there was little in the way of opportunities for recreation or sports for the industrial labourer or worker in Canada's primary industries. For example, Metcalfe (1976) points out how manual labourers were almost completely absent from the club movement in Montreal until the late 1890's and how nearly all of the facilities for sports and popular forms of recreation were limited to the middle-class and predominantly English-speaking wards of the city. Where workers clubs did start up (like some of the Mechanics Clubs) they tended to represent labour's highest status occupations (e.g., mechanics, firemen, etc.), and unless organized by white-collar workers they rarely lasted more than a few years. There were even fewer outlets for recreation and games among the factory workers and unskilled labourers. Beyond the taverns and illegal gatherings associated with canal swims, cock fights, and boxing matches, Metcalfe concludes (1978), regular working-class participation in organized recreation in late-Victorian Montreal was negligible.

Yet, for those Canadians who could afford some free time,

commercial forms of recreation and games were proving to be increasingly popular. As I have suggested earlier, commercialism of some type had always been an important part of traditional community games and recreation, but during the latter third of the nineteenth century conditions were ideal for commercial sports to break out of the ideological and legal constraints that had framed them. The first "challenge" series and semi-structured leagues stimulated the monetization of games, and the progressively wide-open and Horatio Alger-like dimension of entrepreneurial activity in Canada reinforced the idea of the overriding importance of success in all walks of life, including the playing field. More importantly, the adulation and national pride associated with new "professional athletes" like Ned Hanlan (see Cross, 1974: 225) helped to integrate play more formally into the market place and partially legitimate it as an era of open competition and entrepreneurial activity. Yet, however such developments influenced spectatorship and offered limited careers in organized sport to individuals with exceptional abilities, the nineteenth century did not, in any organizational sense, represent the triumph of rational meritocratic values in the world of sports and games. Commercial sport was generally chaotic and in constant conflict with amateurism, and as late as the turn of the century the Victorian legacy of the "gentleman-amateur" continued to dominate as the axis around which the standards of play revolved.

This conflict between amateur and more commercial forms of sporting activities at the turn of the twentieth century raises some interesting questions about the relationships of ideology to changing conditions of social organization. Amateur and commercial approaches to sport shared certain structural similarities but differed markedly in ideology. For example, the controllers of the major amateur agencies objected to commercialism primarily on the basis of four principles: (1) commercialism was supposed to debase play by allowing the representational character of play to take precedence over the act of playing itself; (2) commercialism was seen to emphasize instrumental ends more than traditional means; (3) commercialism was viewed as inflaming passion rather than inculcating the value of restraint; and finally (4) commercialism was seen to be closely associated with gambling, drinking, and frivolity, all of which offended bourgeois Protestant sentiment.

Yet, given the effects of industrial development and democratization, many of the clubs, teams, and individual competitors who were associated with the major amateur organizations had a good deal of trouble living up to the ideals that amateurism defined. As clubs proliferated and as many of them became increasingly involved in intense local rivalries, challenge series, and more formalized leagues, they often became transformed from "exclusive" to "open" and finally to "gate-taking" organizations in a manner similar to the British rugby clubs studied by Dunning and Sheard (1976). At the same time, while it was still in no way ideologically legitimate for a gentleman to want to win above all else, "scientific play" was beginning to rival "fair play" as an accepted standard for judging the sporting experience (see Weiler, 1974). The move from an emphasis on "fairness" to an emphasis on "technique" within amateurism itself seemed to make some of the distinctions between amateur sport and commercial sporting activities less real and more arbitrary. The development of superior technique, whether pursued as an end in itself or as a means to an end, essentially has only one outcome – improved performance.

These changes introduced a difficult and highly ambiguous situation within the definition of amateurism, for they suggested on the one hand that sport, as an apparent derivation of play, was essentially a *democracy of ability*, yet on the other hand sport was a *subordinate* area of life where the development of ability could only be pursued on a casual and part-time basis. In other words, the guardians of the amateur ethos had embraced and assimilated some of the advancing sentiments of nineteenth century utilitarianism, but only within the limits imposed by a conservative view of social organization which stressed moral rather than rational utility (see Gruneau, 1975: 129-32). The use-value of amateur sport lay in its contribution to personal growth and development whereas the use-value of commercial sport came to be increasingly defined in economic terms. But, as Metcalfe (1976) has pointed out, over the last two decades of the nineteenth century there was increased bureaucratization in sport which facilitated differentiation between the executives in the major amateur sport organizations and the players themselves. Given this development, it seems the case that the meritocratic side of the amateur equation was being overly credited at the level of actual play, thus introducing a situation where many clubs defined themselves nominally as amateur, but began to converge progressively with more commercialized forms of sporting activity.

The consequences of this convergence were extremely significant. Influenced by the success of commercial sport in the United States, and finding the elite in the major amateur sport organizations inaccessible and unresponsive, members of the open and gate-taking clubs created organizational alternatives to domination by middle- and upper-class business and professional men. The organizers of the first professional leagues in baseball, lacrosse, and later, hockey included promoters and fast-buck artists, local athletic facility owners, small manufacturers, and local businessmen. In short, they were a far more broadly-based group than the more established businessmen and professionals who controlled the major amateur organizations. However, the leadership in commercial sport itself began to crystallize after the first decade of the twentieth century as team owners and league organizers moved from an entrepreneurial to a corporate orientation.

Corporate Games/State Sport
The period of entrepreneurial development in sport and popular recreation described thus far paralleled an intense period of broader entrepreneurial activity in Canadian society. Despite the recessions of the latter third of the nineteenth century, the Canadian economy continued to expand and open up avenues of mobility within the class structure. Michael Bliss (1974) argues, for example, that most of the capitalists who dominated the Canadian upper class after the turn of the century had begun their careers as clerks and sub-contractors a generation before. Bliss may overstate the degree of actual mobility into the Canadian upper class during this period and his argument should not be taken to imply that great inequalities of condition had dissolved by the turn of the twentieth century, for if anything these inequalities had become more pronounced (cf., Copp, 1974); but

there can be no denying that substantial mobility did occur as Canada went through a dynamic phase of industrial growth and entrepreneurial capitalism. In the sport world, many of the upwardly mobile clerks and white-collar workers, who identified with the Victorian values of the middle class and saw in sport an agency which helped strengthen temperance and the business-related virtues of hard work and dedication, moved into executive positions in the amateur sports organizations as they worked their way toward increased power and privilege. At the same time, as I have tried to indicate, commercial sport opened up as an area of business opportunity and mobility for less privileged members of the bourgeoisie and even to considerable numbers of skilled labourers.

This period of intense and open entrepreneurial capitalism in Canada did not last much beyond the First World War. The increased involvement of established financial capitalists in certain areas of the industrial sector featuring the greatest degree of growth and the accelerated rate of American direct investment in other areas of the industrial sector worked, in the shape of corporate concentration, to solidify a more stable and rigid class structure. As Wallace Clement (1975: 73) suggests, the period of open competitive capitalism which is so commonly depicted as occurring within the transformation from feudal or colonial systems to industrial capitalist systems was generally ended by the establishment of a highly structured bureaucratic approach to production, an accompanying emphasis on specialization within the division of labour, and the overall shift to modern corporationism.

In the world of commercial sport the effects of such developments can be measured by two basic changes. First, as clubs and individuals entered into market relationships with one another in and through sport, it became a necessity to incorporate formally clubs and sport businesses. The number of federal charters on record issued to sport organizations of various types rose from one, in the period between 1890 and 1910, to thirty, in the period between 1911-1920.* Secondly, there developed a growing recog-

---

*Data cited from Canadian Public Records, Division Holdings Inventory (Sport), The National Archives, Ottawa.

nition of the need to create mechanisms that could regulate economic competition between teams and protect the developing labour and product markets in sport. In the early years of organized commercial sport (the period between 1870-1910) promoters and team owners usually acted in an individualistic entrepreneurial fashion and struggled for dominance in the labour and product market surrounding professional athletic activity. Such struggles were ultimately counter-productive since they made it difficult to keep leagues together for any period of time. Arguments over gate receipts, stadium and rink sizes, and franchise rights posed continuing threats to financial success in the sports business. While professional sport in itself was popular, individual teams developed and faded with almost predictable regularity.

The first major shift from an entrepreneurial to a corporate orientation in the Canadian sport world occurred with the formation of the National Hockey League in 1917. By the 1920's hockey had replaced lacrosse as Canada's major team sport, and by 1930 the owners of the NHL franchises had learned, after years of bidding wars for players, that profit maximization could only be hampered by unrestricted individual economic competition. In other words, as Colin Jones (1976) indicates, the owners recognized that in order to maximize individual profits they had to maximize joint profits. The period following this realization has been characterized by concentration and growing league control over both the product and labour markets in hockey. At the same time, as the league solidified it consolidated massive capital gains based on the appreciation of franchise values and on windfall profits. By contrast, Canadian professional football developed within the ambiguity of amateurism that I described earlier and was in constant contact with university sports programs. Most of the "professionalizing" forces in football developed in the West and reflected a strong American influence, but the CFL did not undergo a partial move to profit-maximizing corporationism until after 1950.

The question of American influence in Canadian sport is an important one, for it seems clear that the United States quickly imprinted its own metropolitan influence on organized commercial sport. Sports in the United States were often more "progressive" in their attachment to more fully developed industrial bourgeois values and American society generally provided a favourable environment for an emphasis on democratized and more commercialized forms of sporting activity. The under-representation of petit bourgeois and working-class interests in the control of amateur sport in Canada could be compensated for by involvement with American sports clubs in bi-national commercial enterprises. Attendant to this, an excessively rigid amateur code did not always allow for the type of sporting involvement that captured the interest of the Canadian working-class community. The rapidly developing rational and semi-meritocratic ideology of bi-national commercial sport was especially compatible with petit bourgeois and working-class interests and aspirations and dramatized their growing commercial strength.

But for the working class, the change from the bi-national player-controlled or club-oriented commercial sport of the late nineteenth century to the slick American-dominated corporate sports of the present day has been a betrayal of any liberating transformative promise. As commercial sports grew in popularity and developed market relations to outside business interests, as wealthy patrons of commercial teams increased their influence, and as cartel structures were created in the sports world, relationships between commercial sports and the working class tended to become progressively exploitative. Actual working-class influences on decision-making became limited as mobility into executive positions became restricted to individuals with capital, and working-class athletes generally became transformed from journeyman players to contractually bound labourers.

For the most part these trends continue to be evident features of modern corporate sport, but there have been some interesting fluctuations in them. For example, modern team sports have emerged out of a period of extremely repressive work conditions in the 1940's and 50's to a point where athletes (or, more correctly, *top* athletes) are usually guaranteed high salaries and a measure of financial security through increased pensions and deferred salary payments. Occupations in the sports world have also gained a good deal of respectability and this change, complete with its connotations of executive houses in the suburbs, is indicative of a process that Charles Page (1973) has wryly referred to as the "embourgeoisement" of pro athletes.

Another fluctuation has been a gradual move from the individual, family, or small corporation patterns of team ownership that asserted themselves during the 1920's and 30's to increased interlocking with larger corporations that often have little to do with sports. This pattern was partially stimulated, as Okner (1974) has noted, by the tax advantages that a professional sports franchise might offer a large corporation (although many of these advantages have been successfully challenged in recent years), but in Canada the pattern seems also to have been related to a desire by business to support popular, highly visible public activities for promotional purposes. Beyond the obvious financial advantages and promotional opportunities that are presented when breweries own large percentages of baseball teams, or when broadcasting companies own professional sports teams, team ownership can also be peddled as a "service" that is being provided to the community. In any case, modern trends in the ownership of professional teams appear to point increasingly in the direction of the full-scale integration of sports into more diversified corporate interests.

It should be noted that the movement of commercial sports from small-scale entrepreneurial efforts, to family-based or individually owned corporate enterprises, to involvement in the periphery of the empires of Canada's dominant corporations is sometimes seen as an indicator of progress. Work conditions in commercial team sports have improved, the argument runs, and the ruthless pursuit of profit has been mediated by a broader corporate social responsibility. But is this view of progress an accurate one? I think not. What has really occurred is simply that commercial sports are only now beginning to become subject to the liberal concessions of welfare capitalism. Meanwhile, the lines of power and control in commercial sports are becoming even more closely tied to Canada's corporate elite and its structural alliances with American capital.

We may note the following examples of such alliances. Boards of directors of most Canadian professional sports teams (except for a few teams in the CFL where control lies in the hands of business and professional interests in the local community) maintain readily identifiable ties with indigenous Canadian capital in the areas of finance, trade, the food and beverage industry, and transport and communications, but (again excepting the CFL) the major leagues that these franchises operate within are controlled by American interests. Hockey and baseball, in particular, represent a classic dramatization of the doubly exploitative nature of Canada's association with the American metropole. The accumulative interests of Canadian capital in areas where these interests have always been strong are enhanced by their association with organizations where control lies in American hands. And, whereas Canadian capital is involved in a profitable relationship that maintains patterns of dependency, the interests and forms of cultural expression of most Canadians remain largely under-developed. This is not to say that Canadians as a whole have lost control of commercial sports to the United States; rather, as Clement (1977: 20) points out in the case of the Canadian economy, it is doubtful if any real collective control by Canadians has ever been present. With few exceptions, modern commercial sports have always been owned and controlled by private individuals (or at least by a representation of individuals from middle- or upper-class fragments in communities) and have represented the organization of the interests of these individuals in corporate entities that function in an international capitalist system.

This brings us rather directly to a consideration of the relationships between commercial sport and organized labour – in theory the traditional opponents of bourgeois power. In one of the few attempts to understand sporting activities in the context of labour and class conflicts, Kiviaho and Simola (1974) have noted how working-class sports clubs in late nineteenth century Finland were given considerable support by the Finnish labour movement (also see Steinberg, 1978; Wheeler, 1978). Opportunities for working-class sports participation were stimulated and working-class club teams provided widespread entertainment. The necessity for these labour-oriented sports organizations arose partially in response to the exclusive character of Olympic amateurism but also as a natural part of an attempt to support and encourage working-class culture.

There is some evidence that the potential for similar developments existed in Canada even though the Marxist component of the Canadian labour movement never developed to the extent that it did in many European nations. Bruce Kidd has recently noted, for example, how during the depression years of the 1930's the Canadian Labour Party sought to support working-class sport through the creation of a Workers' Sports Association (WSA) that was to sponsor teams, offer instruction, and provide support for holding demonstrations and athletic exhibitions. The WSA also supported a team picked to compete in the ill-fated "People's Olympics" that were to be held in Barcelona in 1936 as a worker's alternative to the Berlin Olympics (Kidd, 1977; 1978).

However, the ideological focus of the Canadian Labour Party's approach to sports is not clear from Kidd's preliminary study. Even though radical workers' papers like the *Daily Clarion* and *The Worker* occasionally pointed out that organized sports (especially commercial sports) were "a racket," they nonetheless gave them ample coverage in their sports pages. As one editorial noted, sports supposedly provided "the only enjoyment the masses get under the rotten conditions that exist at the present time" (Kidd, 1977: 35). Indeed, there does not appear to be much evidence that any significant attempt to articulate a distinctly working-class approach to sports ever occurred. Kidd points out, for example, that the radical working-class press tended to limit its discussion of alternatives in sport to little more than wistful discussion of the opportunities for sports participation that supposedly existed in the Soviet Union.

It is not completely within the limits that I have set for myself in this essay to attempt to explain the inability of Canadian labour to offer workers an alternative to the dramatic appeal of commercial (and, to a lesser extent, amateur) sports. However, a few hypotheses might be noted. First we must recognize the extent to which the Canadian labour movement, like the industrial sector of the economy itself, was under-developed during the late nineteenth and early twentieth centuries (see Howard and Scott, 1972; Abella and Miller, 1978). Radical independent union organizers were ruthlessly persecuted and there was strong pressure from American unions (primarily the American Federation of Labor) for Canadian labour to ally itself with the American labour movement. The strength of the American influence in the industrial sector of the Canadian economy facilitated the co-opting of Canadian workers by American industrial and trade unions and guaranteed a subordination of Canadian working-class culture to this particular ideology. As Howard and Scott have stressed, this ideology emphasized reproductive interclass collaboration and negotiation rather than the necessity for transformative class conflict. This emphasis in no way implied the complete endorsement of existing social conditions but it contained a tacit acceptance of the essential structure of capitalism and a notion that all workers might ultimately gain access to middle-class life styles. As part of the negotiations with labour under these terms, sports programs and industrial recreation increased markedly and gained considerable acceptability in the world of industry. The responsibility for many of these programs, however, was most often taken by management rather than by labour.

Thus far I have argued that an interest (primarily a fan interest) in commercial sports of various kinds and different types of industry-supported recreational activities have emerged during the twentieth century as the prime outlets for the play impulses of most members of Canada's working class. On the other hand, organized amateur sports have tended to retain a strong association with the middle and upper strata of Canada's dominant class. Even today, when sporting activities appear to be substantially more democratized than earlier in this century, a number of studies (see Curtis and Milton, 1976; Gruneau, 1975 and 1976) have documented a positive correlation between active sports participation and high socio-economic position. Of course, this pattern does not hold as closely in all pastimes – activities with clearly pronounced working-class cultural traditions like boxing and weight-lifting tend to maintain a connection with their past; but, as a general principle, elite athletics and the high-skill levels of amateur sports tend to draw on advantaged groups in the Canadian reward structure. Where democratization has occurred, it has been limited primarily to the expansion of athletic opportunities within the various strata of Canada's dominant class, a situation I have elsewhere labelled the "bourgeoisification" of amateur sport (Gruneau, 1976). While all of this has occurred, working-class athletes have tended to remain under-represented at elite levels and the very poor, the chronically unemployed, and other marginal groups in this country are virtually non-existent in the sports world.

But this whole issue of opportunities for participation is much less important than the question of opportunities for control and the accompanying problems of power and unequal social conditions. There now may be greater opportunities for working-class participation in semi-commercialized amateur sports but there has definitely not been any substantial improvement in working-class control over sports and recreation policies. The growth of the Olympic movement in Canada after the 1920's and the accompanying prestige associated with international sport has continued to guarantee a high degree of exclusivity at the executive levels of the major policy-making organizations. One may expect this, of course, in such Victorian carryovers as the Canadian Olympic Association, but even in our major voluntary sports associations the predominance of upper and middle status interests within Canada's dominant class is revealed starkly.

In a study of a sample of executive members of over twenty of Canada's national sports associations, Beamish (1978) has found that over 50 per cent of executives in 1975 had fathers who had been employed in professional, managerial, or technical occupations. Over 75 per cent of the executives were themselves currently involved in similar occupations. Moreover, the executives were invariably located in the major urban centres – Toronto, Vancouver, Ottawa, and Montreal. Beamish points out how such patterns are clearly linked to the logic of capital in Canada and the distribution of advantages in Canadian society. Most workers are locked into rigid production schedules, many must moonlight to make ends meet, and there is little time or incentive for voluntary participation. Also, as Beamish (1978: 25) explains, there is little in their work to prepare them for such tasks. Many Canadians are involved in non-creative, non-administrative work that does not provide them with the kinds of skills that are easily transferable to the spheres of voluntary administration. Moreover, the bureaucratization of sport and sport's increasing ties to state political structures virtually guarantees the exclusion of all but a narrow stratum of Canadians.

The issue of the role of the state in sports and recreation that

Beamish raises is complex and cannot be considered here in any detail. It should be noted, however, that over the past twenty years the involvement of the Canadian state in the "play" of its citizens and even in "the business of play" has increased markedly. What I mean by "involvement" here is a turn away from directly discernible control-oriented policies in popular recreation, and equally discernible non-control policies in commercial sports, to more welfare-oriented programs ostensibly designed to increase the quality of life in Canada and expand opportunities for the pursuit of athletic excellence. Thus, we now have a bona fide federal ministry of sport and numerous provincial counterparts to it, a national lottery whose proceeds supposedly help in the development of Canadian sport, a National Administrative Centre to house the amateur associations, and the full-scale development of programs designed to certify coaches and athletes.

In the absence of research on sport and the state in Canada, explanations for these developments can only be speculated upon. One argument might be that the increased involvement by the state in recreation, fitness, and sport appears simply as an inevitable part of the expansion of the social rights of citizenship that have been characteristic of most of the western liberal democracies over the last fifty years. This growth of state-supported social rights, most of which have been won by the underclasses in the face of considerable opposition, has accompanied a gradual shift in the socio-political emphasis of liberal democratic states: a shift from the role of direct agent for the accumulative interests of capital to the role of legal and cultural guardian of liberal-democratic ideology.

State-sponsored recreation and sport programs have a good deal of social value for large numbers of individual citizens, yet they also have important political implications. At least, by suggesting incorrectly that the state acts on behalf of all citizens, these programs indirectly serve the long-term interests of Canadian capital. As Leo Panitch (1977) explains, it is only by convincing Canadians that the state does not simply operate at the *behest* of the accumulative interests of capital that it can properly function on the *behalf* of capital. The apparent concern by state agencies for the "democratization" of sports, or for the expansion of recreation opportunities for Canadians, may be well-intentioned or even progressively reformist, but the structural consequences of these reforms seem likely to strengthen state (and, indirectly class) power.

Yet, it is possible to make too much of the rise of "welfare-statism" as an explanation for the expanded involvement of the Canadian state in the organization of sports and recreation. Panitch argues, for example, that even today Canada is little more than a "middle-range" spender on welfare programs. Moreover, in the case of recreation and sports, there has been much less formal attention paid to recreation with an emphasis on "fun" than to fitness, organized sports, and athletic success. A physically "healthy" society is supposedly a more productive society (with lower absenteeism, higher job satisfactions, fewer strikes, etc.) and there is a strong case to be made that the current "fitness boom" merely represents the resurgence of long-standing regulative traditions in Canada that have always been class-based. In the case of athletic success, we are now caught up in an international sport system where state-supported athletes appear to have become little more than ideological labourers, symbolic agents for liberal democracy who oppose the representatives of communism and the Third World in a contest to affirm who has the "healthiest" socio-political system. The unquestioning pursuit of the sports record that develops from this has featured a rationalization of games and sports that goes far beyond Johan Huizinga's wildest fears.

III   SUMMARY AND CONCLUDING COMMENTS

In this essay I have attempted to review a number of theoretical issues relevant to the study of power and play in Canadian society and to link these to a general discussion of some changing relationships between power and play in Canadian social development. My analysis has focused primarily on the treatment of regulated play, games, and sports as dramatizations of social life that have had reproductive or transformative effects. Implicit in this analysis has been an attempt to compare these dramatizations with the transformative promise that appears embodied in the essential character of simple play.

The framework utilized to explore these relationships in Cana-

dian social development is based on a consideration both of inter-
and intra-class conflicts and on patterns of domination and
dependency. I began by noting how in early nineteenth century
Canada the dramatic representational value of traditional play
and game forms essentially had reproductive consequences.
However, given changes in Canadian society the game forms and
sports of the lower strata of the Canadian bourgeoisie grew to
rival the hegemony of traditional play. The disciplined enjoyment of games contained a bourgeois transformative ideal whose
corollary was the control of underclass amusements and the
expulsion of play from the workplace. Further elaborations of
class formations in Canada primarily centred on changes in
industry and production and led directly to the evolution of this
ideal into the exclusionary practices of amateurism. Organiza-
tion-sponsored commercialism, by contrast, dramatized growing
petit bourgeois values and the spread of entrepreneurial ethics
beyond the dominant class in a form that members of the dominant class found unpalatable. At the same time, commercialism
offered the Canadian worker an expressive statement that contained the promise of greater autonomy and collective expression. This promise, however, was a chimera. Commercial sports
developed quickly into a celebration of capital accumulation and,
despite providing an important dimension to working-class
culture, they have done little more than offer workers an
apparent cultural reproduction of the forces that dominate them.
   This is just one way in which the forms of cultural expression
in our modern era appear to have become caught up in the ascen-
dant features of capitalist liberal democracy. Other examples
come readily to mind. Amateur sports have bureaucratized and
have become an important part of state policy in the cultural and
welfare areas, and commercial sports have become fully integrated into the "acceptable" world of corporate social responsibility. In other words, at the institutional level, sports in
modern Canadian society have taken alternative collective meanings and promises in play and games and have largely rendered
them to the area of a non-decision.* Money values are affirmed as

*This is not to say that "personal" meanings always align with "institutional"
ones, or even that the prevailing forces of social reproduction in modern
sports are always accepted and internalized by individuals. However, the

legitimate and inevitable in commercial sports, and sports participation in state programs rarely stimulates or encounters alternative socio-political views.

In an earlier paper (Gruneau, 1975) I have argued that, as institutional-established activities which are ostensibly related to play, sports contain a fundamental contradiction between egalitarian and meritocratic ideals. Play stresses freedom, equity, and fairness, but in its association with games and sports it also stresses skill and inequalities of result. However, the promise of play is to order these various modes of human expression in a specific way; hierarchy, results, and domination in the real world of play are always limited by higher rules of egalitarianism that stress dignity more than domination and equal conditions as well as equal opportunities. Man "the player" (Homo Ludens) may thrive on competition but he only approaches his potential when this competitive emphasis is mediated by structural arrangements that feature autonomous self-expression, equality, and respect. For some, the promise of realizing this potential is enough to sustain them and for others the structurally defined and culturally supported approximations of this promise pass for the real thing. The nature of this approximation in modern Canadian society is embedded in the logic of our particular version of capitalist liberal democracy. What passes for play these days is a confusion of the classical line of mediation between play and sport: in most of our modern games and sports merit and success rule and egalitarianism struggles as a second sister. The most bitter irony of all, however, is that in state socialist societies, supposedly dedicated to egalitarian ideals, the same imbalance has come to rule.

It is tempting to conclude on this pessimistic note, for it seems so apparent that the public representational character of our modern games and sports has been effectively mobilized in the defense of bourgeois culture. But we should recognize that at the private, personal level the meanings of games and sports do not

range of possible meanings consciously incorporated into the organization of sports and forms of popular recreation is extremely limited. Alternative meanings and standards for sport involvement (e.g., those which stress fun over fitness or contemplation and self-development over skill acquisition) do not receive institutional support.

always align with the reproductive features of their public counterparts. An appreciation of the essential drama of the contest
and the attempt to realize the promise of play in our private lives
helps individuals cope with the injustices of a society that corre-
lates dignity and personal worth with abstract notions of skill
acquisition, efficiency, and productive capacity. That such coping
generally fails to challenge the sources of domination in social life
(it is accommodative rather than transformational) is tragic but
not hopeless. Hope remains in the fact that bourgeois hegemony
is far from complete and far from immune to the possibilities of
change. Older cultural traditions which stress the non-utilitarian
character of games have yet to die out completely in Canadian society and it seems inevitable that newer collective meanings and
creative developments in games will continue to emerge in the
struggle for consciousness. However, to be transformative rather
than merely accommodative, the pursuit of these alternatives has
to be moved out of the private spheres of meaning and into the
public domain. Here, the promise of realizing our playful
capacities to create new games in a new society waits only for the
social force that will give it substance.

REFERENCES

Abella, I., and D. Millar
1978 The Canadian Worker in the Twentieth Century. Toronto.
Acheson, T. W.
1972 "The Social Origins of the Canadian Industrial Elite,
1880-1885," in D. S. Macmillan, ed., Canadian Business
History. Toronto.
Althusser, L.
1971 Lenin and Philosophy and Other Essays. London.
Arnstein, W.
1973 "The Survival of the Victorian Aristocracy," in F. C.
Jaher, ed., The Rich, the Well-born and the Powerful. Urbana, Ill.
Aronowitz, S.
1973 False Promises. New York.

Bailey, P.
1975 "Rational Recreation: The Social Control of Leisure and Popular Culture in Victorian England 1830-1885." Ph.D. dissertation, University of British Columbia.
Beamish, R.
1978 "Socio-economic and Demographic Characteristics of the National Executives of Selected Amateur Sports in Canada," *Working Papers in the Sociological Study of Sports and Leisure,* Vol. 1, No. 1, Queen's University, Kingston, Ontario.
Bliss, M.
1974 *A Living Profit: Studies in the Social History of Canadian Business, 1883-1911.* Toronto.
Brohm, J. M.
1978 *Sport: A Prison of Measured Time.* London.
Burnet, J. R.
1961 "The Urban Community and Changing Moral Standards," in S. D. Clark, *Urbanism and the Changing Canadian Society.* Toronto.
Careless, J. M. S.
1967 "Frontierism, Metropolitanism, and Canadian History," in C. Berger, ed., *Approaches to Canadian History.* Toronto.
Clement, W.
1975 *The Canadian Corporate Elite.* Toronto
1977 *Continental Corporate Power.* Toronto.
Copp, T.
1974 *The Anatomy of Poverty: The Condition of the Working Class in Montreal, 1897-1929.* Toronto.
Cosentino, F., and M. Howell
1971 *A History of Physical Education in Canada.* Toronto.
Creighton, D.
1956 *The Empire of the St. Lawrence.* Toronto.
Cross, M.
1974 *The Working Man in the Nineteenth Century.* Toronto.
Curtis, J., and B. Milton
1976 "Social Status and the 'Active' Society," in R. Gruneau and J. Albinson, eds., *Canadian Sport: Sociological Perspectives.* Toronto.
Dunning, E.
1976 "Industrialization and the Incipient Modernization of

Football," *Stadion,* I (1).

Dunning, E., and K. Sheard
1976 "The Bifurcation of Rugby Union and Rugby League: A Case Study of Organizational Conflict and Change," *International Review of Sport Sociology,* 11 (2).

Gruneau, R.
1975 "Sport, Social Differentiation and Social Inequality," in D. Ball and J. W. Loy, eds., *Sport and Social Order.* Reading, Mass.
1976 "Class or Mass? Notes on the Democratization of Canadian Amateur Sport," in Gruneau and Albinson, eds., *Canadian Sport: Sociological Perspectives.* Toronto.
1978 "Elites, Class and Corporate Power in Canadian Sport: Some Preliminary Findings," in F. Landry and W. Orban, eds., *Sociology of Sport.* Miami.

Guay, D.
1973 "Problems de l'integration du sport dans la société Canadienne 1830-1865: Le cas des courses de chevaux," *Canadian Journal of Sport and Physical Education,* IV (2).

Guttmann, A.
1978 *From Ritual to Record: The Nature of Modern Sports.* New York.

Hearn, F.
1976 "Toward a Critical Theory of Play," *Telos,* Winter, No. 30.

Hoch, P.
1972 *Rip Off the Big Game.* New York.

Hodgins, J. G.
1910 *Schools and Colleges of Ontario 1792-1910,* Vol. 1. Toronto.

Houston, S. E.
1972 "Politics, Schools and Social Change in Upper Canada," *Canadian Historical Review,* III (3).

Howard, R., and J. Scott
1972 "International Unions and the Ideology of Class Collaboration," in G. Teeple, ed., *Capitalism and the National Question in Canada.* Toronto.

Howell, N., and M. Howell
1969 *Sports and Games in Canadian Life.* Toronto.

Huizinga, J.
1955 *Homo Ludens.* Boston. (Originally published in 1938.)

Jobling, I.
  1976 "Urbanization and Sport in Canada, 1867-1900," in Gruneau and Albinson, eds., *Canadian Sport: Sociological Perspectives*. Toronto.
Jones, J. C. H.
  1976 "The Economics of the National Hockey League," in Gruneau and Albinson, eds., *Canadian Sport: Sociological Perspectives*. Toronto.
Kidd, B.
  1977 "Canadian Participation in the People's Olympic Games of 1936," presented to annual meeting of North American Association for Sport History, Windsor, Ontario.
  1978 "Canadian Opposition to the 1936 Olympics in Germany," *Canadian Journal of History of Sport and Physical Education*, IX (2).
Kiviaho, P., and M. Simola
  1974 "Who Leads Sport in Finland?" *Eripainos Sosiologia*, N: 05-6.
Lasch, C.
  1977 "The Corruption of Sports," *The New York Review of Books*, April 28.
Lower, A.
  1930 "The Origins of Democracy in Canada," *Canadian Historical Association Reports*.
  1958 *Canadians in the Making: A Social History of Canada*. Toronto.
Loy, J., and A. Ingham
  1973 "Play, Games and Sport in the Psychosociological Development of Children and Youth," in G. L. Rarick, ed., *Physical Activity: Human Growth and Development*. New York.
Mallea, J.
  1975 "The Victorian Sporting Legacy," *McGill Journal of Education*, Vol. 2.
Mann, M.
  1970 "The Social Cohesion of Liberal Democracy," *American Sociological Review*, 35 (June).
Marx, K., and F. Engels
  1975 *Marx and Engels' Collected Works*. London.
Metcalfe, A.

1976 "Organized Sport and Social Stratification in Montreal: 1840-1901," in Gruneau and Albinson, eds., *Canadian Sport: Sociological Perspectives*. Toronto.

1978 "Working Class Physical Recreation in Montreal, 1860-1895," *Working Papers in the Sociological Study of Sports and Leisure*, Vol. 1, No. 2, Queen's University, Kingston, Ontario.

Miliband, R.

1977 *Marxism and Politics*. London.

Moir, J. S.

1967 *Church and State in Canada, 1627-1827*. Toronto.

Naylor, R. T.

1975 *A History of Canadian Business*, 2 vols. Toronto.

Novak, M.

1976 *The Joy of Sports*. New York.

Okner, B.

1974 "Taxation and Sports Enterprises," in R. Noll, ed., *Government and the Sports Business*. Washington.

Page, C.

1973 "The World of Sport and its Study," in J. Talamini and C. Page, eds., *Sport and Society*. Boston.

Panitch, L.

1977 "The Role and Nature of the Canadian State," in Panitch, ed., *The Canadian State: Political Economy and Political Power*. Toronto.

Roxborough, H.

1966 *One Hundred – Not out: The Story of Nineteenth Century Canadian Sport*. Toronto.

Rigauer, B.

1969 *Sport und Arbeit*. Frankfurt.

Ryerson, S.

1973 *Unequal Union*. Toronto.

Sennett, R.

1978 *The Fall of Public Man*. New York.

Shotter, J.

1973 "Prolegomena to an Understanding of Play," *Journal for the Theory of Social Behaviour*, 3 (1).

Steinberg, D.

1978 "The Worker's Sport Internationals, 1920-28," *Journal of Contemporary History*, 13 (2).

Stone, G.
1973 "American Sport: Play and Display," in Talamini and Page, eds., *Sport and Society*. Boston.
Thompson, E. P.
1967 "Time, Work-discipline and Industrial Capitalism," *Past and Present*, 38, December.
1968 *The Making of the English Working Class*. Harmondsworth, England.
Weber, M.
1968 *Economy and Society*, eds. G. Roth and C. Wittich. New York.
Weiler, J.
1974 "The Idea of Sport in Late Victorian Canada," presented to annual meeting of Canadian Historical Association, Kingston, Ontario.
Wheeler, R. F.
1978 "Organized Sport and Organized Labour," *Journal of Contemporary History*, 13 (2).
Wilkinson, R.
1964 *Gentlemanly Power: British Leadership and Public School Tradition*. New York.
Wise, S. F.
1974 "Sport and Class Values in Old Ontario and Quebec," in W. H. Heick and R. Graham, eds., *His Own Man: Essays in Honour of A. R. M. Lower*. Montreal.
Wise, S. F. , and D. Fisher
1974 *Canada's Sporting Heroes*. Toronto.

PART III
Control and Coercion

EDITOR'S INTRODUCTION

The essays in this section are more explicitly related to power and its manifestations in the forms of force and coercion. Because of the clarity of this relationship compared to its complexity reflected in the previous essays, little by way of explication or interpretation is required. The essays, as it were, speak for themselves.

The essential importance of this section lies not only in the inherently innovative and provocative nature of the essays, but in the contrast in use of theoretical approaches. Thus, the book concludes with distinct yet related essays, presented in the contexts of two basically different theoretical approaches. A conflict approach to the analysis of "A Critical Perspective on Law in the Canadian State: Delinquency and Corporate Crime," by Snider and West, contrasts with what is essentially an order perspective utilized by Willett in his "Social Control and the Military in Canada."

Both essays are significant contributions to the Canadian sociological literature. Snider and West, in discussing the legal system and crime and delinquency, place the topic in its historical context, a refreshing departure from the approaches taken by the bulk of studies on similar topics; moreover, they relate the legal system, and juvenile delinquency and corporate crime, in the context of political economy, and present a comprehensive treatment of law and crime in Canada. Their essay provides an important basis for orienting other studies in similar directions, and exemplifies how a common theoretical framework (in this instance, conflict theory) and a macroscopic approach can show the interrelationship between different institutions and widely disparate facets of social behaviour. In so doing, they have provided valuable insights into how the other essays in this volume could be viewed as "base-points" of orientation that could apply to areas far beyond those implied by the topics.

Willett's essay is perhaps the first comprehensive sociological discussion of the military in Canadian society. I agree with Willett that it is bewildering indeed that such an important topic, which lies at the very roots of an understanding of the basic nature of social order and social control, has been virtually ignored by conflict and order theorists alike. In spite of the dearth of studies, Willett provides a useful review of the available literature, and, by taking issue with both order and conflict perspectives, provides a basis for new directions in theoretical approaches. Essentially, however, Willett is more critical of the conflict perspective, especially in its facile assumption that the military is simply the guardian of the power-elite. The relationship between the military and other institutions is far too complex to allow for such general and unsubstantiated assumptions. Willett does see some potential merit in a conflict orientation, but suggests that as it stands it leaves much to be desired and far too much has been presumed.

While conflict theorists would disagree with some of Willett's conclusions, particularly the proposition that the military is not directly supportive of the dominant political economy, they should welcome his challenge to the conventional wisdom of the conflict orientation because it is instructive for all of those who are all-too-ready to embrace an ideology based on false premises or merely inferential data. Willett's essay and his recurring order thesis, in conjunction with the explicit conflict analysis of political economy contained in Part One, serves appropriately as a closing comment to this volume. I hope that this contrast will be considered as part of the dialectical process which may eventually be seen as a distinctive feature of this volume.

CHAPTER SIX

A Critical Perspective on Law in the Canadian State: Delinquency and Corporate Crime*
by D. Laureen Snider and W. Gordon West

Because of academic specialization, parallel developments in different areas of the social sciences frequently remain unarticulated even though they partially overlap in addressing the same topics. In the last decade, a revived political economy of Canada has become the dominant analysis of our society. It has most recently been fruitfully joined with another tradition concerned with developing a theoretical explanation of the modern state. Although conflict (critical, Marxist, or "new") theories of crime have recently become popular with a number of younger Canadian scholars, criminology has remained largely isolated from these developments. In spite of their common intellectual origins, and continued affinity, there has been no Canadian work integrating these three bodies of literature into a distinctively relevant theoretical approach to Canadian law, crime, and delinquency.

In order to develop such a synthesis, we would need a theory which has an historical perspective derived from the Canadian political economy tradition, a recognition of the central role and conflicting functions of the contemporary state, and an incorporation of the best and most relevant recent criminological thinking. As a preliminary effort toward this goal, we will

*The theoretical sections result from our joint efforts; primary responsibility for the sections on delinquency and crime rests with West and Snider, respectively. We would like to thank Paul Grayson, Ken Menzies, Richard S. Gruneau, Gary Burrill, Roger Dale, Dan Glenday, and especially Mary Morton for comments and suggestions on earlier drafts. Our thanks also to Amy Vance, Shirley Fraser, Barb Nicol, Fran Reinders, and Sue Patterson for typing assistance.

attempt to illustrate the power and utility of such a perspective in an empirical examination of two quite different criminological topics: juvenile delinquency and corporate crime.

I TOWARD A THEORY OF CANADIAN CRIME AND DELINQUENCY

Mainstream Criminological Research in Canada
Until very recently Canadian criminology has had a very weak institutional base. Isolated researchers have worked in scattered government offices and various social science departments in universities. Only within the last decade have centres been firmly established in the research branches of various federal and provincial ministries, in the criminology departments in the Universities of Montreal, Ottawa, Toronto, Alberta, and Simon Fraser University and in other social science departments which regularly communicate. Most native-born Canadians interested in criminology or the sociology of law have therefore gone abroad to obtain advanced training.

Thus we have assimilated intellectual traditions of French, British, and American scholars, returning home to dispense the metropolitan wisdom which has underwritten our marketability. Unfortunately, theoretical approaches not only explain phenomena; they also define the phenomena to be explained, since such ideas in part reflect the social and political assumptions and concerns of the societies within which they are developed. Criminology in Canada has frequently been prey to such incautious importation of ideas developed elsewhere. For instance, we have borrowed promiscuously from French ideas about society's functioning in a manner analogous to an organism composed of "the people" when even the most casual observer realizes we are many peoples; from American notions about the potential for integrating into a liberal, free enterprise economy individuals differing in racial, ethnic, and economic backgrounds and about the potential for "correcting" individual human deviation through progressive efforts on the part of the state, when Canadians confront each other less as individuals than through their ethnic groups and institutions; and from British expertise in administering systems of control through massive civil service bureaucracies directed by central governments when our constitution fragments such control through three often opposed levels of government.

Uncritical application of theories which might be useful for defining and analysing phenomena in one society to explain phenomena in a different societal context is obviously fraught with hazards. We must pay more attention to the backdrop of historical specificity provided by Canadian society, not only to end our intellectual isolation, but to comprehend the phenomena more adequately.

Secondly, there has been an overwhelmingly correctionalist focus to Canadian studies of crime. Government-based funding of most research and the lack of independent university centres until very recently have encouraged a liberal reformist ideology which has tended to avoid analyses that question underlying social structures or the function of the contemporary state. Criminology by and large has focused on crook control, as research funded by the federal and provincial ministries of justice and its administration have been primarily interested in highlighting street crime and law reform, rather than political corruption and corporate malfeasance. Burgeoning legions of treatment personnel (psychiatrists, psychologists, social workers, and probation officers) serve to expand state control by supplementing, rather than supplanting or replacing, the efforts of the traditional agents of control, the police and custodial officers (Ericson, 1978). This basic orientation has denied the existence of fundamental structured conflicts while simultaneously treating evidence of such opposition as individual pathology.

Thirdly, and consistent with assuming the objective universality of concepts and the efficacy of piecemeal social engineering and correction, we have been quite positivist and overly empiricist in our research. There is less a lack of research in Canadian criminology than a lack of systematic theoretical analysis or integration. There exist a number of studies on facets of imprisonment (e.g., Mann, 1968; Waller, 1974) and of the groups most at risk of being incarcerated (e.g., Boydell, 1972). With a few recent exceptions (e.g., McDonald, 1976; Tepperman, 1977; Greenaway and Brickey, 1978), it is rare to find empirical studies that draw out the implications of the findings for an analysis of the structure of the society which has given rise to the phenomena under scrutiny.

We will outline in the following section how these deficiencies in Canadian criminology might be redressed. Greater cognizance of the Canadian political economy tradition would ground our research in a general analysis of our own society; this is sharpened by recent work on the state, which has a direct if implicit critique of correctionalism; and critical theories of crime seem most appropriate and consistent.

The Political Economy of Canada
The Canadian state has a long history of appropriating monies belonging to all Canadians and using these to aid the wealth and expansion of a select few, the corporate elite. Whether those who own and control the major economic resources are native or foreign, members of a mercantile or manufacturing elite, British or American, the fact is overwhelmingly clear that they have been able to dominate and control the political elite, those who supposedly represent the needs and interests of average citizens in provincial and federal governments, in the majority of cases. Indeed, government officials and politicians often saw the interests of the corporate rich as identical with the interests of all, so no overt domination or persuasion was required. We will not delve into the history or the significance of this phenomenon here, as it has been well-covered elsewhere (see Ossenberg, this volume; Glenday, this volume; Davis, 1971; Frank, 1972; Glenday *et al.*, 1978; Naylor, 1973; Myers, 1972; Laxer, 1973).

This political economy tradition can be best understood in relation to the recent works on the nature and role of the state in capitalist societies. Interest has focused on: (1) defining the extent of the state; (2) describing and explaining its relationship to society and to social classes; and (3) describing and explaining its role and functions. Analysts seek to understand, in short, why the political elite and government organizations in general act so consistently, even in countries governed by socialist parties, in the interests of those who own and control the key economic resources of that country.

By "the state," we mean the political elite and government (prime ministers, and cabinets at the federal and provincial

levels, plus municipal officials with key territories or responsibilities), the civil service and administrative bureaucracies
(including important agencies), the military and police, the
judiciary and courts, and the public media and education systems
(cf., Miliband, 1974: 50). The Canadian case immediately illustrates some peculiarities in its federal structure and division of
powers. This has direct impact upon criminological and legal
research in that the central government has the basic law-making
powers concerning crime, while the provinces and municipalities
are charged with enforcement. This has generated rather unique
tensions when coupled with federal wealth and relative provincial poverty. Analytic strategies for understanding overcrowded
prisons, difficulties in reform, and the popularity of diversion
begin to be suggested within such a framework. Writings analyz-
ing the functions of the state (O'Connor, 1973; Panitch, 1977) and
the tension between the need to help the ruling class accumulate
capital (for investment and other uses) while simultaneously
legitimating the status quo by instituting reforms to pacify the
noisiest and most dangerous groups without resorting to
"undue" coercion (with its potential of destroying legitimacy), all
help us understand the actions of the agents of social control in
the Canadian state.

Conflict Criminology
This analysis of Canadian society and the Canadian state suggests
the particular appropriateness of conflict theories of crime and
delinquency. The Canadian situation is worth examining, not
only to test general propositions from this perspective, but also to
examine those uniquely raised within it. Cross-national comparisons, for instance, take on a new form when conceived as
metropolis-hinterland comparisons (Hagan and Leon, 1977).

As expressed in British and American writings, this perspective
can be generally characterized by its: (1) skepticism of individualistic theories of crime causation, such as those of Lombroso,
Sheldon, Freud, etc.; (2) seeing legal agencies as motivated by the
conscious use of law to maintain a status quo that disproportionately benefits the powerful; (3) disputing the claim of criminal law to represent community consensus on values; and (4)
utilizing criminal statistics as indices to the workings and biases

of the agencies generating them (Sykes, 1977: 39-40). Studies in this framework have been concerned with: (1) showing why *behaviours* that threaten the economic elite are defined as criminal while other anti-social or harmful acts are not so defined (Chambliss, 1975; Liazos, 1977); (2) discussing how the *laws* discriminate against the poor and powerless to the benefit of elite groups (Carlin and Howard, 1965; Cloke, 1971; Galanter, 1974; Reich, 1973); and (3) showing that harsh *sanctions* are given to the powerless while the powerful escape nearly unscathed (Snider, 1978; McDonald, 1976; Chambliss, 1967; Jankovic, 1978). Interpretations have varied, but most often those who run the state, usually designated the political elite, have been seen in this literature as tools of the economic elite, who use their control over the domestic use of violence (through the police) and its extranational use (through the military) to further the interests and dominance of the economic elite.

While these formulations have considerable isomorphism and resonance with the Canadian political economy tradition and analyses of the state, they need to be grounded and modified by reference to the specific history and structure of Canadian society if the inappropriateness of earlier transplanted theories is to be avoided. Having argued that there is need for such a macroscopic conflict analysis of crime and social control, we therefore propose to illustrate our argument through discussion of two substantive areas: juvenile delinquency and corporate crime. The examples we have chosen demonstrate the utility of reconstruing existing information regarding law-violation in the broader Canadian historical context, of reconceiving social control efforts in terms of the selective application of coercion in the service of the state's ameliorating social conflict, and of calling attention to concerns that other perspectives gloss over entirely.

II JUVENILES IN JUSTICE

The Historical Origins of Canadian Juvenile Justice
Contemporaneously with the developing interest in conflict criminology and the political economy tradition, there has been a new interest in the historical beginnings of Canadian juvenile justice. Although this research is still sparse and has been carried

out more by historians, educators, and lawyers than by sociologists, many of the issues addressed are those raised by a political economy perspective, and the analyses overwhelmingly tend to support the utility of the perspective.

There is a dearth of material on the social conditions experienced by most Canadian children before the turn of the century. We can, however, make somewhat risky extrapolations in guessing that patterns documented elsewhere for children in other countries are at least suggestive. Aries' (1962) work on children in France, for instance, probably depicts the broad outline of childhood in New France. Mediaeval children, he argues, were treated much more as small adults, as indicated by their dress, games, ages of confirmation, and legal status. They often worked from age seven side by side with older members of the community, or were apprenticed to neighbouring craftsmen or teachers. There were movements in the 1700's, however, which sought to redefine childhood as innocent, in need of special protection and special training regarding discipline.

English material (e.g., Musgrove, 1964) strongly supports the argument that this change from mediaeval status coincided quite directly with the industrial revolution and the accompanying urbanization and migration. Musgrove argues that the burgeoning middle-class professionals, unable easily to pass on their trades directly to their offspring, transformed the public school to this purpose. Concern over child labour, training for a widening democracy, and job competition resulted in Factory Acts restricting child labour. Universal compulsory education acts followed, as much to control "street arabs" as to educate. Johnson (1976) has indicated how school curricula were carefully engineered to reproduce the existing class order.

These patterns from the imperial centres were probably used by early Canadians in their dealings with their own children. Although the young continued to play a much more central economic and social role in rural areas, by the late 1800's the larger Canadian cities experienced many of the same problems with youth as did French, British, and American ones (Sutherland, 1976). Burgeoning slum areas, the enforced idleness resulting from the passage of anti-child labour legislation, and fears of impending social disorder through epidemics and street crime focused attention on the working-class young. Poverty and diverse behaviour that in rural areas had been bearably supplemented by neighbours and relatives, and had been relatively hidden, became much more apparent in the cities.

Children had also come to the forefront of English-Canadian public discussion through the widespread immigration of homeless British children during the last decades of the nineteenth century. This practice simultaneously relieved the waif and urchin problem for Britain and added extra labour to the Canadian farm economy. Sutherland's quotation from a contemporary source, "Adoption, sir, is when folks get a girl to work without wages" (1976: 9), indicates the mixing of potentially humanitarian concerns with the imperialist redistribution of excess labour from the British metropolis to the labour-short Canadian hinterland.

The growing youth problem clearly coincided with changes in the wider social order. The late nineteenth century was a time of real economic growth as Canadian industry and trade became established (Myers, 1972). As the economy grew, and urbanization increased, the occupational structure changed, and women were left at home more to look after children alone. Whereas during early industrialization, children were exploited grossly for low wages, their partly humanitarian exclusion from the labour market by the end of the nineteenth century had made them an expendable surplus population, a nuisance with which something had to be done.

This displacement of workers is one of the recurrent problematic contradictions within capitalism. Higher profits can be made by using more machines and fewer workers to produce goods. Constantly expanding markets can absorb such excess labour, which usually consists of the least skilled segment of the population, but there are limits to such expansion. Another "solution" to this problem, then, is to relegate part of the work force to non-productive status. Because of the humanitarian sentiments aroused by their formerly gross exploitation for low wages, the perceived need to train the young as workers and citizens, and the need to acculturate "foreign" children, the young have been increasingly singled out (with the old) for this marginalization (Schwendinger and Schwendinger, 1976: 14). Although the economic system is best seen as the creator of this problem population, the intervention of the state to create institutions (schools and reformatories) to deal with it provides a primary example of government attempts to ameliorate contradictions, simultaneously assisting in the accumulation of profit, the engendering of legitimacy, and the exercise of coercion. Universal, compulsory public education thus became a major political issue throughout the nineteenth century and comprised the main effort to deal with this problem population. Special correctional facilities began to be developed, however, to assist the schools in creating a disciplined and literate work force. Both the schools and corrections were publicly financed, relieving industry of the burden of training and disciplining future workers.

Leon (1977) indicates that periods favouring reformatory treatment of young offenders, industrial school treatment, and probation treatment preceded the formal passage of the Juvenile Delinquents Act by decades. In 1857, an Act for Establishing Prisons for Young Offenders and an Act for the More Speedy Trial and Punishment of Young Offenders were passed. Other institution-providing legislation followed in the succeeding decades, but by the end of the century the leading "child-savers" had come to challenge the institutions by viewing the family (either natural or foster, with or without professional probation worker support) as the best situation for rearing law-abiding citizens (Sutherland, 1976: 108 ff.).

By the 1890's, Sutherland documents, notions about the good family had become so clearly articulated that Children's Aid Societies felt morally justified in breaking up families which did not conform (1976: 18). There seemed to be general agreement among the middle-class "child-savers" that working-class slum conditions of poverty were largely responsible for juvenile misbehaviour: "the distinction in states between *neglected* and *criminal* in effect translated as *potentially* vs. *actually* criminal" (Houston, 1972: 236). An ideology of social engineering infused these early reform efforts, which were strongly linked with other social reforms of the period, such as suffrage and abolition.

The passage of the Juvenile Delinquents Act in 1908 brought these various efforts to culmination and established an organized system of probation and juvenile court as well as the formal status of delinquency. Offences by juveniles against the Criminal

Code, provincial statutes, and municipal by-laws were to be heard in such courts, as well as all cases involving juvenile sexual immorality or other similar vices, and any other offences or conditions (e.g., neglect, very widely defined, Sutherland, 1976: 97) which could result in committal to training school. Trials were to be conducted by special judges, in separate courts and in private. Probation officers were given special investigatory powers, and procedural rules were minimal; no automatic right to appeal was present. Dispositions ranged from warning and release to indeterminate sentences with the guilty remaining under the court's jurisdiction until age twenty-one. Dispositions were not linked to the gravity of the offence but were tailored to the child's needs. The vagueness of this legislation, its lack of due process, the inclusion of a wide range of juvenile status offences (e.g., truancy), and wide dispositional powers have subsequently allowed much of its humanitarian potential to be undermined in its implementation.

Although, as Hagan and Leon state, many reformers and organizers of the Children's Aid Societies, the institutions, and the juvenile courts were respectable middle-class persons, it is also quite clear from the analyses of Leon (1977) and Sutherland (1976: 14-15, 112, 120) that they were strongly supported by members of the elite (government commission members, doctors, senators, newspapermen, judges, provincial cabinet ministers, clergy, etc.), despite the puzzling disclaimers in Hagan and Leon (1977: 590). Leon discusses how some "conservatives," especially police magistrates, saw the Juvenile Delinquents Act as too lenient, but he also notes that almost nobody expressed concern about the increasing deprivation of civil liberties. The battle between the social workers and police was clearly a battle for jobs and jurisdiction entailed in passing the legislation. In winning this competition, juvenile justice was partly detached from the adversarial legal system and became part of an administrative welfare problem. We are left to guess how the (mainly working-class) parents and children felt about this.

The Evolution of Delinquency

It is perhaps impossible ever to give a full account of the effects of the delinquency legislation. It is apparent that new institutions were established and new standards of dealing with neglected and delinquent children became normative. Probation officers were empowered by the 1908 legislation to investigate the situations of neglected, dependent, and delinquent youth, and often "solved" cases without bringing them to trial. This obviously extended the scope of their efforts (Sutherland, 1976: 130), the additional interference being offset by the informal non-court nature of the process. Contrary to the claim of Hagan and Leon (1977), based on ambiguous Toronto data, Sutherland presents evidence that the number of youngsters incarcerated in various types of institutions kept pace with the population growth (1976: 146-9).

Juvenile courts, probation officers, Children's Aid workers, and others, however, clearly did not prevent or cure the delinquency problem. But there are a number of interpretations available to explain the steady increase in official offenders coming to police attention. Those who assume a constant modus operandi for the control agents argue these data indicate a growing incidence of juvenile misbehaviour. One may then argue that the preventative and curative programs have failed and should be eliminated or replaced by alternatives, or one could argue that these programs are working but are not sufficiently supported and funded to be truly effective. Yet a third interpretation is possible, which does not make the assumption that officials operate so consistently that police statistics give us a reliable measure of delinquent rates but are the result of increasingly vigilant and restrictive social control (Sutherland, 1976: 144) by a growing sector of state employees (Armstrong, 1977).

Coincident with increasing pressures to deal with excess labour, it is evident that youth have generally been enclosed in a more restrictive social status (Schwendinger and Schwendinger, 1976). Compulsory education legislation still requires children and adolescents to attend school until they are sixteen years of age. Within educational institutions, they are defined as students and are subjugated to the administrative authority of teachers and principals (Berkeley et al., 1978). Although their civil rights in these settings have been somewhat expanded recently (e.g., in dress code decisions, Goldstein, 1970), they are still subject to relatively arbitrary rules and hindered by the expense and time-consuming nature of any attempted rectification through the courts. Since job opportunities are increasingly tied to age and a stream of educational experience, subjection to mystifying and often invalid testing is an assault on liberty and social pressures to remain in school persist far beyond the legal minimum age of leaving.

Juveniles are still denied the franchise (political power) and are subjected to special closed courts, police, and provisions in different laws. Their everyday behaviour is significantly constrained, as young people have many more laws to obey. Juvenile courts lack elementary safeguards of due process. Judges have access to confidential information on defendants before they are convicted, hardly a situation to uphold the "innocent until proven guilty" principle. Given that they thus have far more laws to break and are more easily convicted in such courts, it is not surprising that young people are predominant in crime statistics. At least fifteen per cent of the juvenile offences are for status crimes (such as truancy, runaway, curfew, alcohol, sexual intercourse, incorrigibility, etc.), actions for which only juveniles are liable. By these offences, juveniles *who act as adults* (*not* those who reject adult values!) break the law. In addition, forty to fifty per cent of incarcerated juveniles in the last decade in Ontario were placed in training schools under "needy children" clauses, rather than for any criminal offence. Such treatment of both neglected and delinquent youth in the same institution has been justified on the strength of the argument that delinquency-prone conditions could be identified and treated. It is unclear that such children get care or rehabilitation: they certainly get confined and controlled in inadequately funded programs.

Self-report studies of delinquency over the last two decades have revolutionized the interpretation of official statistics. Police data indicate that most official delinquents are working-class by a ratio approaching 5:1 compared to middle-class youth. Self-report studies reduce this ratio to 1 1/2:1 (Box, 1971) and when other variables are controlled indicate that social-class background only accounts for a very small proportion of the variance in delinquent behaviour (around five per cent). Although some predominantly working-class crimes are likely seen as more reprehensible (e.g., violent assault), other serious acts (such as theft) reveal no class differences large enough to account for the differential handling, and are a much larger proportion of the total number of crimes.

Interaction or labelling theory suggests that a considerable proportion of miscreants are singled out at each stage of the legal funnel (citizen notice, police apprehension, commitment for trial, sentencing, incarceration) because of "subsidiary characteristics" such as being working-class. Although some research indicates a lack of bias in day-to-day police operating procedures (e.g., Hagan, 1975), other research indicates that more subtle biases exist in deployment, supervision, etc. (Nease, 1966; Box, 1971). The accumulation of a number of small biases at each stage of the certification process results in some groups being unfairly singled out as predominant in the delinquent population (Haldane et al., 1972). Interaction theory thus suggests the necessity of examining delinquent careers. Working-class children are more likely to be precocious or to regard themselves as autonomous in their dealing with middle-class officials such as teachers or policemen (Werthman, 1969, 1971; West, 1975b). Greenberg (1977) suggests some youths seek similar character-establishing acts undertaken in situations of risk, which are either crimes without victims or acts of relatively low social costs (e.g., gambling, drug-use, fighting, and minor property offences such as shoplifting and vandalism). Vaz (1966) indicates how middle- and upper-class Canadian youths involved in similar behaviour avoid arrests.

In addition to obvious working-class characteristics, then, this lack of deference to authority may result in excessive labelling of some youngsters, which may close some legitimate activities to them. After arrest, they will be more closely supervised by officials (such as policemen, teachers, and probation officers) who are thus more likely to notice further misdeeds. Unless a youth has acquired substantial commitments, attachments, and beliefs by late adolescence, his lack of bonds may combine with such labelling to impel him on a career as an adult criminal (West, 1978; Greenberg, 1977).

Some organizational research tends to confirm these explanations, although material on police courts, probation, and training schools is scarce and difficult to interpret. Nease (1966) and Haldane, Elliot, and Whitehead (1972) indicate that the labelling suggested by Cicourel (1968) and Emerson (1969) also occurs in Canadian juvenile courts. Erickson's work (1975) on the role of the defence lawyer in juvenile courts indicates that less than half the judges and social workers in court expect the defence to represent only the child, and instead feel that "he should not get the child off, he should consider the child's best interest," presumably defined by the court.

While young people are treated more harshly in some ways and have fewer legal safeguards, it is probably true that citizens, the police, and the courts are more likely to exercise discretion in releasing more of them without full legal sanction (especially for offences perceived as minor juvenile pranks). This strongly suggests that adolescents, besides being *officially* more prominent, are *actually* more deviant than adults, a claim that self-report statistics on delinquency and criminal behaviour tend to corroborate, scanty as these are for older age groups (Byles, 1969; Christie, 1965).

The most successfully verified explanation of delinquent behaviour, control theory (Hirschi, 1969; Box, 1971), predicts that individuals who lack conventional commitments (e.g., jobs), constraining attachments (e.g., to family), and socially approved beliefs are most likely to commit crime. Ironically, adolescent status places its incumbents in such a position and hence directly encourages delinquency. Control theory would seem to account for high delinquency, since adolescents are loosening attachments to families of origin and haven't yet established such relations with families of procreation; begin to question their subordination in schools while not yet having commitment to stable employment; feel fewer harsh consequences from juvenile law; and are first beginning to question stereotyped moral beliefs. Given the weakness of self-report data on different age groups, such an explanation must remain tentative, but it seems quite plausible that even if juveniles were subject only to adult law in adult courts, their dependent social situation would thus likely encourage them to be more criminal than adults. The very marginalization of youth, then, dialectically reinforces their character as a problem population.

Canadian empirical research that is available corroborates the American documentation of control theory. Le Groupe de

Recherche sur l'Inadaptation Juvenile, working out of Montreal (LeBlanc, 1975; Caplan, 1977; Biron, 1977), Linden and Fillmore (1977) using Edmonton data, and Byles (1969) in Toronto report remarkably consistent findings across regions and ethnic groups. Reviews of the literature (West, 1975a; Ross, 1977) on the effects of school failure, a major indicator of lack of commitment to a legitimate institution, further specify that this factor has an extraordinarily high predictive weight in explaining delinquency (occasionally accounting for over fifty per cent of the variance).

The overwhelming majority of male juvenile offences involve property. Theft is a prototypical crime of concern, as some eighty per cent of the specifically identified violations of the Criminal Code are property offences, with the rate being three times higher for juveniles than for adults (Statistics Canada, 1969). Of all thieves successfully prosecuted, about forty per cent are juvenile, and the modal age is 15-17 years. This should hardly be a surprising finding. Ross (1973) and others have established strong correlation between unemployment and property crimes. Private industry in Canada has simply proven unable to absorb the post World War II "Baby boom" and especially its successors as they hit labour market age. Almost half of the unemployed in Canada are under twenty-five, and the rates of unemployment for teenagers are two-and-a-half to three times higher than the national average (Committee on Youth, 1971). Lack of income, of course, also means that the young command less private space, and are more open to police surveillance.

A work role is essential in a capitalist economy in order to provide spending power as a consumer. Liberal economics have always attempted moral justification on the grounds that individual consumers articulate their wants in the marketplace, increasing demand for desired commodities and encouraging production in those areas as investors seek profit. Legal and social restriction on employment, however, effectively prevents half the Canadian population from functioning effectively in the marketplace (even ignoring the effects of long-term capital accumulation, tariffs, advertising, corporate wealth, etc.). The market economy thus fails to meet the needs of the young, even on its own terms.

Contemporary Contradictions and Directions

In the past decade and a half, young people have caused considerable concern to dominant groups in society. The swelling of the school population by the post-war baby boom stretched educational resources and provincial treasuries, filling classrooms and forcing a reconsideration of the goals and methods of education. Their increased numbers allowed the young to assert their own interests as popular culture peddlers catered to them (Hall and Jefferson, 1975). Their own experience of affluence led to questioning of traditional lifestyles and experimenting with new ones, sometimes centred on threatening alternatives such as drugs. As the baby boom and its successors have passed through school age they have hit an already overladen job market, swelling the ranks of the unemployed. Endless government commissions on education (e.g., Hall and Dennis, 1968), youth (e.g., Committee on Youth, 1971), drugs (e.g., Le Dain, 1970), and the economy have attested to the problems that youth represent in our society.

This has been equally true in the legal area. As they have entered the most crime-prone age of late adolescence and young adulthood, our young have dramatically increased the rates of first property, then violent, crime, which have now begun to taper off as the young shrink proportionately (Greenberg, 1977). In response, the various governments have re-examined delinquency and the surrounding statutes. The federal Committee on Juvenile Delinquency in Canada (1965) has been followed by three bills to replace the Juvenile Delinquency Act. These generally have sought to eliminate all status offences (e.g., truancy and sexual morality); maximum three-year sentences would replace the present indefinite terms. The latest proposal suggests raising the juvenile age from sixteen to eighteen, so this group would be protected from any harshness to which adults are subjected in contrast to juveniles, but they would also lose any adult rights which are not extended to juveniles. The oppressed age group would thus be expanded. Children below twelve would lose all vestiges of responsible personhood in being basically deprived of the opportunity for a court trial. They would be relegated to the administration of the same types of welfare bureaucracies that so obviously have failed to uplift the old, the native peoples, the poor, and previous delinquents (Schur, 1973).

The new legislative proposals also suggest the provision for administrative review of any special treatment, and the addition of some safeguards in the trial stage, such as legal counsel, stricter rules of evidence and proof, and appeals (Leon, 1977: 167). These are combined, however, with the idea of screening or diversion procedures, ostensibly to involve minor offenders as little as possible in the justice process. But there is the danger in such procedures of a greatly expanded net, with previously released minor offenders being "treated" with wide discretion and without being found guilty of an offence. Serious problems thus remain in the conjoining of legal and welfare approaches (Grimes, 1978).

Ontario and other provinces have brought legal aid lawyers to juvenile courts, so that due process is informally more encouraged. But such progress remains subject to casual agreements between individual judges and lawyers, rather than being grounded in statutes. And it remains quite unclear whether the lawyer's client is the paying state, the legally responsible parents, or the child itself (Platt, 1969; Erickson, 1975). Ontario has revoked Section 8 of the Training Schools Act, which allowed dependent children (who had committed no crime) to be incarcerated "if no suitable community facility were available." Weiler (1977) makes clear, however, that the revocation of Section 8 still allows such dependency cases to be incarcerated under a formerly seldom-used clause in the federal Juvenile Delinquents Act. This province is planning to reduce its training school capacity from 885 (1973) to 120 beds, substituting more extensive use of community-based group homes.

Within the wider framework of political economy, such changes may perhaps best be viewed as resulting directly from more immediate organizational conflicts and needs. The elite legal profession has been prominent in supporting the changes, coinciding with their increased entry into juvenile court and government policy units. Their concern with stricter definitions and due process has found support among civil libertarians in general and children's rights activists in particular. The increased first-hand knowledge of juvenile justice by middle-class parents whose children have been increasingly arrested has widened this constituency. Social researchers have been near-unanimous in finding that treatment programs are ineffective if not positively harmful (Schur, 1973). Governments have been increasingly concerned during the seventies to reduce budgets (see O'Connor, 1973) and have been quick to seek to slash programs or to transfer the excessive reformatory population to empty training schools by raising the age limit of delinquency from sixteen to eighteen.

As the decade has progressed, the advocacy of children's rights in general has taken a particular turn. Earlier efforts, inspired by the students' and women's movements, were concerned with extending the *freedom* of the children (e.g., regarding school, work, sex, etc.), but later issues have focused on *protection* of children. Such protection of the very young is easily translated into a licence for professionals to intervene (and curtail children's freedoms), and past experience has shown such intervention to be clearly biased against the relatively poor and powerless. Rather than focusing on improving the child's ability to be self-determining, the present concern re-echoes that of the early child-savers' intent on enforcing their established conception of a proper upbringing (Leon, 1977), that is, an upbringing not threatening to perceived elite interests.

The focus of concern and proffered solutions has increasingly centred on the family (and occasionally some institutions), much as it did a hundred years ago. Wider structural problems in the treatment of our youth in educational, political, social, and economic ways are not at the centre of the discussion. Although we seem to be considering retreating from outmoded delinquency prevention or treatment programs, as much to meet budget constraints as in recognition of their failures, none of the alternatives seriously confront either the marginalized position of youth or the marginal positions available for the poorest of them in later life. Yet the young compose nearly half of the officially registered unemployed and experience unemployment rates two to three times higher than their elders.

This utilization of the political economy perspective has cast the study of juvenile delinquency within Canada in a new light. Questions are raised regarding the origins of the legal category, and links are suggested to wider and more profound events taking place in Canadian society; more historical and legal work is obviously needed. Available empirical research materials are set within a wider context of class relations and production modes; the position of young people within advanced capitalist society becomes salient. Control theory and labelling theory explanations of deviant behaviour remain relevant, and can be incorporated within this wider framework. Finally, the political economy perspective suggests how contemporary contradictions regarding the status of the young have fomented discontent with the existing legislation and led to reform bills.

It seems from this analysis that the "youth problem" and delinquency in particular are basically structured by population demographics, labour market crises, the fiscal crisis of the state forcing delinquency program cutbacks, and the near-universal failure of liberal means of crime control. The bankruptcy of most delinquency programs developed over the past century indicates the perils of eschewing such a wider social analysis. Any successful resolution must begin to address the political economy of the young, and of delinquency.

III   THE POLITICAL ECONOMY OF CORPORATE CRIME

Studying crimes committed by corporations yields a good opportunity to examine the relationship between the polity and the economic structure in Canada. Laws against corporate crime have the potential to affect the structure and power of corporations in Canada, cut into their profits, and put key executives in jail. Thus, the corporate elite are interested in and vitally affected by these laws. On the other hand, the political elite are caught between their general dependence on the corporate elite, and their need (in the interests of legitimacy) to appear to be protecting the public against corporate excesses. We have a situation which uniquely reflects the interplay of power and influence between these two elites.

Following the tradition of Sutherland (1949) and Geis (1974), crimes are defined as socially injurious offences for which a penalty has been provided and in which people are directly or indirectly victimized. Corporate crimes, then, are crimes committed by corporate officials on behalf of the corporation, and also crimes of the corporation itself. Such crimes are not synonymous with what have been called white-collar crimes or "occupational criminal behaviours," because the victim of the latter offences, such as embezzlement or fraud, tends to be the corporate employer, whereas the victim of corporate crimes is either the general consumer and/or competitors of the offending corporation.* Some further definitions, in the interests of precision: "corporate elite" (also known as the economic or business elite) refers to the people who own or control the means of production in the society. These are the top executives, chairmen, and board members who own or run the corporate institutions which dominate the Canadian economy. The "political elite" is composed of those who directly control the decision-making processes of the state – the top political authorities and civil servants.

Laws to be Analyzed

Federal, provincial, and municipal departments are responsible for enforcing a vast number of statutes. According to the definition of crime being used in this paper, many of the activities prohibited in by-laws or statutes are criminal acts, and many others are not. (Technically, only acts prohibited in the Criminal Code of Canada are crimes; however, this is a legal distinction with little utility for the analysis of socially injurious acts which have victims and designated penalties for disobedience). A thorough analysis of corporate crime in Canada would look at a fair sample of the laws which govern or create corporate crime at all three levels of government. However, this is impossible right now, since the data, especially at the municipal and provincial levels, are grossly inadequate, and misleading or inaccessible. Only for certain federal laws are usable data collected and available. Thus, the information to be presented, on municipal and provincial laws at any rate, can be deemed no more than a suggestive survey and is limited to Toronto and Ontario, respectively. It is not suggested that the laws of Toronto and Ontario are

---

*These two types of crimes should never be combined into "white-collar offences," as is sometimes done, since it is to the advantage of the corporate elite to have laws governing white-collar offenders promulgated and enforced, whereas their interests are opposed to the creation and enforcement of laws governing corporate crimes.

entirely representative of municipal and provincial laws throughout Canada; however, I would argue that the structural factors governing enforcement operate in a similar manner throughout the country. More rigorous analysis must wait until better statistics or alternate methodologies become available.*

Municipal Laws
According to the British North America (BNA) Act, municipalities are responsible for services such as garbage pickup, parks, libraries, zoning, and police schools, and for issuing licences for everything from dogs to marriages. Large municipalities such as Metropolitan Toronto also provide specialized services such as Homes for the Aged, nursery and day-care centres, public housing, and environmental health services.

Each municipal department is responsible for enforcing certain by-laws, and methods of enforcement vary from reliance on citizen complaint (noise by-law) to the provision of a squad of inspectors (housing standards by-laws). The City of Toronto Department of Buildings Annual Report of 1974 tells us there were 152,796 inspections made in that year, the bulk of which involved Building By-law 300-68 and Plumbing Regulation 647, and By-law 253-67. These regulate, respectively, the construction and renovation of buildings, setting certain standards of quality for materials and type of construction, and stipulate the installation and type of plumbing required. Licences are required before beginning the job and sanctions provided for infractions, as people can be injured, inconvenienced, and killed by unsafe buildings. Under Building By-law 300-68 in 1974, there were 342 convictions, 127 suspended sentences, 42 dismissals, and 76 withdrawn cases. The two aforementioned plumbing regulations (Plumbing Regulation 647 and By-law 253-67) garnered 213 convictions, 55 suspended sentences, 50 dismissals in court, and 80 withdrawn cases. For all by-laws administered by the Buildings Department, 1,281 charges resulted from 152,796 inspections, or approximately one charge per 100 inspections, a very small percentage. Furthermore, 147 of these charges were subsequently

*Data cited throughout are taken, directly or indirectly, from the figures appearing in the official reports of the enforcing agency or department, unless a citation to the contrary is made.

dismissed and 225 withdrawn. Twenty-nine per cent of the charges, then, did not result in a legal sanction of any kind.

What do such figures tell us? The privacy and confidentiality of those charged are so carefully guarded that it is impossible to get their names. Because of this, it is impossible to find out whether (as one would suspect) the bulk of charges were laid against small entrepreneurs, the builders with a few employees who build just a few houses, rather than against the nine developers who are responsible for 87 per cent of the building units put up in Toronto. Circumstantial support for this interpretation comes from the statistician for the Buildings Department, who privately expressed the belief that large companies were less likely to use or allow their contractors to use shoddy materials because it would cost them more in the long run to repair the errors; such tactics, he thought, were more characteristic of "fly-by-night" operators. This line of reasoning presupposes that the consumers of housing (buyers or renters) have not only as much power as those who build and develop areas, but also have the knowledge which enables them to perceive the difference between, for example, high quality, fire-resistant insulation and inadequate cheap insulation. Moreover, this argument assumes that consumers have a free choice on the marketplace and will avoid inferior products. This is hardly possible if all the choices at a certain price level are similarly constructed, or if one is forced by shortages or public housing authorities to accept any structure that is available.

The Housing Standards section "is charged with the responsibility of ensuring that home owners adequately maintain their properties in accordance with the standards set out in By-law 73-68" (Department of Buildings Annual Report, Toronto, 1970: 19). This, and Building By-law 300-68, cover privately owned homes and "absentee landlord" dwellings rented out to families and lodging houses. In 1972 (the last year Housing Standards was administered by the Department of Buildings before being switched to development), 79,108 inspections were carried out, 2,000 less than in 1971, and there were 92 convictions, 168 suspended sentences, 25 dismissals, and 24 withdrawals (Annual Report, 1972: 14-5). However, during the late fall-winter of 1974-75, there were several rooming house fires with fatalities and, as a result of unfavourable publicity about these "fire traps," city inspectors cracked down. From January 1 to March 31, 1975, 106 charges were laid leading to 61 convictions and 36 pending cases, and total fines of $6,805 were assessed.

The Department of Health also is responsible for controlling some types of corporate crimes in the field of public health and pollution. The Department's role in controlling lead polluters is a case in point. Certain industries have been singled out as villains in the controversy, as high blood lead levels of residents in the areas surrounding three lead smelters and refiners were reported by independent medical authorities. The affected areas are working-class districts where old houses sit beside heavy industry in what has been called "the zone of transition" just outside the downtown city core. The 1973 Department of Health Annual Report for the City of Toronto had this to say about their enforcement efforts:

> Since lead pollution from industrial sources had to be considered as contributing to high blood levels, two plants received orders from the Medical Officer of Health. In one case compliance was deemed incomplete and at year's end had not been finalized before the courts. In the other case, compliance could not be achieved by year's end because standards called for in the order had not been set (p. 123).

That description of inaction is a triumph of obfuscation, especially when it is related in the next paragraph that "this one problem took up forty per cent of the time of the two most senior Officials in the Division, thirty per cent of the time of two Senior Inspectors, plus ten to fifteen per cent of the output of the Staff Public Health Inspectors" (pp. 123-4).

What about enforcement of public health regulations on food businesses? The statistics on enforcement provided are pitifully inadequate. There were 99 court cases in 1973, most against retail stores and restaurants, such as "unclean premises" (23), "failure to abate cockroaches" (13), and "insufficient regulation garbage containers" (12). No one was sent to jail; we are not given the total amount of the fines imposed; indeed, we learn only that 67 cases resulted in a fine, 19 were withdrawn, 6 drew a suspended sentence, and 7 were dismissed. Similar and equally useless statistics are provided for 1974, though here we are given the court fines imposed. In 1974 there were average fines of $94.10 for each charge of unclean premises, $94 for "conditions affecting sanitary operation," and $91 for "toilet room defective," down to an average of $25 for defective floor equipment. No names are given out, and citizens are not allowed to examine court documents to find the information. One wonders who such regulations are protecting, the diners or the restaurant owners. As the *Toronto Star* reported:

If you're a restaurant owner who repeatedly violates the Public Health Act, don't worry too much about bad publicity. Though you may be formally charged with disobeying the food premises section of the act, no health board in Metro will release your name, a survey by the Star has shown. In East York and York boroughs, health inspectors have not laid charges under the act for many years and do not believe in doing so. . . . (*Toronto Star:* 15 December 1975).

Provincial Laws
The provincial legislatures are allowed, by the BNA Act, to make only those laws relating to provincial matters. These include education, hospitals, property and civil rights, provincial corporations, licensing and taxation, administering justice, and provincial correctional institutions. The Department of the Environment in Ontario has jurisdiction over much corporate crime; however, its enforcement activities are minimal according to its annual reports in 1973 and 1974. The 1973 report, for example, chronicles the many achievements of industry and the great capital outlays they are making to control pollution. Surely the bias of the regulators should be a little more critical and less apologetic! Only seven charges against five companies were laid under the Ontario Water Resources Act in 1973. This, in a province where eating fish caught in the English-Wabigoon River System has been banned (Indians who continued to do so suffer from the dreaded mercury poisoning disease called Minamata), where acid rain is killing forests, lakes, and wildlife, and where up to 80 per cent of the lakes in a 100-mile radius of industrial

southern Ontario are polluted. The limited statistics available in the annual reports, however, are insufficient to support a more detailed analysis of the record of this department for the purposes of this paper.

The Ministry of Consumer and Commercial Relations and the Ministry of Labour are the major departments administering laws on corporate crime. Consumer and Commercial Relations has multiple responsibilities for a wide range of statutes protecting consumers and controlling corporations. The Business Practice division "operates to promote fair business practices between debtors and creditors; lenders and borrowers; and buyers and sellers" (Ministry of Consumer and Commercial Relations, Statistical Review 1972-1973: 2). As such, this division licenses and inspects certain kinds of merchants with the major sanction, as well as fines, being the removal of one's licence to operate.

In 1973, under the Bailiffs and Collection Agencies and Mortgage Brokers Acts, there were apparently no complaints initiated by inspectors. There were, however, 653 consumer complaints leading to $6,400 "redress," presumably going to the complainants although the term is ambiguous. Similarly, 1,583 complaints about motor vehicle dealers led to $339,170 in redress; 1,074 complaints about real estate and business brokers led to $188,947 redress. The number of inspections is small for an industrial province of some eight million people – ten inspections of bailiffs in 1973, sixty-seven of collection agencies, eighty-one of mortgage brokers, and ninety-four of motor vehicle dealers. However, there were 2,692 inspections of real estate and business brokers. Why are these businesses singled out for this kind of regulation? What is the rationale behind such enforcement policies? None is given in the reports or the legislation.

The Consumer Protection Bureau is a focal point of Ontario's efforts to protect the consumer. The Bureau, as well as disseminating educational information and investigating consumer complaints, enforces the Consumer Protection Act which "provides for the registration and bonding of itinerant sellers, regulates the use of executory contracts, requires full disclosure of the cost of borrowing, regulates advertising, and provides other helpful steps in dealing with consumer complaints or problems" (Statistical Review, 1972-73: 4). In 1973, out of a total of 4,519 complaints, 2,354 were redressed – a recovery of $174.50 per complaint. Only 363 were found unjustified according to the Bureau, but only 86 prosecutions were acted upon in 1973, 52 of which were left over from 1972. This bureau also refuses to make public the names of companies which have accumulated many complaints.

Perhaps the best-known agency in the Department of Consumer and Commercial Relations is the Ontario Securities Commission (OSC). This is the Ontario counterpart of the federal Securities and Exchange Commission in the United States. It is responsible for registering all dealers, salespeople, and advisers dealing in securities in Ontario, and can, on investigation, suspend or cancel this registration where improper conduct is suspected. Its sanctioning powers are relatively wide. Besides the aforementioned power of registration, the OSC, under the Provincial Securities Act, can impose fines or prison sentences.

From the creation of the OSC in 1931 until the early 1960's, only one real prosecution was launched and it resulted in two hung juries (Laprairie, 1975). Now, two Royal Commissions and countless studies later, the federal police force, the RCMP, have moved into law enforcement in the securities field. Figures obtained from the RCMP since 1968 show there have been steadily increasing work loads: 1969 increased 180 per cent over 1968; 1973 was up 23 per cent over 1972; and 1974 was up 89 per cent over 1973. In a comparison of the first six months of 1975 against the same six-month period in 1972, the number of files open has gone from 92 to 140, fines levied from $10,000 to $54,000, and man hours worked from 22,318 to 90,000 (Laprairie, 1975, Part II). However, the impetus and philosophy of enforcement appear to be unchanged despite the increased activity. There is evidence that enforcement agents still see their jobs in terms of catching the con artist promoters who are into a different promotion scheme every six months and make this their main occupation (Laprairie, 1975). Thus by default, they generally ignore the respectable established companies run by the corporate elite. This does not mean large organizations are never charged; however, they are certainly given much leeway by the inattention and conscious or unconscious bias of the policing agencies.

The Department of Labour is responsible for enforcing many laws governing corporate behaviour. Under their rubric are the laws stipulating working conditions (hours, overtime pay, pregnancy leave, and protection against arbitrary dismissal) and minimum wages. There were a large number of complaints (9,316 in 1972-73, 9,100 in 1973-74), most of which seem to have been justified, since a total of 10,352 employers were assessed for arrears in 1972-73, 9,246 in 1973-74 (Ontario Ministry of Labour, Annual Report 1973-74). Total amounts collected and, presumably, distributed to employees, under minimum wage, overtime pay, vacation pay, termination pay, equal pay for equal work, and unpaid wages, were over $2,000,000 in 1972-73 and nearly $3,000,000 in 1973-74, affecting approximately 37,000 workers each year. Employers stealing from employees is thus not uncommon. But only fifteen charges were laid in 1972-73 and thirty-three in 1973-74. Why such a small number? One can only suspect, in the absence of data on who was charged and what the outcome was, that the employers were charged only if they did not pay when requested to do so by the government. Moreover, small employers, without lawyers to legitimate and argue their cases, would be more likely targets for charges than larger ones.

The Industrial Safety Branch tries to ensure that safe working conditions exist in certain industrial establishments and logging operations. Here, we are told "non-compliance with the legislation resulted in thirty-nine charges laid and $38,100 levied in fines" (Annual Report, 1973-74: 11). This seems a small number when one considers there were 71,186 accidents reported that year, sixty-two of which were fatalities. Were they really all due to workers' carelessness or to unavoidable chance? One wonders again when looking at the number of establishments in which unsafe conditions were found and directives left for employers by the inspectors. In manufacturing, for example, 21,908 directives were left, ranging from "failure to guard machinery" (8,108), to "fire escape et cetera" (1,130), to improper sanitation (1,006) or ventilation (909).

The American situation provides an interesting comparison. An analysis of industrial accidents cited by Hills summed up the situation as follows:

The chances of such accidents as mangled arms and broken legs have steadily increased since 1958 and are now reported to be the highest since the Korean War. Although Department of Labour records indicate that federal authorities uncover violations in more than 90 per cent of the factories they inspect, "only about 1 per cent of the companies responsible are ever called to formal account, and barely one in a thousand is ever punished". Preferring a nonaggressive, coaxing, "education" approach, the Department of Labour from 1963 through 1968 issued safety and health complaints against 154 companies and administered sanctions against only 15 of them (Hills, 1971: 183).

Federal Laws
Because of the division of powers in the British North America Act, the federal government has perhaps the most extensive jurisdiction in the area of corporate crime. Most federal departments are responsible for some legislation with criminal sanctions that affect corporate activity. However, concentration here will be on the Department of Consumer and Corporate Affairs, since it keeps and publishes enforcement data and has jurisdiction over the most important corporate offences. The most important of its legislative mandates are the Combines Investigation Act, Food and Drugs Act, Hazardous Products Act, and Weights and Measures Act.

The data are less than complete. Two of the acts – Hazardous Products and Weights and Measures – are recent legislation, and it was not until 1974 that the Department systematically began releasing enforcement data on any of these acts. Prior to this, enforcement activity was reported only in the federal series "Statistics of Criminal and Other Offences" and in annual reports of the department responsible for enforcement. Neither source gave comprehensive, consistent, reliable data: the former lumped many statutes together under the heading "Other Federal Statutes," and reported neither the size of the crime nor the details or sentence, if any; the latter provided only general information on the numbers charged. Thus, there are usable data only from 1974 to the first half of 1976.

The four acts being analyzed provide a cross-section of corporate criminal acts. The Food and Drugs Act prohibits the manufacture, sale, or importing of unclean and/or unsafe food products and drugs, under penalty of a $5,000 fine or three-year maximum prison term if prosecuted as indictable, or a $500 fine and three-month prison term for a first offence if prosecuted in summary form. (Like many acts regulating corporate crime, the Crown chooses, theoretically on the basis of the gravity of the offence, whether a prosecution is to be summary or by indictment). The Hazardous Products Act, as the name implies, forbids the advertisement, sale, or importing of articles declared by the government to be unsafe in some way (such as exploding pop bottles or poisonous baby toys). The penalties are $1,000 or six months or both (summary), or up to two years in prison and/or a fine of any amount (indictable). Associated offences under the same Act, such as obstructing an inspector or making false statements, are punishable on summary conviction by a $500 fine and/or three months in prison.

The Weights and Measures Act is supposed to ensure that consumers/customers receive no less than what they pay for by ensuring that measuring devices are honest and accurate. The maximum penalties are $1,000 fine and/or two years in prison. The Packaging and Labelling Act is also aimed at preventing fraud in the marketplace, by ensuring that all articles sold contain visible and accurate labels telling the amount and nature of the product. For disobeying the regulations concerning the quantity of a product in a container, the manufacturer/importer is liable to maximum fines of $5,000 or $10,000 under summary and indictable prosecutions, respectively. For disobeying related regulations, the maximum penalties are $1,000 and/or six months in prison (summary), or $3,000 and/or one year in prison (indictable).

The most activity, in terms of number of charges laid, has been under the Food and Drugs Act (see Table 1). The size of fines varies widely from judge to judge, area to area, and case to case. There appears to be an increase in the number of convictions registered (from 57 in 1974 to 91 in 1975) and in the total fines assessed ($18,655 in 1974 to $25,975 in 1975), but the average fine per case or per charge has not systematically increased. Thus, it does not appear that the courts are dealing more harshly with these offenders, although 2 1/2 years is too short a time to establish any trends. A factor not revealed in the table is that virtually all the charges are laid against small retail merchants (for example, Monk Fish Market, Montreal; Pulsateri Supermarket, Toronto; Epicerie Michaud Enrig., Rimouski), generally for short volume, adulteration, or substitution of meat or fish products. Prior to 1976, only one major retail chain was convicted (a Dominion store in St. John's, Newfoundland), though in the first six months of 1976, four Loblaws stores, Dominion Dairies, and two A & P stores were charged (all dominant companies). So perhaps some policy changes are being made, but on the basis of the data we now have, it is safe to say that most of the enforcement activity under the Food and Drugs Act has been directed against small businesses.

Table 1
Sanctions for Food and Drugs Act

	Firms or Individuals Convicted	Number of Charges	Total Fines	Average Fine per Case	Average Fine per Charge
1974					
January to June	23	37	$ 4,380	$190.43	$118.37
July to December	34	56	14,275	419.85	254.91
1975					
January to June	40	55	13,675	341.87	248.63
July to December	51	61	12,300	241.17	201.64
1976					
January to June	44	53	10,300	234.09	194.33

SOURCE: Department of Consumer and Corporate Affairs, news releases, October 15, 1974, to September 20, 1976.

The Weights and Measures Act shows a similar enforcement pattern, although convictions have increased dramatically in the 1975-76 period (see Table 2). Fines per charge appear to have been increasing steadily if erratically, though the drastic increase in the first half of 1976 is due to one $46,000 fine against a motor vehicle dealer in Calgary for odometer tampering. In fact, the Act has been chiefly enforced against two businesses: car dealers for odometer tampering and retail merchants (again in small stores) for short weight scales.

There have been far fewer charges laid under the Hazardous Products Act (see Table 3). But of the four charges laid in 2 1/2 years, three have been against major retailers. Despite the sanc-

Table 2
Sanctions for Weights and Measures Act

	Firms or Individuals Convicted	Number of Charges	Total Fines	Average Fine per Case	Average Fine per Charge
1974					
January to June	19	65	$ 4,219	$222.05	$ 64.90
July to December	17	50	2,875	169.11	57.50
1975					
January to June	16	37	14,625	914.06	395.27
July to December	27	60	9,070	335.92	151.16
1976					
January to June	46	183	64,505	1,402.28	352.48

SOURCE: Department of Consumer and Corporate Affairs, news releases, October 15, 1974, to September 20, 1976.

Table 3
Sanctions for Hazardous Products Act

	Firms or Individuals Convicted	Number of Charges	Total Fines	Average Fine per Case	Average Fine per Charge
1974					
January to June	2	2	$400	$200	$200
July to December	0	0	0	0	0
1975					
January to June	0	0	0	0	0
July to December	1	1	50	50	50
1976					
January to June	1	1	250	250	250

SOURCE: Department of Consumer and Corporate Affairs, news releases, October 15, 1974, to September 20, 1976.

tions allowed by the Act, however, and the size of the firms involved (Steinbergs and the T. Eaton Co.), the fines are very small, amounting to far less than the court costs.

The Packaging and Labelling Act will be an interesting one to watch in the future. With an eye perhaps to precedents, the first three cases laid were against the three major food retail chains in Toronto (Dominion Stores Ltd., Loblaws Ltd., and Steinberg's Ltd.) and resulted in substantial fines. In view of the overall record of enforcement of the Department of Consumer and Corporate Affairs, it is unlikely this pattern will be repeated. Note also that it was a year before any charges were laid under the Act (see Table 4).

Table 4
Sanctions for Packaging and Labelling Act

	Firms or Individuals Convicted	Number of Charges	Total Fines	Average Fine per Case	Average Fine per Charge
*	—	—	—	—	—
*	—	—	—	—	—
1975					
January to June	0	0	0	0	0
July to December	0	0	0	0	0
1976					
January to June	3	7	$7,000	$2,333.33	$1,000

*Not proclaimed in effect until January, 1975.

SOURCE: Department of Consumer and Corporate Affairs, news releases, October 15, 1974, to September 20, 1976.

The Combines Investigation Act is the most complex and, in many ways, the most significant of the statutes under analysis. Since thorough history and analysis of its provisions are available elsewhere (Goff and Reasons, 1978; Snider, 1978) I will summarize these findings and relate them to the original contention: that the content and enforcement of the laws reflect the interests of the economic elite.

The Combines Investigation Act (henceforth referred to as the CIA) contains three key parts: sections 32, 34, and 38, which prohibit conspiracies to combine or otherwise restrict trade and forbid anti-competitive trade practices such as the refusal to supply competitors with merchandise needed to compete; section 33, which forbids mergers or monopolies; and sections 36 and 37, which forbid misleading or deceptive trade practices such as false advertising or "bait and switch" sales techniques. The Act has been revised many times since its passage in 1889. The most recent revisions were proclaimed in force in January, 1976, and provide maximum penalties of one million dollars or five years in prison for conspiracy to restrict trade; two years in prison for illegal mergers or monopolies; and five years in prison or $25,000 fines for most other unfair trade practices. As in the other offences discussed, the Crown has the authority to decide whether charges will be processed as summary offences, which carry lighter sanctions, or indictable ones. In addition, the CIA penalties include the removal of patent customs duties, or trademark protection from an offending firm, and the issuing of an Order of Prohibition, alone or in conjunction with other sanctions. (The Order of Prohibition is a legal nicety ordering the company to stop breaking this particular law from now on, with the threat, never yet realized, of a two-year prison sentence for disobedience.)

Excluding the cases prosecuted under sections 36 and 37 of the Act (misleading trade practices), there have been a total of eighty-nine prosecutions between 1952 and 1975 under the other sections of the Act. Of these, fifty-two were under section 32 (conspiracy to combine and/or restrict trade), twenty-nine under sections 34 and 38 (resale price maintenance and predatory pricing), and eight under section 33 (mergers and monopolies). This is an average of four cases per year. (For comparative purposes, in the twenty-two year period between 1949 and 1972, there were 300,771 cases successfully prosecuted for theft in Canada; see Snider, 1977.) Of these eighty-nine prosecutions, eight were acquitted of all charges and two were discharged at a preliminary hearing. Twenty-two of the corporations were assessed an Order of Prohibition only. This amounts to a second chance for the offender, since the judge is implicitly saying, "We'll let you off this time, but don't do it again." No one was imprisoned; no one has ever been imprisoned for an offence under these sections of the Act. Thus, for only fifty-seven offences over the twenty-two year period was the offender even fined. Nor were the fines overwhelming: they averaged $7,000-$8,000 per company, but varied widely from $300 to $50,000. An interesting point not apparent from the bare statistics is that the Department of Justice often refuses to prosecute *despite* the recommendation of the investigating experts, the Restrictive Trade Practices Commissioners. This occurred in over ten per cent of the cases investigated between 1952 and 1975 (eleven cases), and is all the more surprising given the great caution of the Restrictive Trade Practices Commission in recommending prosecutions, as revealed by the very low proportion of charges pressed in relation to complaints received. In many years only two per cent of the files opened following complaints led to formal enquiries, and very few of these formal enquiries resulted in charges being laid. The Restrictive Trade Practices Commission has consistently *not* recommended that charges be laid unless they were certain they had a strong case (Snider, 1977: 179-80).

Sections 36 and 37 of the CIA refer to misrepresenting the price of a commodity being sold. These sections were put into the Combines Investigation Act in 1966 (see Table 5). Prior to this they were in the Criminal Code, and enforcement was virtually nil under the auspices of the Attorney General of each province. The increase in the number of files opened and charges laid from 1966 to 1973 is striking. The percentage of files which culminate in charges, however, has decreased dramatically. Some decrease is inevitable because it is likely that only the most flagrant and dramatic cases resulted in the mobilization of the law prior to 1966, whereas in recent years more complaints have been initiated by consumers unfamiliar with legislation. (It must be noted that files were opened whenever a complaint was made, until 1974-75.) However, it is apparent that for the vast majority of cases investigated no charges are laid.

Tables 6 and 7 look in more detail at the number of cases processed and the sanctions assessed, taking sections 36 and 37 separately. The unit of analysis employed is the case, not the charge. There are often five or six charges laid in a particular case, and the defendant or defendants typically may be fined $100 on each of two charges, acquitted on one, and have the other three withdrawn by the government. This would appear as one case with one $200 fine in the tables. Per charge, the fines would appear even lower – the mode or most common fine per charge is $100 under section 36 and $200 under section 37. Even per case, the

Table 5
Percentage of Files Resulting in Charges:
Sections 36 and 37 of the Combines Investigation Act

	1966 -67	1967 -68	1968 -69	1969 -70	1970 -71	1971 -72	1972 -73	1973 -74
Number of files opened	15	42	33	412	2520	2872	3470	4387
Number of charges laid	4	10	16	38	92	102	65	110
Percentages of files resulting in charges	26.6%	23.8%	48.4%	9.2%	3.6%	3.6%	1.8%	2.5%

SOURCE: Report of the Director of Investigation and Research, Combines Investigation Act, 1966-74.

fines are very minuscule. However, there seems to be a tendency toward assessment of more severe sanctions for false advertising offences. The maximum fine of $25,000 (before the amendments took effect on January 1, 1976) was assessed only once, in 1973, but there were three fines of $5,000 and one of $8,000 in 1974. There was no parallel trend for cases under section 36, misleading price representation; taking inflation into account, the average fines were probably lower than in the late 1960's.

Another noteworthy change is the declining use of alternate criminal sanctions in sentencing in recent years, and the greatly increased use of the Order of Prohibition. Although nobody actually served any time in jail under sections 36 and 37 (until December 12, 1974, when a Dartmouth, Nova Scotia, man served nine months of a two-year sentence in a federal penitentiary), the alternate penal sanctions serve the important function of reminding both the defendant and the court that these are criminal offences. This is true even though those who were most likely to receive optional penal sanctions were the small entrepreneurs in non-established or "disreputable" businesses such as fortune-telling or weight-reducing salons. When any major company was involved, the charge was likely to be against the corporation, not against individuals *and* the corporation, and the sanction was typically a fine and/or an Order of Prohibition. In only one case was restitution ever ordered, and, again, the defendant was not a

Table 6
Enforcement Record and Sanctions for Misleading Price Representation
(Section 36)

Year	Number of Cases	Number of Cases Convicted	Average Fine	Suspended Sentence	Acquittal	(Per Case) Withdrawn or Dismissed
1962	6	5	$520	1 (fine option)	1	0
1963	6	3	$591.66	1 (fine option)	1	2
1964	2	1	$200		0	1
1965	5	5	$190	2 (fine option)	0	0
1966	6	6	$283.66	0	0	0
1967	5	5	$180	1 (no fine)	0	0
1968	16	14	$218	0	2	0
1969	31	23	$318	1 (fine option & 1 15 days or fine option)	5	3
1970	29	29	$245	0	0	0
1971	34	28	$232	0	3	3
1972	28	23	$211	0	2	3
1973	21	20	$258	0	1	0
1974	26	20	$327	1 10-day term with fine option	4	2

SOURCE: Canada, 1973, 1974, and 1975: Annual Reports of the Director of Investigation and Research, Combines Investigation Act.

powerful corporation but an individual in Montreal. He was given a two-year suspended sentence and placed on probation with the condition that he refund $9.95 to each of approximately 400 people who had purchased his useless electronic TV antennae. This is equivalent to a $4,000 fine and a public lesson. In the same year, under the same section of the Act, the T. Eaton Company was assessed a $200 fine, General Mills Canada Limited was fined $750, and Robert Simpson Company was fined $5,000. No executives were charged in any of these three cases, and no alternate sanctions were meted out.

Table 7
Enforcement Record and Sanctions for False Advertising (Section 37)

Year	Number of Cases	Number of Cases Convicted	Average Fine	Suspended Sentence	Acquittal	Withdrawn/ Discharged/ Dismissed (per case)
1970	11	7	$330	0	4	0
1971	55	45	$461	0	5	5
1972	60	47	$620	1 (fine option)	5	8
1973	54	47	$1,789	0	4	3
1974	78	63	$959	(1 day in jail/ 120 days in jail/ keep peace 1 year/with fine option; 2 years suspended plus restitution)	4	11

SOURCE: Canada, 1973; plus 1974 and 1975: Annual Reports of Director of Investigation and Research, Combines Investigation Act.

The Enforcement Record: Some Observations

In essence, this is the enforcement record of various government agencies regarding corporate crime. It is certainly obvious, especially when comparing these figures to enforcement of traditional crimes, that far fewer criminals are caught. We have seen that a small number of cases are prosecuted for corporate crimes relative to the size of the population "at risk," that is, the approximately one million people in Canada who have jobs which put them in a position to commit these offences. There are two possible explanations for this: one, that businessmen commit fewer offences than other segments of the population, since they can easily be successful by using legitimate means (Merton, 1936), or, two, that their crimes are less often looked for, discovered, or prosecuted. Since the first explanation has been discredited by all the available evidence (Geis, 1968; Sutherland, 1949; Chambliss, 1975), we will concentrate on the second.

Several reasons for this lack of enforcement activity can be suggested. Some of these are: (1) the budgets of the agencies responsible for enforcement are very small, relative to the amount spent on "conventional" crimes, and have often not kept pace with inflation (Goff and Reasons, 1978: 112-113); (2) the regulators have tended to identify with those they are regulating and do not press charges if they can avoid it; and (3) the legislation, especially in the case of the Combines Act, is so poorly written, and the judges often so ill-informed, that securing convictions is a long, expensive, and often unsuccessful process. Thus, enforcement efforts generally have been weak and enforcers have simplified their tasks by focusing their efforts on small entrepreneurs and marginal enterprises and leaving alone the dominant companies which are structurally and politically crucial (Goff and Reasons, 1978; Snider, 1978).

I would argue that the real issue is *why* such barriers to enforcement, which are obvious to the most casual observer, have not been dealt with. Governments act very quickly and decisively when they wish to, when they feel their own interests are threatened. Witness, for example, the fast government passage of an Order-in-Council on September 21, 1976, to make it illegal to discuss details or possess documents connected with an international uranium price-fixing cartel the Canadian government was involved in; or, examine the speed with which legislation to break the Winnipeg General Strike in 1919 was passed—it went through the House of Commons in twenty minutes and received royal assent before an hour had passed (Brown and Brown, 1973: 41-42). Why, then, has serious political muscle not been put into reforming acts governing corporate crime? Why have regulators not been subjected to an intense educational/political program to counter the dominant ideology that corporate criminals are harmless? Or why haven't radicals and consumer activists been hired? Most obvious of all, why have enforcing agencies been starved for funds?

The answers lie elsewhere and are related to the dominance of the economic elite, both directly through its control of the life chances of all Canadians, and indirectly through its overwhelming ideological control. Thus the political elite do not want and cannot afford to jeopardize relations with the people who provide the bulk of the campaign funds for the two major parties. Moreover, the health of the economy depends on the "good will" of a small number of corporations and corporate executives, since they have been permitted – indeed, encouraged – to take control of a vast percentage of Canada's economic resources. If they decided to relocate their factories elsewhere, the politicians as well as many workers and low-level executives would suffer. And the corporate elite are very powerful ideologically, affecting how people in general define and interpret issues. Versions of reality which coincide with the views of the corporate elite are termed "legitimate" and "responsible," while versions that conflict with these are deemed irresponsible or dangerous (Hall *et al.*, 1978). Even a labour or reform-oriented government would face overwhelming odds in any attempt to deliver even-handed justice to rich and poor alike by curbing the excesses of the corporate elite. However, the weakness of the working class in Canadian politics and the strength of the corporate elite and their state allies have allowed this situation to develop to the point where corporations, in effect, control the regulators. (See Stanbury, 1977, for a description of the success of the corporate elite in completely changing the proposed revisions to the Combines Investigation Act, so that a move purporting to strengthen this legislation resulted, many years later, in legislation weaker in many respects than the previous Act.)

The evidence discussed herein suggests that the content and enforcement of laws against corporate crime reflect the interests of the economic elite. They appear to be in alliance with the state to preserve the status quo, which disproportionately benefits the few as opposed to the many in Canada today.

IV CONCLUSIONS

It is our contention that, although we have not had the space to thoroughly develop the theoretical linkages, this analysis of delinquency and corporate crime illustrates the utility of employing a conflict theory in understanding deviance and control in Canada. Further development of this approach should bring criminological work into closer conjunction with what we believe to be the most cogent analyses of Canadian society. The fact that a conflict approach is most compatible with these analyses lends additional relevance to the paradigm. We hold that part of the strength of this approach derives from an academic division of labour, where work from other disciplines than sociology contributes significant insights. Correlatively, a conflict approach to Canadian crime suggests how a major gap in political economy – the study of legitimation and coercion – can be addressed through a fresh examination of topics which are central to criminology. The test of a general theory is its ability to satisfactorily explain particular empirical cases. Richard Ericson's (1974) most serious criticism of the "new criminology" (Taylor, Walton, and Young, 1973) is its inattention to empirical verification in favour of a preoccupation with promoting a sociology whose ends are political equality and emancipation. Our contention is that data do exist in the Canadian context to support the conflict perspective, and it has been our purpose to marshal some of this evidence. If such arguments serve to further the ends of equality and emancipation, we regard this as a virtue rather than a fault of the pursuit.

REFERENCES

Aries, P.
1962 *Centuries of Childhood.* New York.
Armstrong, H.
1977 "The Labour Force and State Workers in Canada," in L. Panitch, ed., *The Canadian State.* Toronto.
Berkeley, H., C. Gaffield, and W.G. West, eds.
1978 *Children's Rights in Canada: Educational and Legal Issues.* Toronto.
Biron, L.
1977 "Social Investment and Delinquency," presented to annual meetings of Canadian Sociology and Anthropology

Association, Fredericton, N.B.
Box, S.
1971 *Deviance, Reality and Society.* Toronto.
Boydell, C., *et al.*
1972 *Deviant Behaviour and Societal Reaction.* Toronto.
Brown, L., and C. Brown
1973 *An Unauthorized History of the RCMP.* Toronto.
Byles, J.
1969 *Alienation, Deviance and Social Control.* Interim Report on Unreached Youth, Ministry of Education, Toronto.
Canada, Department of Consumer and Corporate Affairs
1950-75 *Report of the Director of Investigation and Research, Combines Investigation Act.* Ottawa.
1973 *Proposals for a New Competition Policy for Canada, Bill C-227. Ottawa.*
Caplan, A.
1977 "Attachment to Parents and Delinquency," presented to annual meetings of Canadian Sociology and Anthropology Association, Fredericton, N.B.
Carlin, J., and J. Howard
1965 "Legal Representation and Class Justice," *U. C. L. A. Law Review,* 12 (January): 381-437.
Chambliss, W. J.
1967 "Types of Deviance and Effectiveness of Legal Sanctions," *Wisconsin Law Review* (summer).
Chambliss, William, ed.
1975 *Criminal Law in Action.* Santa Barbara, California.
Christie, N.
1965 "A Study of Self-Reported Crime," *Scandinavian Studies in Criminology,* I.
Cicourel, A.V.
1968 *The Social Organization of Juvenile Justice.* New York.
City of Toronto, Department of Buildings
1970-74 *Annual Report.* Toronto.
City of Toronto, Department of Public Health
1973-74 *Annual Statement.* Toronto.
Cloke, K.
1971 "The Economic Basis of Law and State," in R. Lefcourt, ed., *Law Against the People.* New York.

Committee on Juvenile Delinquency
1965 *Juvenile Delinquency in Canada*. Ottawa.
Committee on Youth
1971 *It's Your Turn*. Ottawa.
Davis, A.
1971 "Canadian Society as Hinterland Versus Metropolis," in R.J. Ossenberg, ed., *Canadian Society: Pluralism, Change and Conflict*. Toronto.
Emerson, R.
1969 *Judging Delinquents*. Chicago.
Erickson, P.
1975 "Legalistic and Traditional Role Expectations for Defence Counsel in Juvenile Court," *Canadian Journal of Criminology and Corrections*, 17 (January): 78-85.
Ericson, R.V.
1978 "Penal Policy in Canada: The Method of our Madness," in W.K. Greenaway and S.L. Brickey, *Law and Social Control in Canada*. Toronto.
Frank, A.G.
1972 "The Development of Underdevelopment," in J. Cockcroft, A. G. Frank, and D. L. Johnston, eds., *Dependence and Underdevelopment*. New York.
Galanter, M.
1974 "Why the Haves Come Out Ahead: Speculations on the Limits of Legal Change," *Law & Society Review*, 95.
Geis, Gil, ed.
1968 *White Collar Criminal: The Offender in Business and the Professions*. New York.
Geis, Gil.
1974 "Upperworld Crime," in A. J. Blumberg, ed., *Current Perspectives on Criminal Behavior*. New York.
Glenday, D. , H. Guindon, and A. Turowetz, eds.
1978 *Modernization and the Canadian State*. Toronto.
Goff, C., and C. Reasons
1978 *Corporate Crime in Canada*. Scarborough, Ontario.
Goldstein, S. R.
1970 "Reflections in Developing Trends in the Law of Students' Rights," *University of Pennsylvania Law Review*, 118.
Greenaway, W. K. , and Stephen L. Brickey

1978 *Law and Social Control in Canada.* Scarborough, Ontario.

Greenberg, D.
1977 "Delinquency and the Age Structure of Society," *Contemporary Crises*, 1: 189-223.

Grimes, R. E.
1978 "A Theoretical Overview of the Canadian Juvenile Justice Legislation: An Exercise in Avoidance Behaviour," presented to annual meetings of Canadian Sociology and Anthropology Association, London, Ontario.

Hagan, J.
1975 "Policing Delinquency," in R. Silverman and J. J. Teevan, eds., *Crime in Canadian Society.* Toronto.

Hagan, J., and J. S. Leon
1977 "Rediscovering Delinquency: Social History, Political Ideology, and the Sociology of Law," *American Sociological Review*, 42: 587-98.

Haldane, L., D. Elliott, and P. Whitehead
1972 "Particularism in the Sentencing of Juvenile Delinquents," in C. Boydell *et al.*, eds., *Deviant Behaviour and Societal Reaction.* Toronto.

Hall, E., L. Dennis *et al.*
1968 *Living and Learning.* Toronto.

Hall, S., and T. Jefferson, eds.
1975 *Resistance Through Ritual: Youth Subcultures in Post-War Britain.* London.

Hall, S., C. Critcher, T. Jefferson, J. Clarke, and B. Roberts
1978 *Policing the Crisis: Mugging, the State, and Law and Order.* London.

Hills, Stuart L.
1971 *Crime, Power and Morality.* Scranton, Pa.

Hirschi, T.
1969 *Causes of Delinquency.* Berkeley.

Houston, S.
1972 "The Victorian Origins of Juvenile Delinquency: A Canadian Experience," *History of Education Quarterly*, 12: 254-80.

Jankovic, Ivan
1978 "Social Class and Criminal Sentencing," in *Crime and Social Justice: Issues in Criminology*, 10 (Fall-Winter): 9-15.

Johnson, Leo A.

1974 *Poverty in Wealth: The Capitalist Labour Market and Income Distribution in Canada.* Second and revised edition. Toronto.

Johnson, R.
1976 "Notes on the Schooling of the English Working Class 1778-1850," in I. R. Dale *et al., Schooling and Capitalism.* London.

Laprairie, Carole
1975 "The Development of Sanctions for Stock-Market Manipulations in Ontario." M. A. thesis, Centre of Criminology, University of Toronto.

Laxer, James
1973 "Introduction to the Political Economy of Canada," in R. Laxer, *(Canada) Limited: The Political Economy of Dependency.* Toronto.

LeBlanc, M.
1975 "Upper Class Versus Working Class Delinquency," in R. A. Silverman and J. Teevan, eds., *Crime in Canadian Society.* Toronto.

Le Dain, G., *et al.*
1970 *Interim Report of the Commission of Enquiry into the Non-Medical Use of Drugs.* Ottawa.

Leon, J. S.
1977 "New and Old Themes in Canadian Juvenile Justice: The Origins of Delinquency Legislation and the Prospects for Recognition of Children's Rights," *Interchange,* 8 (1-2): 151-75.

Liazos, A.
1977 "The Poverty of the Sociology of Deviance: Nuts, Sluts and Preverts," in J. Galliher and J. McCartney, eds., *Power, Crime and Criminal Law.* Homewood, Ill.

Linden, E., and C. Filmore
1977 "A Comparative Study of Female Delinquency," presented to annual meetings of Canadian Sociology and Anthropology Association, Fredericton, N. B.

Mann, W. E.
1968 *Society Behind Bars.* Toronto.

McDonald, Lynn
1976 *The Sociology of Law and Order.* Montreal.

Merton, R. K.

1936 "Social Structure and Anomie," *American Sociological Review*, 3.

Miliband, R.
1974 *The State in Capitalist Society*. London.

Musgrove, F.
1964 *Youth and the Social Order*. London.

Myers, G.
1972 *History of Canadian Wealth*. Toronto. (First published, Chicago, 1914.)

Naylor, R. T.
1973 "The History of Domestic Foreign Capital in Canada," in R. Laxer, *(Canada) Limited, The Political Economy of Dependency*. Toronto.

Nease, B.
1966 "Measuring Juvenile Delinquency in Hamilton," *Canadian Journal of Corrections*, 8.

O'Connor, J.
1973 *The Fiscal Crisis of the State*. New York.

Panitch, L., ed.
1977 *The Canadian State: Political Economy and Political Power*. Toronto.

Platt, A.
1969 *The Child Savers*. Chicago.

Province of Ontario, Ministry of Consumer and Commercial Relations
1973 *Statistical Review, 1972-73*. Toronto.

Province of Ontario, Ministry of the Environment
1973 *Annual Report 1972-73*. Toronto.
1974 *Annual Report 1973-74*. Toronto.

Province of Ontario, Ministry of Labour
1973 *Annual Report 1972-73*. Toronto.
1974 *Annual Report 1973-74*. Toronto.

Reich, C.
1973 "Law and the Corporate State," in W. Chambliss, ed., *Sociological Readings in the Conflict Perspective*. Reading, Mass.

Ross, M.
1973 "Economic Conditions and Crime: Metropolitan Toronto." M. A. thesis, Centre of Criminology, University of Toronto.

Ross, R. R.
1977 "Reading Disability and Crime: In Search of a Link,"
Crime et/and Justice, 5 (1): 10-22.
Ryerson, Stanley
1968 Unequal Union. Toronto.
Schur, E.
1973 Radical Non-Intervention. Englewood Cliffs, N. J.
Schwendinger, H., and J. Schwendinger
1976 "Delinquency and the Collective Varieties of Youth,"
Crime and Social Justice, 5: 7-25.
Snider, D. L.
1977 "Does the Legal Order Reflect the Power Structure: A Test
of Conflict Theory." Ph.D. thesis, University of Toronto.
1978 "Corporate Crime in Canada: A Preliminary Report," Ca-
nadian Journal of Criminology, 20 (2): 142-68.
Solicitor General
1976 Protective Security. Ottawa.
Stanbury, W. P.
1977 Business Interests and the Reform of Canadian Competition
Policy, 1971-5. Toronto.
Statistics Canada
1969 Criminal Statistics. Ottawa.
Sutherland, E. H.
1949 White Collar Crime. New York.
Sutherland, N.
1976 Children in English Canadian Society. Toronto.
Sykes, G.
1977 "The Rise of Critical Criminology," in J. Galliher and J.
McCartney, eds., Power, Crime and Criminal Law.
Homewood, Ill.
Taylor, I. , P. Walton, and J. Young
1973 The New Criminology. London.
Tepperman, L.
1977 Crime Control. Toronto.
Vaz, E. W.
1966 "Self-Reported Delinquency and Socio-Economic Status,"
Canadian Journal of Criminology and Corrections, 8: 20-7.
Waller, I.
1974 Men Released From Prison. Toronto.

Weiler, K.
1977 "Unmanageable Children and Section 8," *Interchange*, 8 (1-2): 176-93.
Werthman, C.
1969 "Delinquency and Moral Character," in D. Cressey and D. Ward, eds., *Crime, Delinquency and Social Process.* Evanston, Ill.
1971 "Delinquents in Schools," in B. Cosin, R. Dale, G. Esland, and D. Swift, eds., *School and Society.* London.
West, W. G.
1975a "Adolescent Deviance and the School," *Interchange*, 6 (2).
1975b "Adolescent Perspectives: On Being a Greaser, Freak or Straight," presented to annual meetings of Canadian Sociology and Anthropology Association, Edmonton, Alberta.
1978 "The Short-term Careers of Serious Thieves," *Canadian Journal of Criminology*, 20 (2): 189-90.

CHAPTER SEVEN

Social Control and the Military in Canada
by Terry C. Willett

A salient feature of social analysis since 1945 has been an aversion to the view that coercive force underpins social order at all levels. The consensus theories that dominated Western sociology until the 1960's suggest that people act according to shared beliefs about what is best for the common good: these beliefs are not drummed in and enforced, but are induced by educative debate. Persuasion and freedom to choose afterwards are seen as good; direction and enforcement are bad, as epitomized by the twin taboos of our times, authoritarianism and regimentation. Conflict theory, on the other hand, does not turn the other cheek to coercive force, since force is seen as a major concomitant of power, whether or not it is subtly concealed. Hence it is curious that conflict theorists after Marx have virtually ignored the social meaning of the military as the embodiment of ideas about coercive force and the structures created to make those ideas work. Perhaps this is because both consensus and conflict theorists confuse what is and has been with what should be. Both seem to reject the view that coercive force is one of the necessary conditions of social order and they seem ready to ignore current events all over the world which support this position.

Consequently, Canadian sociologists have shown little or no interest in the military; indeed the literature on it is negligible and research is almost non-existent.* This is surprising since Canadian society has been influenced greatly by citizens who also were soldiers; moreover, it is unique in having a military

*A notable exception to this is the work of R. F. Hamilton and J. Wright, *New Directions in Political Sociology* (Indianapolis, 1975).

organization in which the navy, army, and air forces are unified. The reasons for this disinterest are obscure: one may be the generally pacifistic climate in schools and universities since 1960, as indicated by the elimination of cadet corps in most educational institutions in Canada during the 1960's, but more likely is the absence of any overt threat to Canada since 1945 and our good fortune in never being conquered or occupied by a hostile power since becoming a nation. So it is tempting to take the easy way and regard Canadians as an "unmilitary people" living in relative harmony and shielded from the sort of traumatic upheavals to which other, less fortunate societies have become accustomed.

But a conflict perspective should not allow such complacency. It sees consensus as a superficial façade behind which there is a constant struggle to dominate by powerful groups with vested and particular interests. It postulates that power and force are much the same thing, and that they are concentrated in the hands of a few whose interests are identified by them as being in the public interest. Whether we call that few an elite or a ruling class is important since there is a distinction; a ruling class is usually conceived as both owning and controlling the means of production, whereas an elite may own nothing, though it may have absolute control by manipulating the conditions in which owners can act. Whichever rules, the military is seen as their obedient instrument for imposing their will on any who would resist it; also, it is inferred that military leaders are sometimes themselves members of what Mills (1956) called a "power elite" whose interests they share in maintaining the existing order and resisting change.

A radical version of conflict theory sees the military and the power-elite as the muscle of the capitalist system based on an international network of heavy industries and funding arrangements that are the substance of capitalism. Added to this impressive concentration of power is the seemingly sinister interest in arms production and distribution in which there appears to be a vested interest in profiting from war. Hence the vision by many American sociologists in the 1960's of a vast "military-industrial complex" which, on close examination by others, proved to have been insubstantial and overdrawn (Moskos, 1976a).

A critical approach to these theories, and some actual acquaintance with the military, renders all of them to a set of half truths and simplifications, for the relationship between the military and the state is very complicated to analyse in most developed societies, including our own. The military is not necessarily a conservative and rigidly obedient instrument; on the contrary, it can be a dynamic means for inducing and compelling change. It can support revolutionary parties or it can be revolutionary itself, as in Cuba, Egypt, and other countries that have undergone revolution. Moreover, a pronounced feature of late twentieth-century political change is the coup d'état by the military followed by a period of government by its officers. It is naive, then, to see the military anywhere as necessarily favouring conservatism or capitalism.

The State and the Military

R. M. MacIver has defined the state as "an association which, acting through law as promulgated by a government endowed to this end with coercive power, maintains within a community, territorially demarcated, the universal external conditions of social order" (MacIver, 1926: 22). In this definition the operative terms are "coercive power" and "social order" since these aspects are the special concern of the military and the police as the agencies of social control operating in the name of the state.

Consideration of the condition of the world as it is now, and as it has been throughout history, leaves little doubt about the omnipresence of armed force as the epitome of power, i.e., the ability of a nation to get what it wants, despite opposition. Indeed, current events in 1978 suggest that there are many who agree with the African guerrilla leaders, Nkomo and Mugabe, that "power lies in the barrel of a gun." Perhaps that is why all nation-states which claim any independent status maintain armed forces of one kind or another in addition to police.* Despite the pacifist arguments that without armies there would be no wars, none seem to want to go beyond ritual in testing this

*Evidently this holds for potential nations also; e.g., Prime Minister Lévesque stated recently that a sovereign Quebec will have its own military forces as "all nation states have them, and there has to be something to maintain the peace when all other means have failed" (*Le Soleil*, 26 July 1977).

hypothesis; one might say the same about reactions to the view that without criminal law and police there would be no crimes.

Of course, there are other reasons than offence or defence for maintaining armed forces, for they are status symbols which, with flags and anthems, express the meaning of the nation to its members as well as to the world outside. This is evident among most of the new nations of Africa and Asia, despite their inability to afford them.

Though changes in the organization and technology of coercive force have been remarkably rapid in recent years, the principles by which force has been applied remain the same. These are two and they are essential in distinguishing the special nature of the military in relation to other agencies of social control. The first is the principle of *graduated force*, which can be expressed graphically:

Minimum	Force		Maximum
Force/Threat	*Symbolic Hurting* e.g., fines, sanctions	*Actual Hurting* e.g., taking hostages, punitive raids.	*Killing* e.g. war, capital punishment

This shows several degrees of force, which, theoretically speaking, are applied according to the amount of threat perceived by the state to its security or to the key values that constitute its particular "way of life." It will be evident that this can apply equally to internal and external threats. Where there is a police force, it is usually able to handle situations requiring symbolic hurting or actual hurting; but beyond that point on the continuum, and up to the use of maximum force, the military may be used because they are especially trained and equipped for that purpose.

The second principle is *economy of force*, according to which it is unwise and wasteful to use more force than is necessary to achieve an aim. The instruments of coercion are now extremely expensive in every respect, but perhaps least noticeably so in their potential to increase the risk that their use may worsen a situation to the point of disaster. This principle governs the remarkably persistent belief in deterrence as an economical means of applying coercive force, since it depends substantially on the credibility of threat and the hope that this will be enough in itself to coerce. Hence, in most modern states, extreme force is used rarely, if ever; there is reliance for as long as possible on the cheapest form of coercive control – bluff.

The State, the Military, and the Police
To some extent these two principles explain the marked difference between democratic and totalitarian states in the organization and use of the police and the military. It may be assumed that democratic governments are more sensitive to popular feelings than are totalitarian ones; hence, democratic states are reluctant to use degrees of force beyond symbolic hurting and risk the often serious consequences of political overkill. Totalitarian states, on the other hand, may be more inclined to use higher degrees of force and rely more on intimidation than on popularity.

Differences in military organization depend on a complex relationship of factors affecting control of the unique amount of force at the disposal of the military and, to a lesser extent, of the police. Besides the universal concern of states about attack from external sources, there are marked differences according to the extent to which attacks from within are feared, including those that might come from the military and police themselves. All of these will, in varying degrees, influence the ways in which constitutions set out the organization of these agencies and the checks and balances applied to their power (Andreski, 1964). Whether there is conscription for a mass army or reliance on volunteer regular forces is not only a matter of tradition or efficiency; this also indicates the extent to which governments can trust the citizens to carry arms and to which it is thought necessary to spread the tight controls of military law through the social structure. The latter is found more often in totalitarian states, where the military and police are often integrated with prison and intelligence organizations (as in the USSR) to make coercive control by the state as pervasive as possible. In democracies, on the other hand, there is often an egalitarian and patriotic motive behind conscription, as in Switzerland and Sweden where bearing arms is a hallmark of full citizenship for men, as well as a means of stressing the egalitarian policy of the state. Other democracies eschew conscription during peacetime as being consistent with the immorality of compulsion, except as a last resort, as in Britain, Canada, and the United States. Typically, these states rely on a mixture of paid volunteers in full-time regular service and others who serve part-time.

It should not be supposed, however, that reliance on voluntary forces ensures that they will not be used oppressively, since the state may make service appealing to particular classes with a vested interest in its survival. Such policies may be so subtle as to make detection difficult. In contrast is the more obvious policy of states, usually dictatorships, that cannot trust their own nationals and recruit mercenaries with no interests other than serving their paymasters; in these cases, however, care is usually taken to isolate these from civilian society to prevent "contamination."

None of these organizational and constitutional arrangements is a certain insurance against the coup d'état. These appear to be increasingly frequent, especially in the new nations of Africa, but they seem to depend for their effectiveness more on certain conditions being present than on any particular feature of military or police organization. Usually these conditions include the centralization of political power where military force can be concentrated against it suddenly and decisively; armed forces that are highly politicised and disaffected, especially among the officers; a core of leaders upon whose co-operation the "rebels" can rely; and a tradition of coup d'état. These conditions are explicit in the noticeable extent to which insecure governments protect the centres of power (including the radio and television stations) with specially recruited forces of guards, control the political indoctrination of officers, permeate the armed forces with intelligence agents, maintain a separate political police, and keep armed forces and certain police forces isolated from civilian society as much as possible, as in Spain and some countries of Latin America. It also is interesting that some of the latter keep the army, navy, and air force separate so that each can be a check on the others if need be: evidently, Canadian governments since 1967 have felt secure enough not to consider such precautions necessary.

In the democracies, the trend has been toward less isolation and more convergence between the military and civilian society; this is certainly true of Canada, where one writer has warned that the growing "civilianization" of our armed forces might erode their ability to fight in a war (Crook, 1975; Moskos, 1976a, 1976b). Also, there is now less reliance on the military to maintain internal security because police forces have become sufficiently numerous and well-equipped to undertake this task. All states tend to use the military as a last resort to secure internal order, but *when* this is done will vary according to the organization, efficiency, and reliability of the police. Reliability can be a problem when the majority of the police are organized municipally or even regionally, and loyalties are apt to be confused as they were said to be among the mainly Protestant Royal Ulster Constabulary whose allegedly biased activities in the 1960's inflamed an already dangerous internecine conflict. It is in such conditions that some states resort to so-called "third forces," recruited specially for use in internal disorders and equipped to use greater degrees of force than conventional police, though rarely as much as the military. An example is the French special police force, equipped with armoured vehicles, and recruited from rural people who have a notable lack of sympathy for the urban protesters who are their usual targets.

For reasons already stated it is obvious that "third forces" may be viewed with apprehension by governments as well as by citizens. Like mercenaries, they are prone to excessive zeal and to become "laws unto themselves," even to the point of aiding a coup. Paradoxically, such forces defeat the purposes for which they were set up: to avoid overkill and reduce solidarity among the dissidents. Usually these objectives are achieved more economically and effectively by means more subtle (or insidious, according to one's viewpoint) than overt force; these are the intelligence agencies whose growing and controversial role in modern states deserves more than the passing mention I can make of it here. It must suffice to say that no serious student of coercive control can avoid such questions as who should control intelligence – should it be a civilian, a military, or a police preserve, or should it be a shared activity among them all? These questions are discussed ably if inconclusively in relation to Canada by French and Béliveau (1979).

In totalitarian and democratic states an almost universal check against the power of military, police, or intelligence agencies, and against the coup d'état, is the principle of *civilian supremacy*. According to this the head of state and the apparatus of government should be civilian and, under no circumstances, be drawn from serving members of the military or police. Sometimes, however, principle and practice diverge, as when the leaders of coups, or those associated with them, drop their military rank and assume civilian status; for instance, Egypt's President Sadat was once known as "Wing Commander" in President (or Colonel) Nasser's military government. Even when military men are candidates for governmental office, as were Generals Eisenhower and De Gaulle, there is concern about their potential military alliances, though the latter's suppression of an attempted coup by the army in 1961 belied some of the anxiety.

Historical evidence suggests that civilian political supremacy is based on the belief that military men make disastrous politicians, but it shows also that this idea is too simple, for the political ability and effectiveness of men like Napoleon, Wellington, and George Marshall can hardly be doubted. In states upholding civilian supremacy, military men are not supposed to be "political animals," yet it is hard to see how any one of them could become chiefs of staff or heads of their military organization without grasping and manipulating the realities of politics. That the myth persists so strongly tells us much about the emotional context in which civilians perceive the military, and vice versa.

Mutual perceptions have not been researched very much save by Segal, Senter, and Segal (1978) in the U. S., where the armed forces seemed to enjoy a favourable, or at least a not unfavourable, image among nearly 600 respondents surveyed in Detroit during 1973; but, in commenting on this, the authors point to the importance of the reserve forces in affecting civil-military relationships. With these researchers, I see the reserves as a bridge between the military and civilian society that perhaps could have been more developed by the military in Canada, Britain, and the U. S. than it has been. Though this link has rarely been regarded as significant, it would be an error to regard the armed forces as discrete organizationally from the host society, for in most countries there is a network of civilian organizations whose origins, at least, are derived sufficiently from the military to constitute what I call a "military infrastructure." This consists of the so-called Legions of which the Royal Canadian Legion (350,000 members), The Royal British Legion (850,000), and The American Legion (2.5 million) are examples, as are the groups that operate more specifically in the military field, such as the British Army League and the Conference of (Canadian) Defence Associations representing the reserve forces of Canada. In addition there are the cadet corps whose membership (about 18,000 in Canada), though mostly under sixteen years old, is numerous and enthusiastic enough to indicate that interest in things military is more alive than it seems.*

From their size alone, the Legions are of special interest, and here again it is surprising that so little study of them has been done by social scientists that we are left only with mere impressions. These suggest that, though their membership is aging, their branches are collectively quite rich: an asset in a society where wealth counts, and one that suggests that their political clout is (or would be) great if they cared to use it. Moreover, it seems the membership is mainly from the working class and the lower middle class, though here one's personal knowledge is confined to Britain and Canada. That their politics in the countries cited might be inclined toward conservative views is suggested by the Royal Canadian Legion's campaign in 1976 to alert its membership to arrest the suspected decline in traditional values in Canadian society and especially the permissive influences giving rise, in their view, to erosion of the family. The resolutions of the American Legion against amnesty for deserters and draft dodgers after the Viet Nam War are another example. These organizations present an obvious problem for conflict theory, pointing as they do to consensus among a sizable number of the working class, and one would hesitate to attribute this to "false consciousness," especially on the premises of Legion branches.

The infrastructure is important also because it is a means of bringing all members of the military, the police, and the correctional services together socially with the civilian community in which Legion branches are often centres of social life.

*Strengths given are for 1977-78.

This should help to bring into perspective some important distinctions that have to be made in both theory and practice between the military and the police if one is to avoid confusion between the two. At first sight these distinctions seem to depend on the degrees of force each is trained and equipped to use, but this is only to beg the question as to why the differences exist. One answer is that the historical and actual roles of the two agencies are so essentially different that their traditions and self-images are affected quite profoundly. Generally speaking, the role of the military is seen by its members as the defence of the state from threats originating outside its frontiers, beyond which they must be prepared to go and to die. A secondary concern of the military is defence of the state from internal threats so serious that they seem to justify the tacit admission by the government that the non-military agencies cannot cope with the situation. The police, on the other hand, derive their tradition and self-image from the ancient office of "constable," i.e., a civilian appointed to protect the community from threats to peace and order within its boundaries. This is epitomized in the democracies by the legal status of "peace officer" in Canada and England. Hence, the police, where they are separate from the military, are an essentially civilian agency working in a civilian context in which their role and status does not depend on carrying arms, in contrast to the military whose distinctiveness rests almost entirely on the fact that they are an armed force trained and equipped to use maximum force if necessary.

From these essential differences in role and status further distinctions can be made between forms of organization and discipline and between systems of command and control. The military are subject to both military and civilian law in most democracies, including Canada; the police are also subject to civilian law, but their more limited access to powerful weaponry does not seem to demand such a rigorous code of discipline as that of the military. Police organization and systems of command are designed for members who work mainly as individuals in everyday conditions among other civilians, where emergencies requiring group activities are the exception rather than the norm; those of the military are designed for groups working under the stress of battle or of extreme emergency. To clarify a difficult issue, the "scenarios" in the minds of military and police members, against which they see their raison d'être, are very different and help to explain the vehemence with which members of the police deny that they are "military," and with which those of the military deny that they are "police." There are other differences, but as this essay is concerned primarily with the military I will concentrate on the characteristics that distinguish this group. One is the ideology peculiar to the military almost everywhere, in which four concepts have special salience and meaning.

The Ideology of the Military
The first concept is that of *loyalty*, which is rooted in the oath of fealty given by soldiers to their sovereign; among the military this loyalty totally transcends self-interest, and its power is magnified by enabling an identification with the nation itself, which the sovereign personifies. This appears to be so whether the sovereign is a secular president or a monarch whose quasi-sacred status adds the additional mystique of identification with religious authority. The "idea" of loyalty is reinforced strongly by symbols such as flags and national anthems; hence the clarity and power attached to the equally potent "idea" of "nation." Indeed, the nationalism of the military is most striking, and its essential nature can be seen in that the ultimate expression of loyalty is the readiness to sacrifice life. That this is no myth is exemplified by the dedication of the Kamikaze pilots to their sacred emperor, and of the Hitler Youth to their secular Führer. Hence it is unlikely that the confusion about the national identity, which has generated so many courses on Canadian Society in recent years, was shared by members of the military; it is also interesting that the rhetoric about Canadian unity has taken little or no account of the key part the military have played in making it real.

Linked closely to loyalty is the peculiar meaning given by the military to *discipline*. This does not mean punishment but the development of self-control and the ability to call on inner resources of strength when natural inclinations pull in other directions. It also includes the ability to obey orders under stress.

The third concept is *leadership*, which has excited much criticism of the military because the term itself suggests fascism and the encouragement of blind obedience to a leader. To the military, however, it is the mainspring of the capacity to survive and overcome the most adverse circumstances, and even to achieve the apparently impossible. Like so many aspects of military ideology it is subtle and difficult to explain; but in crude terms it might be conceived as the capacity to inspire others to do their utmost when things are at their worst. Like loyalty, with which it is linked closely, it depends essentially on reciprocity. In its ideal form, leadership requires the wholehearted support of one's peers and subordinates and vice versa; the "good" leader is seen as one committed totally to the role, putting it before any kind of self-interest. This is manifest in many ways, for example, the setting of minimum ages for officers to marry and the subtle lack of encouragement to those wishing their families to accompany them "on service." It is implicit also in the view that rank and privilege ought mainly to be a practical means of freeing officers from mundane concerns so that they may give their whole attention to the training and welfare of their subordinates. Unhappily, this is a view that many subordinates and students of military history might question.

These factors can be fused into another and perhaps more powerful concept that the military call *morale*. It is as elusive to define as "personality," but it expresses in vivid terms the prominence in military ideology of combat as the ultimate situation in which these ideological qualities are tested to the full, and to which they are geared. This highlights the distinction between the committed military professional and the civilian whose commitment to his or her job is usually partial and stops well short of personal sacrifice.

Hence, relationships between the military and civilians are often distorted by the very different ways in which each sees their world. To the military, civilian concerns about self-interest and individualism threaten esprit de corps and the capacity to survive in crisis. And to civilians, the military's commitment to the state and to itself may seem to threaten democratic freedom. But even from the superficial sketch given in Appendix A, the perceptive reader might dismiss the Canadian military as too small, too dispersed, and too heavily weighted with administrative units to threaten anything or anyone.* And certainly it stretches the imagination beyond credibility to see it as a powerful and oppressive adjunct to a ruling elite, given the frequent criticism that its equipment is obsolete, reflecting vividly the years of neglect by governments that have seemed to care nothing for the military. Even so, it is not necessary to have sophisticated equipment to break strikes or to suppress riots, nor, for that matter, to stage an effective coup. And it remains that, in terms of coercive power, no organization in Canada would be any match for the military: certainly not the police, a smaller force with more limited strength in weapons. So there remain some important questions about the raison d'être for the military in Canadian society, now and in the future, to which its history is highly relevant.

Some Historical Aspects of Canadian Military
In titling his book *Canada's Soldiers, A Military History of an Unmilitary People*, G. F. G. Stanley (1960) makes a telling point: that for some reasons which may emerge later Canadians do not recognize the deep influence of the military on their society. (Nor do they value it, if its neglect by those who offer courses in Canadian Society is any indication.) Moreover, an overwhelming impression from the evidence of my current research on the role of the Canadian militia in peacetime is that there is little interest in, or knowledge of, the military among the public. Perhaps one of my research informants put things too strongly in saying that "we don't think about the military, we don't think about war, and we don't want to think about either," but there are many instances in which much the same has been said with less emphasis.

This would be understandable if the record were one of which Canadians might be ashamed, and it is perhaps possible that an unsympathetic focus on the few years of real peace since the passing of New France might leave some doubts. For, until 1873,

---

*Appendix A outlines briefly the organization of the Canadian Armed Force in 1978 to help readers appreciate its uniqueness and the extent of the changes described in the following pages.

governments had only the military to deal with problems of internal order in times that were, to say the least, turbulent. Contrary to some views, I see the eighteenth and nineteenth centuries as no less violent than the twentieth, and perhaps more so. Mobs and riots were not unusual in days when recourse to civil law was difficult if not impossible, and threats from powerful and predatory European nations were very real, as were those from an even more turbulent neighbour to the south.

Dating back to the influence of the British regular garrisons of the seventeenth and eighteenth centuries, British military traditions have always been embedded deeply in the Canadian military as exemplified by the great emphasis on the regiment, its territorial origins, the direct link with the sovereign shown by the honorific title "royal," and a paternalistic relationship between officers and other ranks. To this day most Canadian regular and reserve units have active affiliations with British units, and many Canadians have chosen to serve in the British forces in preference to their own (probably because career prospects were better, for one thing). This is mentioned because it calls attention to the distinctive relationship between military units and the sovereign that is symbolized, among other things, by the formal wording of the commissions and warrants held by the officers and warrant-officers, as well as by the colours that, in turn, symbolize the meaning of the unit itself.* This has a lot to do with the absence of the threat of a coup d'état and the strong yet civic sense of loyalty to the monarch-sovereign that seems to be something more subtle than loyalty to the state or a government acting in its name. So there is evidence here to counter the impressions that might be derived from the military's role in aid of the civil power, as outlined below, in that the Canadian military seems neither to have been alienated from the people nor a hated force of oppressors.

Between 1900 and 1914, 1918 and 1939, and again between 1946 and 1950 we find that the citizen force, the militia, was the most visible feature of the Canadian military. The regular force, though growing steadily in size, was an adjunct to the reserves to

---

*The term "meaning" has powerful emotional and indefinable connotations when it is applied to institutions with deeply-rooted traditions in communities and nations, as in this instance.

provide instructors and necessary services. Most militia units were up to full strength and had little trouble in parading 600 men at their weekly drills; moreover, these apparently were representative of all classes in the communities. Continuing a centuries-old function, the military provided an effective means of gaining social status through rank, especially for the middle class, and it brought contacts that led to jobs which were often hard to get otherwise. Among other things, militia units were social clubs with a strong bond to their communities, and their civic meaning was emphasized by their part in civic ceremonies. In many tightly-knit Canadian communities the militia units symbolized civic pride; as one elderly informant put it in referring to a typical small city's relationship with its unit: "in the old days the Rifles was Brockville and Brockville was the Rifles." (The Brockville Rifles, established in 1866, and continuously "alive" to the present, is one of the many militia units carrying the name of its parent community). So, for various undocumented reasons, militia service was not an unpopular activity for the "unmilitary people" in peacetime. The militia was strong everywhere, and no less so in provinces like Quebec and Nova Scotia, which were never distinguished for their devotion to Ottawa. Hence there is reason to think that militia loyalties were strongest at the local level.

Beyond this brief introduction it is difficult to treat the historical material chronologically, given the limited space available, and yet to select from it the aspects that are especially relevant to this analysis. Therefore, I will focus on the military in aid to the civil power, and on its development in wartime; the first is related clearly to the conflict perspective and the questions it raises; the second is essential to understanding the contemporary Canadian military from a sociological standpoint and to generating ideas about its future.

Aid to the Civil Power

Leaving wars and national emergencies for later discussion, it seems credible to see the military as the "long arm of the establishment," and especially of employers during the rather turbulent years of peacetime in the nineteenth century and into the 1930's. According to Gellner (1974), they were called out to deal with strike situations on forty-eight occasions between 1875 and 1933 in addition to a variety of other somewhat mundane problems such as stopping prize-fighting. It seems, however, that none of these were dramatic or bloody affairs by comparison with "civil disturbances" in Europe and the U. S. at the time, and total fatalities appear to have been less than twenty.

As many of these incidents were in urban areas the troops involved came from the urban units of the militia, often consisting of middle-class young men who either served without pay or returned the meagre sums to their regiments to cover the costs of uniforms and equipment. Accounts from the histories of the 17th Royal Canadian Hussars of Montreal (Steele, 1934) and The Queen's Own of Toronto (Morton, 1970a, 1974) record the enthusiasm with which the men of these units responded to orders to stop rioting and violence among striking workers, which they seem to have done without any dramatic losses of life or injuries on either side. No doubt this kind of action made them less than popular with emerging trade unions, but it is difficult to see from the evidence whether the militiamen's action was against the violence and rioting or against the strikes as such. That some other units of the militia, possibly recruited from different strata, took a poor view of strike duties is implicit in the refusal of the Belleville Militia to turn out to deal with a strike of railway workers in 1876; hence the necessity to send for The Queen's Own from Toronto.

Pending the publication of more historical research, little is known about the working-class Canadian's view of these internal security activities. What is known suggests that the use of armed force against citizens in the manifest interests of employers, or to enable the government to suppress legitimate protest, could not have found much favour among what seems to have been anything but a docile population, including the militiamen themselves.* Certainly the use of cavalry-style charges against the Winnipeg strikers in 1919 aroused popular anger, especially as most

---

*It is notable that the British commander-in-chief of the Canadian Army, Major-General J. C. Herbert, reported to the federal government in 1894 that they consider "the degree to which the militia of Canada is affected by the presence in the ranks of men belonging to labour organizations, and as to whether the force which should be a safeguard against internal trouble may

of the victims were war veterans. In fact, the "troops" involved in the latter incident were not military but The Royal Canadian Mounted Police who, owing to a quirk of history, are often confused with the armed forces. Though they were formed as The Royal North West Mounted Rifles, their status as such lasted only a few days, after which they became essentially a police force. They did supply men to serve as cavalry in the Canadian Expeditionary Force to South Africa in 1899 and again in 1914; and they display traits derived from the military, such as the wearing of scarlet and blue uniforms and the commissioning of officers, but these are symbolic only. Nevertheless, many Canadians regard the RCMP as a military force and as essentially different from the "ordinary police." To some extent they *are* different since they are the only federal police force and have widely ranging responsibilities for dealing with subversion and counter-espionage that overlap with military intelligence. But it should be noted that their milieu of operation is a civilian one, and they are not equipped to use maximum force nor, for that matter, any more force than other police in Canada.

The next notable use of the military in peacetime to deal with strikes was the employment of troops to intervene and prevent violence by strikers in Ontario at a Hamilton furniture factory in 1933, but, though again there was no loss of life or serious injury, the effects of the affair were enough to discourage repetition. The Opposition in the provincial parliament made great capital from alleging that the government used military force in the manifest interest of employers, and the only alderman to support the strikers during the disturbances was elected mayor in the subsequent election! (Gellner, 1974: 132)

The last instance to date of using troops in strikes was the perhaps less questionable intervention in the 1969 strike of the Montreal police force. This was again without bloodshed, but it is an important incident for our later analysis because it raises the problems of trade unionism and the right to strike in the agencies of social control themselves.

---

become a danger to the State." Noting also that many armouries were in working-class districts giving easy access to weapons, the General proposed improving the militia cavalry "recruited from the best class of the rural population" and an expansion of the regular force.

As Gellner says, there is no doubt that the political climate had changed so much by the 1930's that a simplistic and unashamedly biased use of troops in aid of the civil power (and of employers) became politically unacceptable. It was also made more difficult since legislation in 1924 made it necessary for local authorities to put requests for troops to provincial attorneys-general; before that mayors had been able to call out the troops themselves. There is some virtue, then, in a procedure which now seems to be unnecessarily bureaucratic and cumbersome when the request by the civil power is to deal with less politically sensitive problems such as blizzards, floods, and fires.

Since confederation, the only internal disturbances regarded by the government as threats to the state have been the Riel Rebellion (1869-70) and the so-called "crisis" of 1970 in Quebec. The former was notable more for the endurance of the troops and the shortcomings of the commanders than for any controversial uses of the military; indeed, the whole affair seems to have been exaggerated as a threat to the Canadian state. The forces engaged were small, even according to the standards of the time. Instances of historical over-dramatization include: calling the three-day action at Batoche between adversaries each less than 1,000 strong a "battle"; and labelling the ten-day containment of less than 1,000 police and civilians in the stockade at Battleford a "siege," though Morton (1970b: 112) has since dismissed it as a farce. It is, however, significant that Riel has become a folk hero since the "turbulent sixties," especially in Quebec where I was shown with pride an original oil painting of him on the walls of an elite militia regiment with the Red River expedition among its battle honours.

This is not the place to give an account of the highly controversial "1970 Crisis"; it has been done elsewhere by Gellner (1974), Pelletier (1971), and much more dramatically by Vallières (1976). The bald facts seem to be that seven battalions of regular infantry – apparently all there were in Canada at the time, according to Gellner – and some units of militia were mobilized against a group of supposed insurrectionists numbering "no more than three dozen" (Gellner, 1974, ch. 4). Incredibly, the infantry had the support of a squadron of jet fighters and the overall impression was of major crisis, especially with the concentration of several thousand police on the city of Montreal. In fact, the entire military force, massive by contemporary Canadian standards, was never in action directly against anyone; in the main it was used to man roadblocks and provide a "presence" as a context within which the police carried out the now notorious number of arrests and searches that, in the end, yielded 35 prosecutions. The militia were confined to the manning of vulnerable points, and some were not trusted to do that, according to officers who told me of the sudden and tactless occupation of their armouries by regulars.

Though the operation seems to have had the support of those Canadians who write to editors and answer opinion polls, there is no question that it was a case of massive overkill, given the evidence that has since emerged. However, despite the pungent allegations of Vallières (1976) that it was all contrived by the federal Cabinet to intimidate the separatist movement in Quebec and maintain the provincial Liberals in power, and that the police and the military were aiders and abetters, the latter seem to have come out of the affair untarnished.

Despite its small scale, the significance of the 1970 affair for the Canadian military should not be under-estimated. If Quebec "separates," the position of the many Québécois in the armed forces (and especially in the militia) may be extremely difficult, especially should the federal government use force to intervene. Serious problems of morale are involved in this matter, and it is regrettable that space compels only passing mention of it here; again, it is surprising that the copious literature on "Unity" should have given so little attention to military aspects of it.

Another important consequence of the October events is their effect on the relationships between intellectuals in politics, the media, and education on the one hand, and the military on the other. The FLQ (Front de Libération du Québec) was tiny, and its attempts at revolution were pathetically inept, but its radical socialism was undoubtedly appealing to intellectuals and others who believe intensely in this type of political philosophy. One has only to mix a little with the military to sense a marked antipathy to radical extremism, with which intellectuals are perhaps identified too readily. The hostility is probably mutual, and it is understandable if there is substance in the view of many intellectuals that the military are still an oppressive instrument of a capitalist elite. From the military viewpoint, however, this feeling may be due more to beliefs held about the attitudes of intellectuals to war, and the links between socialism and pacifism, than to any sympathy with capitalists or elites.

War, the Military, and Canadian Society
Without wishing to play down the formative influences on the Canadian military of its activities in peacetime, the experience of war seems to reduce these events to relative insignificance. Canada has been through at least three major wars in its short history as a federal state: the First and Second World Wars, and the Korean War; though not regarded as a commitment of the nation, the latter involved a substantial military effort. Sociological analysis has paid little or no attention to these massive upheavals, yet they have probably done more to change Canadian society than anything else.

Though one can mention them only in passing, it would be an error to omit the war situations of the eighteenth and nineteenth centuries, mainly because of their effect on relationships with the United States that are highly relevant to the development of the military in Canada, as we shall see later. Until the Civil War, American relationships with Canada were fraught with suspicion stemming from the former's ambivalence to the imperial designs of both Britain and France. More generally, the U. S. was seen by Canadians as an ally of France, and as a potentially hostile power, especially to British interests. Hence, the Canadian military saw nothing strange about being ready to defend Canada against the Americans. The last time this was turned to near reality was in 1866 when pro-Irish irregulars, the Fenians, made sporadic minor forays into Ontario that were notably unsuccessful. There followed a long period when the penetration of Canada by the Americans discounted military means in favour of others more subtle: a process that has continued until today, when the threat of American military intervention in Canada is not salient in military thinking. The issue is not dead, however, and I shall return to it at the end of this essay.

The history of the two world wars belongs elsewhere; here there is no room to do it justice, but only to point to some specific events of sociological significance that have direct relevance to the place of the military in Canada's structure and ideologies. First, they both involved the rapid mobilization of the nation to produce an effort in combat that was not only dramatic but of great practical significance in overcoming the adversary and ending the wars. And this effort was mainly by the citizen soldiers produced from the "unmilitary people." The fighting achievements of Canadians at Vimy Ridge in 1917 and again at Dieppe in 1942 are examples: indeed, it has been said that Canada became a nation on the slopes of Vimy Ridge, though it might be more accurate to say that Canada became recognized as such by the world after that amazing achievement. There can be little doubt that there were no illusions about what it meant to be a nation from the substantial responses of the Canadian people, despite the involuntary nature of Canada's involvement in World War I. It was in the second war that the concept of nation was sealed by the Canadian government making its own unilateral decision to go to war. But, in both conflagrations, the issue of conscription (to fight a war in distant places that some called a "British War") did much to fuel the prejudices and hostility that have existed between Anglophones and Francophones throughout Canada's history.

The bitterness of those who volunteered for overseas service was apparently deep when regarding the tender matter of the so-called "zombies" who would not serve outside Canada; but it is sometimes forgotten that many of the latter were not French Canadians. Another divisive issue that contributed a certain hostility to radicalism was the incidence of strikes in the war industries and the police in which the military intervened. In these cases there seems every reason to see the latter as concerned more with the war effort than with any set of attitudes to industrial action as such, but objectives and the ideals underlying them can easily become blurred, as we have seen in other instances of military intervention. Another issue was that of conscientious objection to military service, which has tended to be most common among intellectuals and which, again, led to bitter feelings among those who "did their bit." It is indeed paradoxical that unmilitary people can be so hostile to other unmilitary people!

However, these "out-groups" and the adversary powers helped to unify Canadians nationally and communally to a remarkable degree. The experience of war also had a marked impact on the social structure of the country; among other things, service in the military increased social mobility as it always has done, and many people in humble positions in peacetime became accredited leaders in war and afterwards when they consolidated their middle-class and upper middle-class status. Also notable was the effect of the wars on the status of women; in both they showed their capacity to stand the full brunt of bombardment and perform heavy manual work, as well as to lead men and women as NCO's and officers. There is some portent for the future in the rapidity with which prejudices against women and other minority groups were overcome when the need to survive was dominant, and even the reluctance to use women in combatant units was broken down in the 1940's by their employment serving the guns of the heavy anti-aircraft batteries defending England against the Luftwaffe. And, to counter the divisions between ethnic groups opened up by the conscription issue, there were the impressive reputations as fighting units gained by French-Canadian regiments, among which the Royal 22nd Regiment (the "Vandouzieme") has become a symbol by which the Canadian nation is known, and by which it knows itself.

It is axiomatic that it takes a war to make the military appreciated, but any truth there is in this was vitiated by the twist of fate and technology that ended the Second World War: the use of nuclear bombs for the first time on Japan in 1945. This did much to influence the growth of anti-military feeling in the West that culminated during the Viet Nam War; it had a profound effect on thought in universities and schools, and consequently among the more highly educated young people.

But the real significance of nuclear warfare was not reflected in the Canadian military, for they began to re-organize for peacetime in 1946 as though the thing had never happened. As before 1939, the militia resumed its numerical and civilian predominance with a strength of 47,500 in 1947 as compared with only 15,500 regulars. Both the Navy and the Air Force shrank in size, but the latter increased its importance as expert in a new technology of war involving the "weapons systems" integrating

Canadian military effort more tightly with the United States than ever before.

The link with the U. S. became closer in the Korean War (1950-55) when the "unmilitary people" seemed to have no difficulty in recruiting rapidly a complete brigade group, plus naval and air support for the predominantly American United Nations Force, thus beginning the several contributions by the Canadian military to that organization. The feat is rather remarkable considering that not even a decade had passed since the end of the Second World War: hardly long enough for unpleasant memories to fade, yet many veterans volunteered. This was, however, to be the end of an era for the Canadian Forces because the strategic planners saw it as the last of the "conventional" wars in which three distinct services would participate in a full-scale non-nuclear conflict; instead they foresaw limited operations which, if not resolved by peacekeeping forces under UN auspices, might lead to a major war between the super-powers using nuclear weapons and other terror-technology. Such thinking was inspired essentially by American power and interests, and it was to have a marked effect on Canadian defence policy and military organization.

First, it priced Canada out of the "big league" of the nuclear powers. Second, it ruled out the old format of reliance on reserves with a small regular force as instructors. Third, it postulated that superiority in technology and equipment would always prevail over the human unit, fighting on inner strength and morale, often despite its equipment. The consequence was a re-organization and reduction in strength of the militia and other reserves, with the largest – the militia – allotted the task of coping with the consequences of nuclear attack on Canadian cities: in effect, civil defence. But the main insurance against crisis was to be an all-volunteer, regular "force in being" ready for instant use.

The Unification of the Canadian Forces
The concept of a "force in being" (as distinct from a "total force," founded mainly on reserves that can be mobilized) transformed the Canadian military between 1960 and 1970 into a monolithic bureaucracy, almost entirely different from its predecessors or the armed forces of its allies. Though still committed to providing

mobile "conventional" forces for its NATO contingent and for its "peacekeeping" tasks in the Middle East, the emphasis was on co-operating with the U.S. for the defence of Canada, using land bases from which missiles and missile-armed aircraft could operate. The emphasis was to be on rational organization, according to systems theories that made full use of computers and non-human means. The new military was organized no longer for movement, dash, and heroic deeds in close combat, but to operate from offices on fixed bases or from platforms of technology in (and beneath) the three elements of land, sea, and air. The sheer complexity of the system and its huge fixed bases demanded an administrative "tail" that Canadian military planners thought too expensive and, more significantly, too irrational if triplicated for each of the Navy, Army, and Air Force. This was one reason for unifying the three services in 1967. There are others, such as the desire of former Prime Minister Lester Pearson and Paul Hellyer, his ambitious Minister of Defence, to create something unique; a perceived need to reduce inter-service rivalry; and especially the wish to bring the military into line with the rest of the state system, thus enabling greater political and fiscal control over it.

By 1970 Canada and the other NATO powers had adopted what is now called the "total force concept"; this envisions, as before, a professional force in being, but–and here is the differ-ence–dependent on highly trained reserves that can be mobilized quickly to augment the regulars. Though the new concept revived the emphasis on the importance of the reserves and changed the role of the militia from civil defence to that of playing its part in a field army, the situation was very different from the period before 1939. Then, the bulk of the military force available to the government for external and internal duties was part-time and essentially amateur: mainly a militia of about 86,000 men rooted in communities and drawn from all classes of men. And the units were real "regiments" of approximately 600 men. Now, on the contrary, the main insurance is a small professional force of about 78,000 men and women, of which only 20 per cent are in combatant units and at least half of these are outside Canada in Europe, Cyprus, and Egypt. The militia is still the largest of the reserves, but its strength was down to under 17,000 in 1978 and each of its units could muster no more than 150 men and women. Perhaps it is as well from the government's standpoint that they have more substantial and better trained police forces to maintain internal order, though it would seem that these are stretched to the limit by their routine tasks.

It should now be evident that another marked change between the present and the period before 1939 is the almost complete disappearance of the military force from internal security in peacetime: October, 1970, and a handful of small-scale operations to provide a "presence" to quell disturbances in penitentiaries, are the few exceptions to this. Indeed, it would be no exaggeration to say that, inside Canada, the military are on public view rarely, save on occasional (and much appreciated) ventures to help local authorities cope with floods, forest fires, and blizzards. With the notable exception of the combat group in Europe, it would seem that most of the Canadian military have been employed since the Korean War on essentially peaceful kinds of work of which "peacekeeping" in Cyprus and truce supervision in the Middle East (and briefly in Viet Nam) are known best.

Less obvious, but of considerable importance inside Canada, has been the role of the military in promoting bilingualism as essential in a force composed of such high proportions whose mother tongue is either English or French, but not always both. And there is the more recent and highly publicized extension of posts in the armed forces open to women, though at present these are restricted to support and administration as distinct from combat.

Generally, then, this socio-historical survey has shown an increasing emphasis on the peaceful, constructive, and humanitarian character of the Canadian military, rather than a trend toward militaristic sabre-rattling or ruthless oppression in the name of some self-conceived law and order. To those concerned about the threats of agencies of social control to the liberty of Canadians, this should be reassuring. But the essential nature of military institutions to which I referred early in this paper cannot be overlooked: the military have a unique access to and knowledge of coercive force, and they are not police. And, they are still the last resort of the state to keep order when all else has failed, so we have to ask what to expect if that happens, given what we know of the military as it is now. Unfortunately, what we know now about the Canadian military largely has to do with its organization and structure. Little is known about its social composition: a serious deficiency, as the way in which social control is carried out depends greatly on the kind of people who do it. "Structures makyth men" (and women) only up to a point!

The Social Base of the Canadian Military
What is known about the Canadian military suggests that its age structure is dominated by those under thirty years old, especially in the combat units, and also in the militia whose "other ranks" are predominantly students under twenty. Officers tend to be older, but in these ranks the recent tendency has been to squeeze out those over forty unless they have some qualifications that are difficult to replace by younger people. The same is true of warrant officers and NCO's, of whom the regulars and the militia are very short. Indeed, the shortage of mature NCO's in the militia is a problem, given the preponderance of very young soldiers; this is one of the several ways in which the military of today differs from formerly when there was an effective distribution of age and maturity among the various ranks, though physical standards have always favoured those under thirty.

Traditionally the military has been a male domain and the advent of women is recent; in Canada it has been strictly controlled in peacetime, despite the massive utilization of women in the two world wars (though as "auxiliaries," a category that excluded them rather subtly from full membership). Now they are about 4.6 per cent (4,700) of the regular force and about 19 per cent (4,000) of the reserves, though there is reason to think that these proportions could increase considerably if ceilings were not set for the proportion of women, especially in the combat units of the militia. But, as stated above, women are restricted to administrative and support roles throughout the military. Generally, they tend to be educated more highly than the males and to come from higher socio-economic groups (especially in the militia); but, as with their numbers, opportunities for promotion are so restricted that few can rise above captain, and the most senior woman is a full colonel.

The distribution of ranks among women differs markedly from

that among males, where the trend has been sharply to increase the proportions of senior ranks among officers and other ranks. And the proportions of officers to other ranks has increased also. Hence one finds the same tendency for "chiefs to outnumber Indians" as in the other government services; and it is notable that the lowest rank of private has been reduced to one of probationary status, since promotion to corporal is now virtually automatic after about one year's service. This illustrates the general tendency for previously sought-after status to be eroded by making its attainment general and relatively easy. However, the gap between commissioned officers and non-commissioned ranks remains, especially in the regular force where it is still reinforced by the much higher educational standards of most officers, many of whom are graduates of The Royal Military College or of civilian universities, though an increasing proportion come from the ranks, especially in the technical and administrative elements. Thus, the old social-class division – in which officers came from the upper-middle and middle classes and the other ranks from the manual workers – still prevails in the regular force, mainly in the combat arms. The class distribution of the reserves is more egalitarian than in the regulars; in the militia many non-commissioned ranks are filled by young people with university or high school education from middle-class backgrounds, and it is not uncommon to find units where the socio-economic characteristics of the other ranks are much the same as those of the officers.

The contrast between the old and the new militia is marked in terms of social class. The former recruited its officers from the leading families and professions in the community directly to commissions, and the other ranks came from a spread of lower level occupational groups, most of which were blue-collar. Now the officers are usually civil servants or teachers, and few are self-employed or professional men and women: they are, in common parlance, "very much middle-class" like the other ranks. Indeed, the upper class and the stable, mature, working class have almost disappeared from the militia. The regulars and the militia are proud of the rising levels of education and social class in the ranks, despite the price paid in terms of high turnover as young people leave to advance their education in civilian employments, which still have a greater appeal than military life.

The ethnic composition of the military is indicated by what is known of linguistic divisions. By 1976 Anglophones were still predominant at 80 per cent of all regulars, but in the preceding decade the Francophone proportion increased by 32 per cent to 20 per cent of the whole. This reflects some success in the aim of the military to achieve the same relative proportions as in Canada's population (approximately 28 per cent French- and 72 per cent English-speaking), but with a strong emphasis on bilingualism. This is reflected in the increased proportion of bilingual Francophones in the highest ranks, and by the emphasis that bilingualism is essential to promotion; yet, it is still evident that the Francophones are found in disproportionate numbers among the non-specialized lower ranks (Cotton, 1976; Coulombe, 1972). It is uncertain what the proportion of Anglophones to Francophones is in the reserves, but there are indications that Anglophones are slightly more predominant than in the regulars with 82 per cent answering a "reserves-wide" research questionnaire in English and only 18 per cent in French (Goodfellow, 1976).

Summarizing this slight but important information, we can say that the Canadian military is young, as it always has been, but increasingly so, with an officer corps based more broadly in the lower-middle and middle classes. It seems that the proportions of females and Francophones are increasing, with most of the latter possibly in the combat arms (these are usually the ones with fewer specialist trades). There is still a difference in socio-economic status between officers and other ranks, but the militia does not reflect this and does show quite striking changes from the past in presenting a homogeneous picture of highly educated middle-class males and females in all ranks. Attrition rates are high in both regular and reserve forces, so we might infer that a continuous exchange is going on between the military and the civilian sectors of our society, thus increasing slowly the convergence referred to earlier. Such a summary brings us close to sociological analysis or commentary, which we now are in a position to begin.

The New Canadian Military: A Sociological Commentary

As Cotton *et al.* (1978) have observed, "the Forces emerged from the turbulent sixties as an expensive military establishment, smaller in size and with a highly differentiated occupational structure dominated by technical and administrative specialist roles." Observation of the Canadian military nowadays leaves no doubt that Cotton is correct. It reveals drastic changes from the kind of military force that one might assume to be perceived in a society bred on historical images that are now out of date. As in the United States and to a lesser extent in Britain, it is proving hard to maintain armed forces, especially in the combat elements, without conscription. The reasons for this are mainly sociological, and they may prove to be increasingly difficult to counter.

One reason is that the proportion of the male population of military age in Canada apparently is falling. Also, urbanization is increasing and so is the measurable standard of education, and both are known to affect recruiting to the regular force adversely. The recruiting base is therefore shrinking, and it may be unresponsive to approaches that cannot convince aspirants that the military offers a career that is not short, nor of limited use in civilian life (Cotton, 1976). Another reason is the apparent remoteness of war, or even the threat of it. Thus, the purpose of the armed forces may be unclear to Canadians, and especially to the young whose education has ignored their existence. Other problems in maintaining the armed forces include the loss of freedom and the distaste many young people have for the arbitrary discipline thought to be stressed, with some over-emphasis on the minutiae of dress and hair length.

The impact of these problems has been greatest on the combat arms, where it is increasingly difficult to attract and retain manpower in the face of the growing importance of the more static administrative tail. Indeed, the appeal of administrative work, with its adaptability to civilian life, is being used deliberately by policy-makers to maintain recruiting and as an inducement to combat soldiers who are promised transfer to the "tail" for the latter part of their service. The values of the military seem to be changing from according the highest status to combat roles (once a prerequisite for high rank) to placing equal emphasis on those dependent on administrative skills. This is having a profound effect on lifestyles and the ways in which authority is conceived, as the armed forces become more bureaucratic and civilianized.

The process through which these changes have evolved is illustrated clearly by the theoretical scheme proposed by Max Weber to explain the emergence of what he thought to be the ultimate in the forms of authority by which states are ruled: *bureaucratic authority*. According to Weber there are three types of authority that follow in sequence through history. The first he called "charismatic," in which power is made legitimate by some supernatural source that he called the "Gift of Grace"; he showed that this kind of legitimation was usually claimed by great religious leaders and the heroic warrior-kings who founded royal dynasties. The second was derived from the first since successive generations of rulers may not have the personal charisma of their ancestor; in these cases authority becomes "routinized" and reliant on established traditions. The right to rule is inherited or "ascribed" as distinct from being earned or "achieved." Finally, there is the third type of authority, derived not from mystic sources but from a code of law administered by rulers whose positions are achieved by selection according to qualifications, as distinct from heroic or intangible qualities. For Weber the central feature of bureaucracy was the "bureau," or office, as the source of authority, and not the personality of the individual occupying it; incumbents might change, but the office would continue unaffected and efficient if filled by qualified persons (Gerth and Mills, 1946). Hence, the individual is seen as virtually faceless and purely professional, since the idea of the "office" requires only certified knowledge and precise consistency of performance; it excludes idiosyncratic or colourful individuality as disrupting the smooth running of a rational system, and it permits no departure from all-pervading rules and precedents.

It is evident that Weber's scheme is a direct contradiction of the principles of patronage and privilege that make civic or military government corrupt and inefficient, but it is also inconsistent with an organization oriented to crisis and emergency, such as combat. In the military, rigid conformity and control by faceless seniors, whose capabilities rest mainly on a capacity to "work the system" produce the kind of "efficiency" that invites disaster. The truth of this as it applied to a modern army at war is demonstrated in two important books by Gabriel and Savage (1978) and Hauser (1973); their analysis of the American defeat and shame in Viet Nam has some telling lessons for the future. The applicability of Weber's model is admittedly controversial, but there is evidence from my current research on the militia that it fits. This may be reassuring or not, according to standpoint and one's idea of what the military is for.

Since unification there is no question that the militia has been dominated by a desire to be professional and to model itself on the regular force for which current policy requires it to supply "packages" of manpower or individuals whenever or wherever needed. Life in units is dominated by rigorous training and administrative programs, the latter identical with those of the full-time regular force; there is little time for public parades, civic or social activities, and one might say with some truth that many militia units have dropped out of sight in their communities. Also, there seems to be little or no consideration of what all the activity is for, except to "support the regular force." There seems to be little thought about the demands of future war, and internal security is excluded from training. The view of my respondents is that "we're just not trained to do it" and, though there are exceptions, there has been a marked influence from the events at Kent State in 1970, where four students were killed by U.S. national guardsmen during an anti-war demonstration. Criticisms of bureaucracy are very salient, especially of the regulars as being "more like a civil service than an army"; also, there is some poignancy in the comment of one respondent that reflects the views of many that "the only type of war that's real to us is the paper war!"

The common complaint that regular and reserve units are over-burdened with paperwork raises the vexed issue of the use of women in the military to "free the men from admin." This is one reason given for opening more posts to females. However, the burden on the men has not been reduced. Nor, according to protagonists of a more open policy to admitting women, would this make much difference either, even if it included combat roles. The grounds of the resistance to women are well-known: that fighting is a job for men and always has been; that fighting capability would be weakened as men would be more concerned over the safety of their female "buddies" than with the job in hand; that romantic attachments would make regimental life traumatic, especially in isolated places; and finally, that this would be one more step towards a "civilianization" incompatible with the demands of war. Much more plausible, however, is the probability that objections to using women in combat are explained by the link between warrior-status and social status; the denial of warrior-status to women, and their apparent acceptance of it in peacetime, seems to be one of the important justifications for the conventional stereotypes limiting their power and responsibility outside the domestic context. As possibly the first barrier to equality with males, it might be the most resistant to removal (Harris, 1975).

But all these objections are speculative and unproved in practice, since no modern armed forces (including Israel's) employ males and females equally, and all exclude women from direct combat. So we have no idea what a mixed armed force would be like. Possibly its adoption in Canada would ease the growing problem of recruiting from a declining population of males, especially as I have found many instances of units turning away numbers of well-qualified females anxious to join. It is questionable to assume that females civilianize the military because they can be jealous guardians of military traditions and are known to be strict disciplinarians when in authority. (Indeed, their zeal might well exacerbate the shortage of male applicants even further!)

So far it may be thought that the fears of the effects of civilianization are unjustified, but something of their real substance emerges when the issue of trade unionism in the military is raised. Trade unions now exist in the military organizations of several countries, e.g., Sweden, West Germany, Belgium, and the Netherlands.

The consequences of these developments for the operational employment of the military may be profound. The demands of active service are clearly inconsistent with those of a static bureaucracy, as are those of trade unionism with the essential features of military ideology. Signs of things that could come are visible already from developments in the police, who, with the notable exception in Canada of the para-military RCMP, are unionized to the point of using the strike; the same is true of prison staff, though in this case there is an interesting difference since they are under the auspices of large unions that include civil service workers of many kinds. The police are organized in "brotherhoods" which consist entirely of police.

As noted earlier, there has been reluctance since 1933 to use the regular or reserve military in industrial disputes during peacetime, and preference to rely on the police. But the growing unionization of the police and an increasing solidarity with the ethos of organized labour could cause the police to refuse involvement with industrial unrest in any way. Given this possibility, it would seem that the only safeguard against governments using the military to intervene is to preserve the RCMP's resistance to unionization, or to rely on the unlikely eventuality of police forces in general eschewing strike action. It may be tempting to see the armed forces as a more feasible solution to this problem than they were before 1939, because of the changes in them since then and their well-advertised expertise in peacekeeping abroad; but there are still some formidable objections to such an answer.

Clearly, members of the military have a perennial distaste for being used as police because they are trained to work in groups and to base their methods on their weapons. Hence, they view their use as inappropriate in settings that constrain or even forbid them to manifest these essential characteristics. Peacekeeping, as it is required under the United Nations, is just such a setting. Typically, in Cyprus, they are equipped to fight as soldiers but are forbidden to do so despite often extreme provocation by the two belligerents, whose activities they have to frustrate as best they can. And there is a surfeit of the duties the military find most irksome and boring: guarding and surveillance. When excitement and danger come there is a peculiarly unpleasant aspect: the high probability that whatever is done will be disastrously wrong and will attract criticism by those in the media whose main concern is to create drama and attach blame. Sometimes movement outside bases is curtailed and the soldiers' natural tendency to compensate for family deprivation by making friends with civilian families is inhibited. Without undue elaboration, it is police work without any of its advantages, especially for the troops who have to do the job as distinct from those who plan and administer it from comfortable headquarters (Moskos, 1976c).

In circumstances like the above it would be surprising if the so-called "constabulary role" was popular with the military. But its disadvantages pale into insignificance when compared with the internal security duties that British soldiers are now undertaking in Northern Ireland among people who are indistinguishable culturally from themselves. Such a situation adds an additional stress to a difficult situation, because detachment is harder and sympathy more likely with all its risks of bias. And the consequences of error or impetuousness are even more grave, since unfamiliarity with the cultural context cannot be an excuse.

I mention this comparison before touching the question as to whether the skills learned in peacekeeping abroad enable the Canadian military to do the job equally well at home. It is difficult to answer since there is a profound difference in the two situations, as the British dilemma in Northern Ireland shows. Involvement in political or industrial disputes nowadays is likely to be quite different from half a century ago; whatever the opinion about levels of education among the troops between now and then, the greater exposure to the media will ensure that the soldiers of today are more informed about all sides of the problem than their predecessors were. Moreover, the same facilities will ensure that their actions are seen all over the country, especially if their bluff is called and they are belittled by their inability to use the force they represent. Such problems are unlikely to become troublesome in such contained situations as dealing with disturbances in penitentiaries; they arise especially when the members of the military can identify, even a little, with the "opposition."

The hazards of sympathetic identification are well-known to military commanders, and explain the reluctance to use troops in situations close to their homes. This is not difficult where units have distinctive ethnic or territorial affiliations, as the militia do, but Canada's unified force is not organized on this basis except for the French-Canadian units. Hence, the difficulties and the dangers of using the military in confrontations with their own citizens remain, especially when unions and political parties take sides. And the problems are compounded if the military themselves become unionized and possibly immobilized by considerations of "solidarity." In such an instance governments have no legitimate agency of control for maintaining order, and the temptation would be to turn to para-military forces, such as the so-called "third forces" mentioned earlier. The trend toward doing this is already evident in the increasing use of private security and police organizations, which now outnumber the regular police forces in Canada. Since Magna Carta, private armed forces with loyalties only to particular paymasters, and even to particular governments, have always been feared because of their reputation for ruthless oppression and abuse of power. So much for the view that the lessons of history are irrelevant!

Conclusion

On the evidence presented it is difficult to see the Canadian military as a threat to liberty within the state or to the state itself. It is also hard to see it as an obedient machine, functioning mindlessly to oppress the masses in the interests of capitalist or totalitarian power. In this regard it is instructive to compare the use of the Canadian military in the 1970 "crisis" with that of the Soviet Army in Hungary during 1956 when heavy weapons were used without restraint and civilian casualties were heavy. It is useful also to compare the status and overt power of the military in the USSR and other countries of the Warsaw Pact with the power and status of the Canadian military. The comparison speaks for itself, but it also highlights a proposition that is fundamental to a credible theory of social control: that the key values of a state are made manifest in the ideologies and organizational behaviour of its agencies of social control whose special concern is with the use of force in crisis, i.e., the military, the police, and the penal services. The sequence in which they are cited here is accurate historically for all developed societies; hence the necessity for understanding the military if the basic nature and processes of social control are to be grasped at all.

If I have seemed to present a serene situation, it would be misleading and dangerous to settle for such a view. In the highly volatile political situation that is approaching, with the possibility of some Canadian provinces seceding from the federation, the position of the military will be delicate to say the least.

Another consideration is the latent threat of military intervention by the U. S. In this regard it is interesting to compare Canada's position in terms of military capability with that of the satellite powers of the Warsaw Pact. The dominant position of the U. S. armed forces is clear, and it is probable that they would be used should political power in Canada shift drastically toward anti-capitalist socialism (or the reverse, if the U. S. became a socialist state). This is not the place to discuss the probabilities of conflict with the United States or any other power since this has not been an essay on strategy or its options. It is mentioned here only to remind readers of a factor that must condition realistic sociological thinking about the Canadian military.

Primarily, however, these final reservations about being complacent are stressed to make one point: that, in actuality, power and authority in modern states are balanced as delicately now as they have been throughout history. The exponents of civilian supremacy and of peace can never afford to forget how easily the balance can be upset.

Appendix A
CANADA'S ARMED FORCES:
A BRIEF ORGANIZATIONAL SKETCH

By 1979 Canada had the only armed forces in which the three traditionally separate elements of the military – the sea, land, and air forces – were unified into one monolithic Canadian Force (CF). Its established strength in 1978 was 79,443 regulars (including 4,700 women), committed to varying terms of continuous service, and about 21,200 (4,000 women) in the formed units of the reserve force who have no contractual commitment for any period. Like most modern armed forces the majority of its members are in staff, support, and administrative work, and only about one in five of the ranks below officers were in combatant units in 1977 (Cotton et al., 1978). The truly combatant element is therefore relatively small and distributed widely among West Germany where it supplies a combat force of about 3,000 to the NATO forces, Cyprus and the Middle East where it contributes about 1,700 to the United Nations peacekeeping force, and Canada itself where a combat group of some 3,000 is "ready to move" anywhere in the country or to reinforce units abroad. For these tasks the regular force is notoriously low in strength, and it relies heavily on temporary reinforcements from the formed reserves, notably the militia (the reserve army with about 16,600 all ranks in 1978), though the naval reserve (3,070), air reserve (890), and communications reserve (1,750) make contributions also. Its equipment is for "conventional" operations. The CF has no nuclear capability at present (1979).

The Canadian Force is strictly under civilian control by the Cabinet through its Minister for Defence and his Ministry of National Defence, composed of both military and civilian staff. The Minister is advised by the top-ranking officer in the CF, the Chief of Defence Staff (CDS) who is appointed alternately from each of the three elements into which the CF is organized for combat roles: sea, land, and air. The policies devised in the Ministry are implemented by the "functional" commands: Maritime, Mobile, Air, Communications, and Canadian Forces Europe. Units and headquarters live (often collectively) on a number of large static Canadian Forces Bases, which employ a considerable number of civilians; hence, in Canada and abroad these bases contribute substantially to opportunities for employment of all kinds. All ranks must be Canadian citizens over the age of 18 and under 55 without criminal records.

More detailed information on the structure of the Canadian military can be found in the *Annual Yearbook of Canada*, as well as in several other sources.

REFERENCES

Andreski, S. L.
  1964 *Military Organisation and Society.* London.
Cotton, C. A.
  1976 *Francophone Military Career Participation in Canada.* Canadian Forces Applied Research Unit, Report 76-4. Toronto.
Cotton, C. A. , *et al.*
  1978 "Canada's Professional Military," *Armed Forces and Society,* 4 (3): 365-90.
Coulombe, P.

1972 "Social and Cultural Composition of the Canadian Armed Forces," in H. J. Massey, ed., *The Canadian Military*. Toronto.

Crook, R. K. N.

1975 *The Armed Forces in the Context of Rapid Social Change*. Operational Research Analysis Establishment, Report R55, Department of National Defence. Ottawa.

French, Richard, and Andre Béliveau

1979 *The RCMP and the Management of National Security*. Toronto.

Gabriel, R. A. , and P. L. Savage

1978 *Crisis in Command*. New York.

Gellner, John

1974 *Bayonets in the Streets*. Toronto.

Gerth, H. H. , and C. W. Mills, eds. and trans.

1946 *From Max Weber: Essays in Sociology*. New York.

Goodfellow, T. H.

1976 *Reserve Forces Study*. Operational Research Analysis Establishment, Report R61, Department of National Defence. Ottawa.

Harris, M.

1975 *Cows, Pigs, Wars and Witches*. New York.

Hauser, W. L.

1973 *America's Army in Crisis*. Baltimore.

MacIver, R. M.

1926 *The Modern State*. London.

Mills, C. W.

1956 *The Power Elite*. New York.

Morton, D.

1970a "Aid to the Civil Power: The Canadian Militia in Support of Social Order 1867-1914," *Canadian Historical Review*, 407-25.

1970b *Ministers and Generals*. Toronto.

1974 *The Canadian General*. Toronto.

Moskos, C. C.

1976a "The Military," *Annual Review of Sociology*, Palo Alto, California.

1976b "The Emergent Military," *Pacific Sociological Review*, 16(2): 255-79.

1976c *Peace Soldiers.* Chicago.

Pelletier, Gerard

1971 *The October Crisis.* Toronto.

Segal, D. R. , M. S. Senter, and M. W. Segal

1978 "The Civil-Military Interface in a Metropolitan Community," *Armed Forces and Society,* 4(3).

Stanley, G. F. G.

1960 *Canada's Soldiers.* Toronto.

Steele, H.

1934 *The Long Ride: A short history of the Duke of York's Royal Hussars.* Montreal.

Vallières, P.

1977 *The Assassination of Pierre Laporte.* Toronto.

Willett, T. C.

1970 "Military Roles in the 70's," in Byers and Gray, eds., Wellesley Paper No. 2, Canadian Institute of International Affairs. Toronto.

Index

Acheson, T.W., 172
Act of Union (1840), economic effects
    of, 41
Aitken, Hugh, 37, 41
Amateurism in sport, 158, 166-76,
    179, 184, 187
Anti-statism, 111
Arcand, Adrien, 84
Aries, P., 205
Armstrong, H., 73
Arnstein, Walter, 165
Aronowitz, Stanley, 150
Audet, Louis-Philippe, 111
Authoritarianism, 81-96 passim
    play as resistance to, 151
Authority, 65
    Trudeau on, 91-92

Baby boom, 213, 214
Ball, George, 75
Beamish, R., 184, 185
Bennett, R.B., 84
Bilingualism, and the military, 270,
    273
Bliss, Michael, 176
Bourassa, Robert, 78
Bourgault, Pierre L., 53
Bowles, Samuel, 107, 117, 139
British North America Act, 42, 43, 50,
    219, 222, 226
Building by-laws, 219, 220
Bureaucracy:
    in education, 139-40
    in the military, 274-76, 277
    in sport, 175-76, 184, 187
Business Week (periodical), 66, 67, 72-
    73
Butler, General Smedley, 82-83, 89

Canadian Labour Congress (CLC), 80,
    90, 93, 96
Canadian Labour Party, 182
Canadian Nazi Party, 84
Capital crisis, 32, 65-99
Capital-intensity of industrial
    production, increasing, 66
Catholic Church, and education in
    Quebec, 111, 112, 121, 122, 125
Caves, Richard, 36, 52-53
CEGEP colleges, 125
Centrale des Enseignants du Québec,
    78
Child-centred learning, 128
Child labour, 205, 206
Children's Aid Societies, 207, 208
Children's rights, 208, 209-10, 212,
    214, 215, 216
Civil defence, 268
Civilian supremacy, principle of, 253
Clark, Joe, 76, 92
Clark, S. Delbert, 20-21, 55
Class conflict:
    and Canadian economy, 32, 36
    and capital crisis, 90
    and education, 113, 115-16, 117
    Marx and Engels on, 15

Myers on, 19-20
and play, 166-68
Ryerson on, 18
Classical colleges, 112
Clement, Wallace, 22-23, 54-56, 177,
181
Coercion, see Force.
Collective-conscience, 16
Combines Investigation Act, 226, 230-
35, 236, 237
Commercialism in sport, 156, 170,
173-83 passim, 187
Committee for an Independent
Canada, 60
Communist Manifesto, The, 14-15
Community colleges, 125, 129
social impact of, 139
socio-economic characteristics of
students, 130-31, 132
Compulsory school attendance, 103,
113, 115-16, 122, 205, 207, 209
Confederation, and Canadian
commercial elite, 31, 42-45
Confédération des Syndicats
Nationaux (CSN), 78, 79
Conflict theory:
applied to Canadian society, 18-24
basic assumptions of, 11
characteristics of, 12
and criminology, 197, 199, 203-04,
215-17, 238
and education, 104, 106-09, 117-18,
120, 132-34, 136, 142
and the military, 198, 246, 247
and sports, 105
Conquest (1763), economic and
political implications of, 37-38
Conscientious objection, 266
Conscription, 250-51, 266, 267, 274
Consensus, and social order, 8
Consensus perspective, see Order
theory.
"Conservatism" of Canadians, 30
Conservative Party, Canadian, 31-32,
56, 59, 84, 92
Conspiracy theories of education, 105,
113-16, 142
Consumer and Commercial Relations,
Ontario Ministry of, 223, 224

Consumer and Corporate Affairs,
Department of, 226-35
Consumer Protection Bureau
(Ontario), 223
Consumerism, and sports, 105
Continentalism, 31-32, 35, 54-61, 75,
76
Control theory, 212, 217
Copp, Terry, 112, 121-22, 123
Corporate crime, 217-38
data on, 218
distinguished from "white collar
crimes," 217-18
federal laws against, 218, 226-35
municipal laws against, 218, 219-22
provincial laws against, 218, 222-26
reasons for lack of enforcement
against, 235-38
victims of, 218
Corporate elite:
and corporate crime, 237-38
defined, 217-18
and political elite, 202-03, 217
and Trilateral Commission, 84-85
See also Economic elite, Canadian.
Corporatism, 89-96
and fascism, 94-96
Trudeau on, 96
Correspondence principle, 107-08,
120, 136
Cotton, C.A., 273-74
Countervailing power, 95, 96
Coup d'état, 248, 251, 253, 259
Creativity, and play, 153, 157
Cricket, 166
Crime:
conflict theories of, 197, 199, 203-04
corporate, 217-38
defined, 217-18
Durkheim on, 16-17
juvenile delinquency, 204-17
See also Corporate crime;
Criminological research in
Canada; Delinquency.
Criminological research in Canada,
200-202
Crisis of Democracy, The, 32, 65, 84-89
Crosbie, John, 76
Cross, Michael, 162

Cultural differences, and educational
behaviour, 135
Cultural expression, play as, 150-51,
152-59, 167, 172-73, 187
Cutbacks:
in delinquency programs, 217
in education, 137
in social expenditures, advocated,
72, 73, 91, 92

"Day of Protest," 80
Debt, governmental, 71, 72
Deficits, 72
Delinquency, 204-17
new legislative proposals, 214-15
political economy perspective on,
202-04, 215-17, 238
and school failure, 213
and social class, 210-11
and unemployment, 213
See also Juvenile courts; Juvenile
Delinquents Act.
Democracy:
and capital crisis, 65-96
and corporatism, 93-96
Crisis of Democracy, 32, 65, 84-89
and economic elite, 32
Democratization of sport, 185-86
Dependency, Canadian, 24, 32, 39
and Canadian power elite, 30, 31
Dictatorship, 65
See also Fascism.
Diefenbaker, John, 59
Discipline, of military, 256
Division of labour, 16
Dollar, Canadian, fall in value of, 71
Dominant-value perspective, on
education, 116, 118, 142
Domination, and games, 148-51
passim, 154, 158, 161, 164, 169,
187, 189
Dubuc, Alfred, 44
Dunning, E., 165, 169, 171, 173, 175
Durkheim, Emile, 16-17

Economic elite, Canadian:
Clement on, 22, 54-56
and Confederation, 31
and corporate crime, 237-38

and democracy in Canada, 32
and education, 32-33, 119-20, 122,
123
and entrepreneurial gap, 52-53, 61
historical development of, 30, 34,
36-50, 60
homogeneous character of, 42
Naylor on, 49-50
Porter on, 21, 54, 55, 119-20
and regional economic disparities,
40
and sports, 22, 105, 180
See also Corporate elite.
Economic nationalism, 56, 59, 61, 75,
76
Economy, Canadian, 29-33
American control of, 31, 45, 52, 56,
70
Edgett, C.E., 84
Education:
as agent of social equalization, 128,
135, 140
child-centred learning, 128
commissions on, 141
conflict approach to, 104, 106-09,
132-34
contemporary issues in, 124-42
and cultural differences, 135
development of, 110-24
and economic elite, 32-33, 119-20,
122, 123
elementary, 110-11, 115, 116, 128
and employment, 87-88, 126-27,
137
expansion of, 118, 124-26, 128, 138
of minorities, 116-17
and mobility, 104, 116, 118, 120,
126, 134-35, 138
order approach to, 104, 106-09
political dimensions to, 103
post-secondary, 125-33 passim, 138,
139
and power, 103, 104, 106-42
and productivity, 126
in Quebec, 111-12, 121-24, 125, 133
radical revisionist theories of, 104,
108, 109, 112-24
secondary, 111, 112, 117-20, 128,
129

separate schools, 111
and social change, 103, 109, 123
and social class, 103-09 passim, 114-20 passim, 123, 128-31 passim, 138
and social control, 103, 104, 117, 122
and socialization, 103, 104-05, 134, 137
Educational development:
radical interpretations, 112-24
traditional interpretation, 110-12
Educational planning:
Crisis of Democracy on, 87-88
and unemployment, 87-88, 137
Educational reform, suggestions for future, 139-42
Egalitarianism in sport, 188
Elite theory, on education, 118
Elites:
in Canadian history, 19-20
Clement on, 22
and the military, 247
and sport, 168, 183-84
Porter on, 21-22
See also Corporate elite; Economic elite; Political elite; Power-elite.
Employment, and education, 87-88, 126-27, 137
Engels, Friedrich, 14-15
"Entrepot":
Central Canada as, 42
defined, 39n
Entrepreneurial development in sports, 176
"Entrepreneurial gap," 36, 52-53, 60
Environment, Ontario Department of, 222
Erickson, P., 212
Ericson, Richard, 238
Expansion of schooling, 118, 124-26
causes of, 138
effects of, 128

Fascism, 81-84
and corporatism, 94-96
and the military, 257
Federal laws, 218, 226-35
Fédération des Travailleurs de Québec (FTQ), 79
Feudal society, games in, 151, 153-54, 156
Finance, and exploitation of staples, 40
Financial Post (periodical), 76
"Fiscal crisis of the state," 68, 70, 71
and delinquency, 217
Food and Drugs Act, 226, 227-28
Force:
Clark on, 20
Durkheim on, 17
economy of, 249
graduated, 249
Marx on, 14, 15-16
Pareto on, 17
Ryerson on, 19
and social order, 8-9, 246-49 passim, 280
use to support norms of power-elite, 10
Ford, Henry, 83
Foreign Investment Review Agency (FIRA), 75
Foreign ownership, 34, 35-36, 45-52 passim, 61, 70, 160, 177
statistics of foreign investment in Canada, 47, 48, 49
Fortune (periodical), 82
Fraser, John, 93
French Canadians:
in the military, 266, 267, 270, 273, 279
participation in post-secondary education, 133
Ryerson on, 18, 19
Front de Libération du Québec (FLQ), 264
Frontier play, 155-56, 161
Fur trade:
and development of Canadian economic elite, 37-39
Innis on, 23-24, 35
Ryerson on, 19

Gellner, John, 260-61, 263
Gintis, Herbert, 107, 117, 139
Government:
aid to business, 68, 72

commissions on youth problems, 214
federal-provincial division of powers, 43, 50, 203
growth in expenditures by, 69
investment, 69
Grant, George, 60
Great Britain:
influences on Canada, 58, 60-61
investment in Canada, 47, 48, 160
Greenberg, D., 211
Gross national product, and capital crisis, 67
Guay, Donald, 164-65
Guerin, Daniel, 81

Halsey, A.H., 107
Hartman, Grace, 80
Hazardous Products Act, 226, 227, 228-29
Health regulations, 221-22
Hearst, William Randolph, 82
Henderson, Hazel, 68-69
Hills, Stuart L., 225-26
Hitler, Adolf, 83, 89, 94-95
Hoch, Paul, 158
Hodgins, J.G., 166
Homo Ludens, 152-55, 188
Horton, John, 11
Houston, Susan, 167
Huizinga, Johan, 152-55, 156, 157, 186
Human capital-productivity theory, 126-27, 137
Hurn, Christopher, 138

Income tax, 70
Industrial accidents, 225-26
Industrial democracy, 89
Industrialization:
and Canadian economic elite, 49-50
and sport, 168-69, 171-72, 175, 177
Inequalities, social:
contrasting views on, 11-12
and education, 103-105 *passim*, 115-20 *passim*, 123, 128, 129, 133-42 *passim*
use of power to maintain, 8-9
Inequalities, regional, *see* Regional disparities.

Inflation, 67, 71, 93
Trudeau on, 92
Innis, Harold, 23-24, 35, 41-42
Institutions of socialization, 10, 103, 104
Intelligence agencies, 252
Internal security, 252, 255, 261-64, 270, 278, 279
Investment capital:
increased demands for, 69-70
and technological competition, 66

Jencks, Christopher, 134
Jones, S. Alfred, 83-84
Juvenile courts, 207-08, 209, 210, 212, 215
Juvenile Delinquents Act (1908), 207-09, 214, 215
Juvenile justice:
historical origins of, 204-08
Juvenile Delinquents Act, 207-09

Karabel, J., 107
Katz, Michael, 108, 115
Kidd, Bruce, 182
King, William Lyon Mackenzie, 77-78
Kinnaird, Jim, 80
Korean War, 268

Labelling, 211-12
theory, 217
Labour costs, and capital crisis, 67
Labour movement:
and capital crisis, 65-96
and commercial sport, 181-83
Crisis of Democracy on, 86
politicization of, 79-80, 81
in Quebec, 78
and tripartism, 93, 96
Labour, Ontario Ministry of, 223, 224-26
Lane, David, 135
Lasch, Christopher, 146, 163
"Law and order," 33
Laxer, James, 74
Leadership:
Crisis of Democracy on, 89
of military, 256-57
Porter on, 22

Legions, 254
Leon, J.S., 207
Lévesque, René, 78, 79
Liberal Party, Canadian, 31, 56
Life-long learning, 140-41
Living standards, see Standard of
    living.
Lower, Arthur, 155, 156, 161
Lower Canada, economy of, 37, 39, 40
Loyalty, of military, 256, 259

MacIver, R.M., 248
Mackasey, Bryce, 73
Manipulation, and social order, 8, 9-
    10
Mann, Michael, 150
Maritime provinces, economy of, 31,
    38-40, 51
Marx, Karl, on power and social
    change, 14-16
Marxist views, of play, 156-59 passim
    See also Neo-Marxism.
McDermott, Dennis, 93-94
McLeod, J.T., 90, 95
Media:
    Crisis of Democracy on, 88-89
    elite control over, 22
    and military, 278, 279
    portrayal of unions by, 32
Metcalfe, Alan, 168, 170, 173, 175
Metropolis-hinterland concept, 23-24,
    30, 31, 49, 160
Miliband, Ralph, 158
Military, 197-98, 246-84
    as agency of social control, 10, 19,
        248, 249
    as aid to civil power, 260-65
    anti-military feeling, 267
    and bilingualism, 270, 273
    bureaucratization of, 274-76, 277
    "civilianization" of, 251-52, 274,
        277
    Clark on, 20
    differences from police, 255-56
    ethnic composition of, 273
    historical aspects of, 258-60
    ideology of, 256-58, 274
    infrastructure, 254
    as manifestation of power, 9, 246-49

    passim
    organizational sketch of, 282-83
    recruitment to, 274
    relationship with civilians, 253-54,
        257-58
    relationship with the state, 248-56
    social composition of, 271-73
    unionism in, 277, 280
    women in, 267, 270, 271, 276-77
Military-industrial complex, 247
Militia, 259-60, 261, 276
    age structure of, 271
    impact of nuclear weapons on role
        of, 267, 268
    in "October crisis" (1970), 264
    and social class, 272, 273
    and "total force concept," 269
Mills, C. Wright, 8, 12, 247
Minority groups:
    education of, 116-17, 133
    and military service, 267
Mishan, E.J., 96
Mobility:
    and Canadian economic elite, 54-55,
        61
    and education, 104, 116, 118, 120,
        126, 134-35, 138
    and foreign entrepreneurship, 55
    and foreign ownership, 35
    in late 19th century, 176-77
    and military service, 267
    and sport, 177
Money supply, expansion of, 71
Montreal, school systems in, 121-22,
    123
Moral reform movements, 162-64
Morale, of military, 257
Morin, Claude, 76
Mosely, General George Van Horn, 83
Multinational corporations, 32, 76
Municipal laws, 218, 219-22
"Muscular Christianity," 165
Musgrove, F., 205
Mussolini, Benito, 94
Myers, Gustavus, 19-20

National Hockey League, 178
Nationalism, of labour, 76-77
    See also Economic nationalism.

National Policy (1878-79), 44-47, 57, 77
Native peoples, Ryerson on, 19
Natural resources, *see* Staple exports.
Naylor, Tom, 49-50, 160
Nazis, 83, 94
   Canadian Nazi Party, 84
   See also Fascism.
Neelands, Donald, 67
Neo-Marxism, perspective on education, 107, 108, 117-18, 120, 135-39, 142
   See also Conflict theory.
New Deal, 81, 92
New Democratic Party, 59, 60
"New morality," 74, 75
Normative-integration, 12
Norms:
   of power-elite, 10
   and social control, 16
Nuclear weapons, 267, 268

"October crisis" (1970), 263-64, 280
Okner, B., 180
Ontario Securities Commission (OSC), 224
Open competitions, 168, 169, 170
Order theory:
   and education, 104, 106-09, 118, 127, 136
   on the military, 197, 246
   and Porter's concept of society, 21-22
   view of society held by, 11-12
Organization for Economic Cooperation and Development, 69-70, 119, 125, 129, 140

Packaging and Labelling Act, 227, 229, 230
Page, Charles, 180
Panitch, Leo, 185, 186
Pareto, Vilfredo, 17-18
Parizeau, Jacques, 79
Parkin, F., 9-10
Parti Québécois, 76, 78
Peacekeeping, 278, 279
Pepín, Marcel, 79
Play:

as creation of culture, 154-59
and creativity, 153, 157
as creator of culture, 152-54
as cultural expression, 150-51, 152-59, 167, 172-73, 187
debasement of, 156
in feudal society, 151, 153-54, 156
in frontier society, 155-56, 161
and labour, 157
Marxist views of, 156-59 *passim*
and power, 103, 105, 148, 149, 158, 159, 160-86
regulation of, 163-65, 167
and reproduction of power relations, 149, 151, 157, 161-62, 166, 187-89
and ritual, 153-54, 163
shaped by social conditions, 147-48, 161-62, 166
and social development, 152-54, 155, 163
and socialization, 150, 151, 154
styles of, 147
as symbolic comment on social processes, 146-47, 148, 151, 156-57, 161
transformative character of, 151-52, 158, 159, 179, 187, 189
as validation of social roles, 150
Police:
   as agency of social control, 9, 10, 19, 248, 249
   Clark on, 20
   differences from military, 255-56
   and internal security, 252, 270, 278
   unionization of, 277, 278
Political economy:
   American influences on Canadian economics and politics, 31, 56-61
   of corporate crime, 197, 217-38
   and delinquency, 197, 202-204, 215-17
   and the military, 198
   and social structures and processes, 29
Political elite:
   and corporate elite, 202-03, 217, 237
   defined, 218
Political pluralism, 23

Political power, Marx on, 15
Politics, Canadian:
  American influences on, 56-61
  British influences on, 58
Pollution, enforcement of laws
  against, 221, 222
Porter, John, 21-22, 54-55, 119-20,
  124, 129, 131
Post-secondary education, 125-32
  passim
  and employment, 138
  minority participation in, 133
  socio-economic characteristics of
  students, 130-32, 139
Power:
  and change, 8, 9, 13, 14, 18-24
  checks on, 95, 96
  and education, 103, 104, 106-42
  distribution of, 7, 29
  governmental, *see*
  Authoritarianism.
  and sports, 103, 105, 148, 149, 158,
  159, 160-86
  theories of, 11, 14, 17
  use to maintain social inequalities,
  8-9; *see also* Force.
Power-elite, 30
  contrasting views of conflict theory
  and order theory on, 12
  methods of social control by, 9-10
  Pareto on, 17
  Porter on, 21-22
  and sports, 105
Power structures, 7-8
  and social change, 8
  Porter on, 21-22
"Prairie nationalism," 59
Prairie provinces, 46
Prentice, Alison, 114
Press, *see* Media.
Presthus, Robert, 90
Private schools, 120, 130, 165, 166, 168
Private sector, *see* Government: aid to
  business.
Productivity, and education, 126
Professionalism in sport, 158, 169,
  170, 174, 176, 178, 180
Progressive Conservative Party, *see*
  Conservative Party, Canadian.

Provincial laws, 218, 222-26
Provincial powers, 43, 50, 203
Public health, 221-22
Public school reform movement
  (Britain), 165-66

Quebec, 24
  education in, 111-12, 121-24, 125,
  133
  labour radicalism in, 78-79
  "October crisis" (1970), 263-64
  separatism in, 24, 79, 264

Radical politics in Canada, 58-59
Radical revisionists, interpretation of
  education, 104, 108, 109, 112-24
Railroad, transcontinental, 41, 42, 44,
  46, 50
Rea, K.J., 90, 95
Rebellions of 1837-38, 166
Recruitment to armed forces, 274
Recurrent education, 140-41
Regional disparities, 23-24, 30, 40, 42
Regulation of play, 163-65, 167, 186
Reproductive character of play, 149,
  151, 157, 159, 161-62, 166, 187,
  188-89
Reserve forces, 253, 269, 272, 273
Restrictive Trade Practices
  Commission, 232
Retention rates, school, 124-25
Revolution:
  Clark on, 21
  Marx on, 14, 15, 16
Riel Rebellion, 263
Ritual, and play, 153-54, 163
Rockefeller family, 77-78
Rockefeller, David, 84
Rodrigue, Norbert, 78
Roosevelt, Franklin, 81, 82, 92
Royal Canadian Mounted Police, 224,
  262, 277, 278
Ryerson, Egerton, 116, 167
Ryerson, Stanley B., 18-19

Satellization of the Canadian
  economy, 70, 71, 76, 78
Schecter, Stephen, 112, 113, 117
Scheinberg, Stephen, 45n

School failure, and delinquency, 213
Schools, *see* Education; Private
 schools; Separate schools.
 play activities in, 167-68
Science Council of Canada, 70-71
Sennett, Richard, 151-52
Separate schools, 111
Separatism, 24, 79, 280
 and the military, 264, 280
 "October crisis" (1970), 263-64
Sheard, K., 165, 169, 171, 173, 175
Shotter, John, 151
Smiley, D.V., 90, 95
Smith, Denis, 57-58
Social change, 7-8
 and education, 103, 109, 123
 and power structures, 8
Social class:
 Clement on, 54-55
 and delinquency, 210-11
 Durkheim's concept of, 16
 and educational aspirations, 129
 and educational expectations, 129
 Marx on, 14-15
 and military, 272
 Porter on, 21
 and post-secondary education, 130-
 32, 133, 139
 and schools, 103-109 *passim*, 114-20
 passim, 123, 128-31 *passim*, 138
 and sport, 105, 160, 169-73, 176,
 177, 181, 183
 and staples theory, 35-36
 structure in Canada, 9, 34, 55-56
Social control:
 and criminology, 201, 203, 204, 209
 Durkheim on, 16-17
 and education, 103, 104, 117, 118,
 122
 "hard" form of, 10
 Marx on, 14-16
 and the military, 197, 246-84
 and recreation, 163, 164-65, 166
 "soft" form of, 9-10
Social costs of technology, 68-69, 71
Social Credit Party, 58-59
Social expenditures:
 cutbacks in, 72, 73, 91, 92
 and social stability, 73

Socialization, 8, 9-10
 and education, 103, 104-05, 134, 137
 institutions of, 10, 103, 104
 and play, 150, 151
 and sports, 158, 166
Social selection in secondary schools,
 129
Social solidarity, Durkheim on, 16
Social stratification:
 and education, 127, 130
 and sport, 168
Sports:
 amateur, 158, 166-76, 179
 associations, 171-77 *passim*, 184
 class and, 105, 168
 commercialism in, 156, 170, 173-78
 passim, 180
 and consumerism, 105
 elite control over, 22, 105, 180
 entrepreneurial development in,
 176
 industrialization and, 168-69, 171-
 72, 175, 177
 participation in, 159
 and power relations, 103, 105
 professional, 158, 169, 176
 state involvement in, 185-86, 187-88
 technology and, 153, 158
Sports clubs, 168-77 *passim*, 181
"Stagflation," 67
Standard of living, and capital crisis,
 32, 72, 73-74, 91
Stanley, G.F.G., 258
Staple exports:
 and capital needs, 35-36, 70
 and entrepreneurial gap, 61
 importance in Canadian economy,
 31, 35, 46, 53, 61, 70-71, 160, 167
Staples theory, 23-24, 30, 31, 35
 and social class, 36
State:
 intervention in the economy, 61
 involvement in sport, 185-88
 relationship with the military, 248-
 56
Status competition, 138
Stevens, Sinclair, 74
Stevenson, Garth, 43
Stone, Gregory, 147

Strikes, use of military against, 261-62, 266, 278, 279
Sutherland, Neil, 109, 206, 207, 209

Tariffs, of National Policy, 44, 45
Taxation:
  and capital crisis, 32, 69, 70, 72
  municipal school tax, Montreal, 121-22
Team sports, 166
Technology:
  and capital crisis, 32, 33, 66, 72
  social costs of, 68-69, 71
  and sport, 153, 158
"Third forces," 252, 280
Thompson, E.P., 164
Timber trade, 39
"Total force concept," 269
Transformative character of play, 151-52, 158, 159, 179, 187, 189
Transportation, and staple exports, 40-42
Trilateral Commission, 32, 65, 84-89
Tripartism, 90-96 passim
Trudeau, Pierre, 58, 73-74, 90, 91, 92, 95, 96

Unemployment:
  and capital crisis, 32, 67, 75, 93
  and educational planning, 87-88, 137
  and politicization of labour, 80
  and youth, 213, 216
Unification of the Canadian forces, 246, 268-71, 282
Unions:
  increasing militancy of, 32, 33, 79-80
  and military, 261, 277
  nationalism of, 76-77
  in Quebec, 78-79
  radical tradition of, 77
  and tripartism, 90
United States:
  economic domination of Canada, 31, 45, 52-53, 56, 70
  influence on Canadian sport, 178-79, 181
  influences on Canadian economics

and politics, 31, 56-61
  relationships with Canada, 265, 268, 281
Universities, 130, 131, 132, 139
Upper Canada, economy of, 39, 40
Urbanization:
  and education, 114
  and military recruitment, 274
Utilitarianism, and sport, 175

Vertical Mosaic, The, 21-22, 54-55, 119-20, 124, 131

Waffle, 59
War:
  Canadian military in, 265-68
  "conventional," 268
  and nuclear weapons, 267-68
  "Weapons systems," 267-68
Weber, Max, 107, 148-49, 151, 152, 154, 275
Weights and Measures Act, 226, 227, 228-29
Welfare state, 73
  and capital crisis, 84
  and labour radicalism, 78
Welfare-statism, 186
Western radicalism, 77
White collar crimes, 217-18
Wilkinson, Rupert, 165
Wise, S.F., 155, 171
Women:
  in military forces, 267, 270, 271, 276-77
  in post-secondary studies, 133
Workers' Sports Association, 182